The Believers
in
CHRIST

PERSECUTION OF THE NAZARENES IN SERBIA

Dr. Branko Bjelajac, PhD

Trilogy Christian Publishers A Wholly Owned Subsidiary of Trinity Broadcasting Network 2442 Michelle Drive Tustin, CA 92780

Mark Daniels the official Book translator from Serbian to English.
Vojislav Batta Vujicic, the official Book translation Editor
from Serbian to English

For information about special discounts for bulk purchases, please contact Trilogy Christian Publishing.

Manufactured in the United States of America

10 9 8 7 6 5 4 3 2 1

Library of Congress Cataloging-in-Publication Data is available.

ISBN 978-1-64088-269-0 (Paperback)
ISBN 978-1-64088-270-6 (ebook)

The translation of this book from Serbian to English was undertaken by a group of brothers from the Apostolic Christian Church - Nazarean of La Puente in California. It is intended for the furthering of the Gospel of Jesus Christ and in memory of their grandfathers, fathers, brothers, uncles, their families, and many others who faithfully served the Lord in our Nazarene faith.

This book is an abridged version of a Ph.D. thesis titled: *THE NAZARENE¹ MOVEMENT IN SERBIA: 1918-1941*, WITH PARTICULAR FOCUS ON THE PERIOD AFTER THE SECOND WORLD WAR², defended by Branko Bjelajac, M.A. on 23 May 2012 at the Evangelical Theological Seminary in Osijek, Croatia, as part of the requirements for award of his doctoral degree (Ph.D.).

The Doctoral Examination Board comprised:

- Professor Dr. Peter Kuzmič, Board Chair – Rector of the Evangelical Theological Seminary, Osijek; Professor of World Missions and European Studies at Gordon-Conwell Theological Seminary, Boston, USA.
- Professor Dr. Paul Mojzes, Board member – Chair of the Religious Studies and Humanities Department at Rosemont College, Philadelphia, USA.
- Professor Dr. Zdravko Šorđan, Doctoral advisor/mentor – professor at the Adventist Belgrade Theological Seminary; General Secretary of the Centre for Tolerance and Inter-Religious Relations, Belgrade.
- Professor Emeritus Dr. Juraj Kolarić, Board member – former professor and dean of the Catholic Faculty of Theology in Zagreb
- Professor Dr. Marcel Macelaru, Board member – associate professor of Old Testament Studies; dean of the Evangelical Theological Seminary, Osijek.
- Assistant Professor Dr. Krešimir Šimić, Board member – assistant professor at the University of Osijek.

---

[1] "Nazarene" is a form more commonly used in Europe than the "Nazarean" (used in the US), corresponding more closely with the Serbian *Nazaren* and hence we have elected to use the former throughout this book.

[2] Original title: *Nazarenski pokret u Srbiji: 1918 - 1941 sa osvrtom na period posle Drugog svetskog rata*

In gratitude for their years of heartfelt support while I conducted my research and traveled and wrote on the Nazarenes, I dedicate this book, with love, to my wife Nada and daughter Ružica.

– the author

The Serbian Nazarenes

> That the Servians[3] as a race are not incapable of religious fervour can be proved not only by their old history…but also by the religious fanaticism of the Servian Nazarenes. These are a Christian sect which, about the middle of the last century, originated in Hungary and spread rapidly among the Servians of that country and less rapidly among the people of the kingdom of Servia… They have no churches and no priests; they repudiate the worship of the Madonna and the Saints as idolatry, and they consider it as the greatest sin to kill a man, and therefore they refuse to bear arms and serve in the Army. In Servia some of them have been condemned to twenty years' imprisonment for having refused to comply with the lawful duty of every citizen to serve in the Army. They have cheerfully undergone that heavy sentence for conscience' sake, never murmuring a word of protest. They are absolutely honest and truth-loving people.
>
> (Mijatovich, 1911:38)

---

[3] Servia; Servians – archaic forms of "Serbia; Serbians" – translator's note (t/n).

CONTENTS

INTRODUCTION

While I was writing my master's thesis, which I defended in 2000 at Tyndale Theological Seminary in Badhoevedorp, the Netherlands, I came to the interesting conclusion that most Evangelical and Protestant churches and movements in Vojvodina and Serbia began their initial ministries with members who were converts from the Nazarene movement. Historical examples testified to the significance of the Nazarenes for each individual denomination: for the establishment of the Baptists in Novi Sad in 1875, later for the Methodists, the Adventists, the Pentecostals and for others who emerged in the late nineteenth and early twentieth centuries. The Nazarene refusal to swear oaths before courts and state officials, as well as their refusal to bear arms—although they were willing to serve as medics or auxiliary personnel—provoked the antagonism and animosity of practically every government. Nazarenes in Serbia were numerically strong but their theology kept them introspective in their attitude and closed to outsiders. For that reason, they declined from a force of more than 10,000 believers (late nineteenth century) to a religious community split into two groups with not more than 2,000 believers (late twentieth century).

These two groups call each other *ona druga strana*, [the other side].[4] This observation suggested an interesting starting-point and a challenge: to carry out serious and systematic research into the period between the two world wars, which is to be presented in this dissertation with the expert academic assistance of my dissertation mentor Professor Zdravko Šorđan, D. Sc.

---

[4] Throughout this book square brackets are used to indicate an in-line translation of the preceding text (t/n).

To date, as a religious community, the Nazarenes have published nothing about themselves in the Serbian language, other than a single anonymous book in 1934. The great majority of materials published about them are from hostile sources and mostly consist of criticism by the state and traditional churches. An in-depth study of the Nazarenes was published in 1943 by Dr. Đoko Stojičić, and in the last ten years, master and doctoral theses have been published by historian Bojan Aleksov—the master's thesis at the Open University in Budapest in English and a doctoral thesis in Germany, also in English. In the doctoral thesis, which has been translated into Serbian, the development of the Nazarene movement is considered over the period up to and including the year 1914.

The period studied in this book (1918-1941) has not yet been researched in any academically relevant way. Other than the sources to be mentioned herein, there have been a few articles published about the Nazarenes recently in Serbian-language journals, but they are mostly concerned with the current situation in individual local communities or ethnic groups. These papers have been published in the journals of JUNIR (Yugoslav Association for the Scientific Study of Religion) in Niš and CEIR (Center for the Empirical Research of Religion) in Novi Sad.

The Nazarenes are without doubt the most persecuted Christian religious community in our country, having frequently come into conflict with the state over their theological principles and due to their numerical strength at certain points in history. Their emergence, their development, their spread first in Vojvodina and then toward the south and their arrival in central Serbia, as well as their resilience in the face of persecution, are subjects that very much warrant further study.

The sources that will be looked at in the course of this paper have not so far been sufficiently researched or analyzed. The texts that are to be found on this subject in the Serbian language are mostly one-sided and critical, with superficial and politically-colored opinions that have for the most part been copied from other writers before them. Only recently have some authors taken a more methodical approach: *Vera i sloboda, verske zajednice u Jugoslaviji* [*Faith and Freedom, Religious Communities in Yugoslavia*], by Dr. Zorica Kuburić, published in 1999, and her relatively recent paper *Verske zajednice u Srbiji i verska distanca* [*Religious Communities in Serbia and Religious Distance*] from 2011, as well as the primarily socio-logical study *Verom protiv vere* [*Faith Against Faith*], by Dr. Radmila Radić, published in 1995 (the latter still containing numerous super-ficial statements).

The geographic territory of modern Serbia saw its first Protestants just twenty or so years after Luther's Theses, during the 1540s, and the reforms of the Habsburg Enlightenment Emperor Joseph II involved the settlement of many Lutherans and Reformers in the territory of what is today Vojvodina, then known as the "Lower Lands" and the "Southern Danube Lands." The Princedom of Serbia recognized the existence of these two confessions fairly early on, and in 1853 allowed the establishment of a Belgrade Protestant parish. The formation of the kingdom of Serbs, Croats and Slovenes (king-dom of SCS) and later Yugoslavia, was a favorable development for the further growth of Protestant churches, and the Nazarenes among them, since the new legislature adopted the old legal frameworks of the Austro-Hungarian Empire and with them the prevailing laws. Protestant missions were free to act in the territory of the SCS and Yugoslavia, and not enough has been written or researched on this subject; I will mention just a few of these missions here:

- The Hrišćanska Zajednica Mladića [Christian Young Men's Association], later the Christian Young People's Association and better known in the west as the YMCA[5] from England
- The Salvation Army together with the Methodists
- The Hrišćanski Studentski Pokret [Christian Student Movement] which was active at Belgrade University from 1911 to 1914
- The British and Foreign Bible Society (until now only suffi-ciently studied in Peter Kuzmič's published doctoral thesis *Vuk-Daničićevo Sveto Pismo i Biblijska Društva na južnoslovenskom tlu*

---

[5] Young Men's Christian Association.

u XIX stoljeću [*The Vuk-Daničić Holy Bible and Biblical Societies on South Slav Soil in the Nineteenth Century*]).

The period of their activity and growth in post-war Yugoslavia is a little better known, mostly because the Nazarenes, owing primarily to their distinguishing characteristic – conscientious objection – were under close observation.

Focus and scope of study

In this study, I intend to research and chronologically present the Nazarene movement among the Serbs in a detailed and exhaustive manner, looking at the emergence, development, and activities of the Nazarenes, as well as the enormous difficulties they had with the authorities in the period under consideration – between the two world wars.

The study encompasses the emergence and development of the movement and its strengths and weaknesses in the effort to determine its scale and significance, its position and status in the kingdom of SCS, and later in the kingdom of Yugoslavia, and the heavy state persecution to which it was subjected. This overview will begin with Samuel Froehlich in 1830s Switzerland, going on to look at the arrival of the movement in the kingdom of Hungary and then at its expansion into central Serbia. This brief overview will then give way to an in-depth study of the Nazarenes in the period between 1918 and 1941.

Research questions and themes

1. By what means did the Nazarene movement reach Vojvodina and later the Serbian population? How did this religious movement fit in with the culture and tradition of the Serbian people? What was the relationship between

the Nazarenes in this region and other Protestant and Evangelical movements? What was their impact?

2. What was the position of the Nazarenes in the period between the two world wars, the impact of state and political circumstances on this religious community and the extent of its persecution by the state and the majority religion in Serbia, the Orthodox Church?

3. What were the theological distinctives of the movement and what led to the schism within it?

Limitations

This research will be limited in the geographical sense to the modern-day territory of Serbia, considered in its historical context in the Austro-Hungarian Empire, the kingdom of SCS and subsequently the kingdom of Yugoslavia, and to a lesser extent the DFJ (Democratic Federal Yugoslavia), the FNRJ (Federal People's Republic of Yugoslavia), SFRJ (Socialist Federal Republic of Yugoslavia) and finally the SRJ (the Federal Republic of Yugoslavia). We might also say that this work, geographically speaking, encompasses the Serbian ethnic borders.

The research will look at Nazarenes of Serbian origin, although not solely, in view of the quantity and content of the existing literature.

The proposed study will also include some other forms of research such as consideration of archival records, though unfortunately only those which were accessible to the author in the period from 2000 to 2006.

One of the more significant limitations will be the lack of literature on the Nazarene movement written from the point of view of the Nazarenes themselves. Because of their theological outlook they did not and still do not publish their own historical data, statistics or synodal decisions, nor do they communicate publicly regarding infringements of their rights. Only in the 2000s did some members of this religious community begin to contact different international organizations such as those defending the rights of conscientious objectors, for example Amnesty International, Keston News Service (KNS), etc.

Another limitation has been imposed by the reservations that the members of this religious community have towards any kind of research, including this, which they see as "mingling with the world." There is also frequent suspicion regarding the motives of researchers, since in the past some of them have proven to be undercover police informers. In this sense any contacts I succeed in establishing for the purposes of this research will be solely with those members of the movement who are willing to communicate with the outside world and provide information on the internal workings of the movement itself in Serbia. I consider this a major constraint, imposed by the attitude of the members of this religious community towards those outside their group.

Assumptions

It is fair to assume that the results of this research when published will do much to shed light on this religious community, which has existed in Serbia (to be more precise, in the ethnic Serbian territories) since the early 1870s. The bibliography that has been compiled along the way will be useful to future researchers as a starting-point for their own further studies.

The Nazarenes were the first denomination to initially come from the West – though in time developing their own unique, local characteristics – to put down roots among the Serbian population and other ethnic groups, and not just in Vojvodina but also, somewhat later, in central Serbia, despite the active opposition of the authorities and the dominant Orthodox Church. It was a movement that spread among the lower classes – the peasants, craftsmen and laborers – who were attracted by the simplicity of its message and teaching. The external expressions of religion that were so dominant in orthodoxy (veneration of icons and saints, crossing oneself, lighting candles for the living and for the dead, liturgy in the (Orthodox)

Church Slavonic language and so on) were rejected in favor of an emphasis on the inner spiritual life (searching one's heart, repentance and humility before God, frequent prayers, reading the Psalms aloud in unison etc.).

The Nazarenes did not have formal church leadership, nor paid ministers and missionaries, as they were primarily Congregationalist in terms of their church structure. Individual believers took on the role of elders – several in each fellowship – although it was possible to discern among them those who preached and lead the local fellowship. To begin with, they met in people's houses, but later they got (or rather fought for and won) permits to build themselves places of worship, many of which are owned today by Evangelical and Protestant churches.

Overview of existing literature

We have already said that there have been no prior academic studies of this religious movement in Serbia in the period under scrutiny. The majority of studies of the Nazarenes were published in the late nineteenth and early twentieth centuries, always penned by their impassioned opponents. One of the earliest authors, Pavle Paja Dimić, published his first work on them as early as 1870, in which he initially calls them "Nazirees" (*nazirei*) – *O Nazireima* [*On the Nazirees*] – with articles published in installments in *Pastir*. He later wrote another book on them, published in 1881, titled *O Nazarenima* [*On the Nazarenes*]. A great critic of the Nazarene movement at this time was Vladimir Dimitrijević, theologian and later doctor of theology, a priest in Pest, Hungary, who published at least four books and a great number of articles and features on this "plague" afflicting the Serbian Church. Another author from this period, Jug Stanikić, published a sixty-two-part feature in opposition to the Nazarenes, in *Srpski Sion* between 1897 and 1899 and in a number of installments in *Hrišćanski Vesnik* between 1902 and 1903.

A publication also worthy of mention is the book *Nazareni* [*The Nazarenes*] by the anonymous author "Hadžija," published in

Belgrade in 1936. It consists of a discussion on various injustices and wrong decisions taken among the Nazarene leadership in regard to conscientious objectors, written by someone who was doubtless high up in the leadership/eldership of the movement.

This period, prior to World War I, ends with the book by SPC (Serbian Orthodox Church) historian Đoka Slijepčević, *Nazareni u Srbiji do 1914. godine* [*The Nazarenes in Serbia up to 1914*], which was published in 1943 in Kragujevac and comprises the only serious study of the Nazarenes before the mid-twentieth century.

In the post-war period the Nazarenes attracted the interest of the state security service, which in 1953 published a study on religious communities in the FNRJ, in which the Nazarenes were singled out for special attention.

Only in the 1990s were two academic papers published on the Nazarenes, one of them by Bojan Aleksov in English, "The Dynamics of Extinction: The Nazarene Religious Community after 1945," a master's thesis defended in Budapest, the other by Sanja Đorđević, a bachelor thesis written at the Belgrade Faculty of Philosophy on the topic of the Nazarene religious community, with a special focus on their church in Zemun. Earlier in 1975, Jakov Makaji had defended a bachelor thesis at the Biblical Theological Institute (BTI) in Zagreb, titled *Istorijat i nauka nazarena* [*History and Teachings of the Nazarenes*].

In preparation for his doctoral thesis on the emergence of the Nazarenes, defended in Germany, historian Bojan Aleksov carried out extensive research. He later (in 2006) published the paper in English under the title "Religious Dissent Between the Modern and the National, Nazarenes in Hungary and Serbia 1850-1914." In 2010 this paper was published in Serbia under the title *Nazareni među Srbima: verska trvenja u južnoj Ugarskoj i Srbiji od 1850. do 1914* [*The Nazarenes Among the Serbs: Religious Friction in the Southern Kingdom of Hungary and Serbia Between 1850 and 1914*]. Aleksov's work, in terms of its theme and its approach, has served as a starting point for this work, since it studies the Nazarenes in the period prior to the one to be considered in this book. The period spent in Hungary, and his academic work in Budapest, enabled the author to review and analyze a large number of Hungarian-language sources, a work significant for the understanding of the Nazarene movement which was then growing in the so-called southern kingdom of Hungary.

In the journal *Religija i tolerancija*, published by CEIR, Novi Sad, in issue 14 (2010) Aleksandra Đurić-Milovanović published an article titled *Multikulturalizam i religijski pluralizam: Rumuni nazareni kao manjina manjine u Vojvodini* ["Multiculturalism and Religious Pluralism: Romanian Nazarenes as a Minority of the Minorities in Vojvodina"]. The younger generation of sociologists of religion have only just begun to study this interesting area. This research is intended to further contribute to the study of this religious community and movement.

Several studies on the Nazarenes in present-day Serbia have been published abroad, in Hungary, Russia, Germany and the US, and these will be consulted in the course of this research, even though all are more than a century old: Karoly Eotvos: "The Nazarenes"; Perry Klopfenstein: "A Treasure of Praise: Nazarenes in Jugoslavia"; V. Olhovskii: *Nazareni v Vengriji i Serbii* [*The Nazarenes in Hungary and Serbia*], and others. One more recent work is that of Bernhard Ott: *Missionarische Gemeinde Werden* [*Becoming a Missionary Church*], written in 1996, in which the Nazarenes in Serbia are mentioned in the context of the work of the HILFE organization from Zurich.

The emergence and existence of the Nazarene movement also caused something of a stir amongst the artists of the time, and several short stories, novels, and treatises appeared in artistic and literary forms, inspired by the existence and beliefs of the Nazarenes. The best known are the short story *Novoverci* [*The New Believers*] by Simo Matavulj and the novel *Nazaren* [*The Nazarene*] by Jaša Tomić. The story *Nazaren* was published in 1995 in the collection *Priče o Rusinima* [*Stories of the Rusyns*] by Stevan Konstantinović.[6]

---

[6] This might be a good point to mention that the artistic "Nazarene movement" that emerged in the early nineteenth century had no direct connection with the Nazarene religious movement. In 1810 in Rome, a group of six German painters began a new artistic movement that primarily focused on portraits and self-portraits, using soft lines and strokes. This school had some influence on

Despite all the works previously listed we can conclude that the Nazarenes, as a religious group and as a unique sociological phenomenon, as well as the restriction of their religious and human rights, have not been studied sufficiently. This is especially true given that they are a religious group specific to this region.

Basic Definitions

When the five German princes and representatives of fourteen free cities submitted their *protestatio* to representatives of the Roman Catholic Church at the Diet of Speyer in 1529, the expression "protestant" was born. Divided amongst themselves and outnumbered by the forces of Catholicism, they found it vital to give form to their unique confession of faith, in the face of efforts by the official church to hold back the advance of Lutheranism, by the introduction of minor innovations and changes. This protest was only one phase in the development of the new religious movement, and in the sixteenth century there were cases where the Lutherans were referred to as "Protestants" and Calvinists as "Reformers," since it was the Lutherans who were "protesting" and the Calvinists who wanted to "reform" things; later though, these movements were amalgamated under a common name.

Today the expression "Protestant" implies much more than just a separation from the Roman Catholic Church, which at the time had an expressly negative connotation. To be a Protestant today means to embrace certain postulates that have been distinctives of the movement since the time of the Reformation. This is why, for example, some High Church Anglicans traditionally do not consider themselves representatives of Protestantism since, they believe themselves to have remained true to the centuries-old "Catholic" system of

---

Serbian painters, especially in the latter half of the nineteenth century, relating to so-called impersonal classicism. See more on this Serbian art-related topic in Šelmić, 1979.

belief. It is also common to hear religious communities with origins in Protestantism to be referred to as churches of Reformed heritage.

Lutheranism, Zwinglianism, and Calvinism might be termed the primary branches of Protestantism, while there are other faiths (church denominations) that are Protestant in terms of their general characteristics. Professor George Williams of Harvard talks of Magisterial Reformation (the general form of Protestantism supported by the civil authorities) and Radical Reformation (comprised of groups which refused to cooperate or have any contact with the civil authorities). Since the term Protestantism is today so inclusive, and carries such a multiplicity of meanings, it is difficult to find a particular confession that would encompass all or most of the confessional traits of the various Protestant movements. However, one can identify certain shared characteristics of the branches of Protestantism that were later also adopted by Evangelical Christianity:

1. *Justification by faith* — This was one of the key issues on which Protestantism (Luther) offered an opinion – that a man's righteousness was not dependent on his deeds but on God's work of salvation in Jesus Christ. This synthetic teaching probably comprises the single greatest difference between Protestantism on one side and Catholicism and Orthodoxy on the other.

2. *Holy Scripture* — Representatives of the Reformation were united in asserting that Holy Scripture was and remains the only authority with regard to doctrine. The early Reformers had great respect for the early church fathers and decisions of the ecumenical councils, but they did not consider them equal in authority to Scripture. The later, more radical Reformers distanced themselves further from tradition, considering Scripture the only significant point of reference.

3. *Relationship between church and state* — Although the early Reformers, Lutherans, and Calvinists (and in part Anglicans) sought to influence statesmen and rulers, and

succeeded in doing so, the Radical Reformation believed that church and state should be separate, primarily in order to avoid Erastianism (state control of the church). It should be noted that all Protestants are not in agreement in regard to this issue, and that there are groups that have organized themselves as state churches, those that reject all forms of collaboration, and all shades of opinion between these two extremes.

4. *Priesthood of all believers* — Protestant doctrine rejects a rigid church hierarchy and a "bicameral" division into priests and monks on one side and the laity on the other. In a general sense, this means that the ministries of preaching and conducting rites among Protestants do not reflect a fundamental division among believers, but only a functional one. This distinction can still be seen, though, especially in nominal Protestant churches. Over time a division has arisen in Evangelical Christianity between trained preachers and the laity, but that division is still merely functional.

5. *Holy Sacraments* — Protestantism decisively rejected the seven Holy Sacraments and introduced two "commands of the Lord" — baptism and communion (the Lord's Supper). However, some Protestants subscribe to the notion of sacrament, while others only to that of command. All Protestants accept the Lord's Supper in both elements (bread and wine) but visible differences persist even today among Protestants over the actual significance of the act. Luther held that Christ was really and bodily present alongside the bread and wine (consubstantiation), Calvin talked of a spiritual but real presence, while Zwingli preferred to emphasize symbolic presence, the importance of fellowship and the need for believers to recall Christ's redemptive death. Today this last view predominates, even though there are those who believe differently, in particular the majority of Lutherans and some Reformed Christians.

In the transition from Europe to the US, Protestantism underwent profound changes. In the eighteenth century, influenced by Puritanism and the Great Awakening, as well as in the early nineteenth century under the influence of a new wave of revival (the so-called Second Great Awakening) growth and reform came about in society itself. Protestantism had a direct impact on the abolition of slavery, the establishment of temperance groups, the growth of entrepreneurial capitalism, the beginnings of the Social Gospel movement and on the civil liberties movement. Under the auspices of the latter, a great many different church and religious denominations began to rapidly emerge.

According to the statistics, today there are around 1.2 billion Protestants and adherents of churches and movements that are Protestant in character.

Evangelical Christianity emerged as a natural progression of Protestantism after a number of religious revivals, focusing its theology on the contemplation and development of the Christian life. Some authors believe that the roots of the Evangelical movement go back to the early Middle Ages and the views of Anselm of Canterbury, Bernard of Clairvaux and others. For the new movement, saving faith, or "conversion" became a key issue, together with the awareness of the individual that God's love was expressed through Jesus Christ. On this subject, Dr. Aleksandar Birviš writes that Evangelical Christianity is essentially a return to the source. It seeks to do the following: (a) to clean away the residue of centuries of adulteration and (b) to appropriate direct revelation in Jesus Christ on the basis of the reliable reports in the Gospels.

Evangelical Christian theology of the early nineteenth century began to emphasize the renewal of church and believer, as well as evangelism (taking the Good News to the whole world), whilst not neglecting the general betterment of society and support for the individual.

By the mid-nineteenth century, Evangelical Christianity began to move away from an understanding of the Christian life as the renewal of the fundamental truths and doctrines of the early church. Instead, the theology of the evangelical movement began to take up a position against growing liberalism and so-called higher (literary) criticism of Scripture, seeing this type of criticism, in tandem with the Enlightenment and Rationalist movements, as systematically tearing apart the fabric of nominal churches and theological seminaries in Europe and the United States. In response, a multitude of new theological learning institutions sprang up, seeking to define modern evangelical theology anew.

In the late nineteenth century, evangelical theology saw growth in the areas of apologetics and ethics, and in the early twentieth century the Pentecostal movement began to also emphasize a new approach to the theology of the Holy Spirit. Evangelical theology began to primarily center around in-depth study of Scripture accompanied by prayer and meditation, with an emphasis on the Gospels. The purpose of this study could be summarized in the questions "How do I know God?" and "How do I worship God?" Special emphasis was placed on life in the fellowship of believers and on acts of love (love for one's fellow man) whilst awaiting Christ's second coming.

The theology further developed with the emergence of specific evangelical denominations, each of which made special emphasis of particular biblical doctrines. Thus, one denomination might place great importance on the methodical and systematic study of Scripture, and the need to approach everything else in our spiritual life in the same way; others specially emphasize the importance of the personal experience of the believer and his or her relationship with the Holy Spirit.

Despite the evident differences, there is considerable theological similarity among evangelical churches. Today there are a great number of Evangelical denominations, among which some differ only in name.

In the latter half of the twentieth century there was a revival and growth of the so-called charismatic movement in Evangelical Christianity, which also included Pentecostal denominations.

In the early 1990s, especially in the US and Scandinavia, some Pentecostal denominations adopted liturgy as their primary form of service, emphasizing the importance of transcendence in the relationship with God.

Today, worldwide, there are around 420 million Evangelical Christians and around 345 million Charismatic and Pentecostal Christians.

The peoples of Serbia, as well as the Serb population in the region as a whole, had contact with Protestantism in the earliest times. Not only did they live in areas where the new teaching was spreading fast (the Srem region, the Podunavlje region, the area around Timişoara etc.), they also quickly became a subject of interest for Protestant preachers, particularly those Serbs who lived in the Turkish-occupied territories (Bosnia and central Serbia). The region that is Serbia today, including Vojvodina and Kosovo, in the period leading up to the twentieth century, was a meeting point of many roads and a "promised land" for a great many craftsmen, soldiers, traders and laborers – mostly Germans, Slovaks, Czechs and Hungarians – among whom there were Protestants, who brought their faith with them in the same way Catholics did.

Regarding the definition of basic concepts referred to in this book, I propose that the term *Protestant church* encompass all those Christian churches that emerged and developed in an organized way in the spirit of the Reformation tradition, separate from the Orthodox and Roman Catholic churches, founded on the basic tenets of Protestantism: faith alone and Scripture alone. I propose we define *Protestant missions* as being Christian mission activities initiated by Protestant churches and by movements that emerged from the Protestant tradition, for the most part in Europe. By the term *Evangelical church* or *Evangelical movement,* I propose we refer to modern churches and movements from the Reformation tradition that arrived in Serbia in the second half of the nineteenth century.

By *Protestants* and *Evangelical Christians*, this book refers to the members and adherents of traditional Protestant churches, and the churches and faith communities that emerged from the Reformation tradition in Serbia, which in terms of their theology and doctrine do not deviate from the fundamental and most important principles of Protestantism. These are as follows: the Evangelical Christian Church of the Augsburg Confession, the Reformed Christian Church, the Evangelical Methodist Church, the Anglican Church, the Christian

Nazarene Community, the Christian Baptist Church, the Christian Adventist Church, the Protestant Evangelical Church, Christ's Pentecostal Church, the Evangelical Church, the Church of God and the Church of Christ Brethren[7]. There are also other individual Evangelical fellowships: Calvary Chapel, the Church of Christ, the Christian Fellowship, the Free Pentecostal Church[8], etc.

By *Nazarene movement,* I propose we refer to the indigenous movement that emerged in the 1830s in Switzerland, the founder and leader of which was Samuel Heinrich Froehlich, and that same movement as it spread to and developed in Vojvodina and Serbia in the nineteenth century and later.

---

[7] Respective Serbian names are as follows: Evangeličko-hrišćanske crkve augs-burške veroispovesti, Reformatska hrišćanska crkva, Evangeličko-metodistička crkva, Anglikanska crkva, Hrišćanska nazarenska zajednica, Hrišćanska baptis-tička crkva, Hrišćanska adventistička crkva, Protestantska evanđeoska crkva, Hristova pentekostna crkva, Evanđeoska crkva, Crkva Božija, Hristova crkva braće (t/n)

[8] Respective Serbian names are as follows: Crkva Golgota, Hristova crkva, Hrišćanska zajednica, Slobodna pentekostna crkva (t/n)

PROTESTANTISM IN SERBIA: THE BEGINNINGS AND EMERGENCE OF DENOMINATIONS

There is a deep-rooted notion that the religious movements that sprang up from the Reformation only arrived in Serbia in the eighteenth century due to immigration and in the nineteenth century due to the work of missionaries. However, historical and literary sources and the accounts of travellers say otherwise.

Pre-Reformation Movements

The region of today's Serbia has since the twelfth century had contact with different protesting groups of believers: the Bogomils were seen in this region, and with them the Waldenses in the thirteenth century, the Hussites in the fourteenth century and, as early as the fifteenth century, Lutherans, Calvinists/Reformers, Hutterites, Unitarians, Sabbatarians, Anabaptists, and others. There are no sources from this pre-Reformation period, except a few details and some assumptions.

> Within the Raška (Žiča) archdiocese and its successors, there were religious movements (secret ones, semi-secret ones and even some fairly public ones). Some of them made efforts to achieve separation from the state religion and to establish separate spiritual bodies. We know very little –

next to nothing – about these movements. Why? Because persecution in the Byzantine Empire was brutal and left no written traces: there are no court minutes and no witnesses ever came forward, as they could be killed after they were finished with. There are references in oral tradition and folklore. Neither is sufficiently reliable for the historian (Birviš, 2010:11 – own translation[9]).

Waldenses

From existing sources, it can be determined that the followers of Peter Waldo – the Waldensian movement that spread from Milan, Italy – sent missionaries to visit the scattered non-conformist churches in the period after 1220. The Waldensian missionaries also travelled the Balkans.

> Their route was marked with new Waldensian churches and the pyres of martyrs. When the Inquisition began to mercilessly persecute them, these missionaries were compelled to conceal the real purpose of their travels. They traveled as silk and pearl salesmen and wherever they had the opportunity they sold that precious pearl, the Word of God, which they always carried with them, usually their own transcribed copies (Golubić, 1973:183).

Apart from the countries of western Europe, these missionaries visited the kingdom of Hungary, Bulgaria, Turkey and other countries. Catholic historians, who speak particularly negatively of the

---

[9]   All English citations of non-English sources should from here on be assumed to be "own translations" by the author/translator in the absence of an existing English translation (t/n).

Waldenses, state that their churches and followers were found even in Constantinople, as well as in Slavonia, Croatia, and Dalmatia (Seventh Day Baptists…, 1910:72).

Contacts with Hussitism

As Dr. Dragutin Prohaska says, there are indications that in the sixteenth century, the Hussites and Taborites joined forces with the Bogumils from Bosnia in warring against the Catholics. But even more interesting is his discussion of the appearance of Hussites in Srem and the "surrounding areas of Bosnia and Rascia" (Prohaska, 1922:437).

Dr. Šidak mentions a number of settlements in Srem and in the Fruška Gora hills that were involved in Hussitism. Kamenica is mentioned, on the right bank of the Danube, near Petrovaradin, where the population was ethnic Hungarian, as well as Bač and Beočin, and Sent Martin. It is interesting to note the observation by historians that wherever there were Orthodox believers, Hussitism took root only among Catholic church members.

In 1432 (or possibly 1431), Constantine the Philosopher, writing his *Život despota Stefana Lazarevića* [*Life of Despot Stefan Lazarević*], conveyed something of the prevailing atmosphere at the peak of the Hussite rebellion, and of the role of the Serbian army in crushing it. King Sigmund sought a small unit from his Serbian vassal to help in the battles with the Taborites. And in the winter of 1421 and early 1422, this unit in fact invaded the west of the kingdom of Hungary.

> When in late fall of 1421, King Sigmund requested military assistance against the Hussites in the Czech lands, Stefan Lazarević responded willingly. A unit of Serbian cavalry, apparently under the command of Timiş Prefect Pippo Spano, was dispatched to a far-off field of war. It took part in fighting during December 1421

and January 1422 (Istorija srpskog naroda, 1994:209).

The organized arrival of the Taborites and Hussites in our part of the world probably did not come until 1437, when a military expedition against the Turks in this part of the world included several companies of Taborites in its ranks. Yet there are many sources which speak from a Serbian perspective of existing Hussites in the region as a problem to be resolved.

Thus, on fifteenth March 1437, Jakov, Bishop of Srem, writes to Pope Eugene IV to tell him that the inquisitor James of the Marches has found many heretics in the Diocese of Srem and surrounding area: "By careful inquisition he has found many heretic priests and laymen perverted by the heretical adultery of the damned Hussites, those who envy the Catholic faith and the Holy Roman Catholic Church" (Kàtona, 1782:773).

Bishop Jakov adds that the heretics have dubbed the Roman Church the "Synagogue of Satan," that they partake of both [elements of the Communion], that they meet at night and that they "might" have wanted to slaughter all the bishops. The letter to the Pope came after some initial disagreements – Friar James had been prevented from working in the area as he did not have orders or approval to do so. Hence the inquisitor had turned to the local bishop asking for written permission to operate (Stanojević, 1928:114). A year later on the eighteenth of July 1438, Bishop Jakov received a similar letter from the authorities in Valpovo, Croatia.

A letter from the prefect of Požega county, Count Vladislav, dated the twenty-fifth of February 1437, talks of the areas in which the inquisitor found Hussites "between the rivers Sava and Danube, and in the surrounding areas in Bosnia and Rascia," and states that in those regions have lived mostly "Rascians, Bosnians and Christians, as well as Hussites for many years."

The reports of James of the Marches speak of the widespread presence of Hussites in Vojvodina, that is, in Srem and Bačka districts. In his 1436 report, he speaks of the Diocese of Kalocsa in Bačka and says the following,

...found many heretics (Hussites), priests and laymen, who were confessing and spreading heresy around the forests, ale-houses and mills, around mountain caves and dens of the earth (Grujić, 1931:438).

From Bačka, Friar James moved on to Srem where he requested support from the Požega district Prefect, Vladislav, in writing, in which we read:

...that in Srem too there are truly many Orthodox (Rasciani), Bogumils (Boznenses) and Hussites (Huzytae) (Grujić, 1931:439).

Also, several documents are preserved which speak of Friar James' struggle against the Hussites around Kamenica and Beočin. In July 1438 in Valpovo, Count Vladislav issued a letter to Friar James in which he writes:

...in Srem, some country towns and villages were for many years infected with adherence to the heretical Hussites...but that this vicar converted them with God's help (Klaić, 1980:51).

However, as Klaić says, despite all of the efforts of Friar James of the Marches, the Hussites survived both in Srem and across Moldavia, as attested to by reports from the 1460s. Another report from August 1439 speaks of the overall climate on the Fruška Gora and in the area as a whole:

He [Friar James] gave the order for the priest of Beočin, Valentin, who had defended the heretics, to be clapped in irons and confined in the jail in Kamenica, and for three heretics (Hussites) to be tied to the stake. As the Hussites were being bound, a tailor, Valentin, from Kamenica (another source says he was a cobbler) leapt on the judge of Kamenica, Jovan and drove him away with unsheathed sword. Then, with the gathered townspeople he freed the bound Hussites from the stake and, having been to the house of the judge, they broke down the door of the jail, freed the priest of Beočin and took off his chains... (Grujić, 1938:438).

As far as the causes and the rise of Hussitism in Srem are concerned, Dr. Šidak, in his article (op. cit.), confirms the words of Ladislav Morovićki, who as far back as 1437 wrote that "the primarily Catholic population was adopting Hussite reformist slogans" and who believed that it had not been Bosnian "Patarene" heretics who had prepared the ground for the introduction of the new teaching. According to Šidak, Hussitism primarily spread along the Danube belt, from Slankamen in the east to Ilok in the west, "through the markets and towns, among merchants, traders and other citizens, most of all in the Hungarian settlements" (Šidak, 1932:5).

A number of Srem Hussites fled to Moldavia under strong pressure from the Inquisition, but there too the Franciscans were soon entrusted with the mission against them. Thus, in Vojvodina, the Hussite movement came into contact with Serbs and Orthodox Christians and was known of and seen in these parts.[10]

---

[10] For further study of Hussitism in this region, the following two details may be of interest: 1) Concerning the Church of St. Dimitrie in Nădlac, Romania, Stevan Bugarski says the following, "...in the 16th century, after the male line of the Jakšić's of Nădlac came to an end, by the efforts of their wives and descendants of a foreign faith, (the church was) adapted and reorganized so that half was used by the Orthodox, half by the Hussites." This church was destroyed in 1695 in fighting with the Turks. 2) In Belgrade on 3 July 1877, the anniversary of Hus's death in 1415 was formally celebrated and a booklet published to mark the occasion, containing his sermons and letters: "Četiristogodišnjica Jovana Husa u Beogradu" [400th Anniversary of Jan Hus in Belgrade], Štamparija N. Stefanovića i Druga, Beograd, 1877.

Reformation among the Serbs

The discussion on Luther in the Slavo-Serbian language in 1534-35

Gavrilo Svetogorac[11] was a writer of the first half of the six-teenth century, a priest of Mount Athos for three terms and a "*pro-tosynkellos* of the Holy Patriarch in Constantinople." As notary of the Protaton in Karyes, Gavrilo translated the history of the found-ing of Mount Athos into the Serbian language, wrote *Život Nifona* [*The Life of Niphus*] and translated two other church books into Serbian: *Ustav za sveštenike pri spremanju za službu* [*Constitution for Priests in Preparing for the Ministry*] and *O službi nad umrlim u Veliku nedelju* [*On the Liturgy for the Dead in Holy Week*]. As well as translation and writing, Gavrilo maintained a theological corre-spondence in the Slavo-Serbian language with Lacko of Măcești, logothete of the Hungarian king John Zápolya. "In refuting Luther ('Luftor'), Gavrilo also speaks ill of the Catholic church" (Đ.S.R., 1958:432).

Of the two letters to Gavrilo and his two known replies, only the last letter with questions and a letter with responses missing its end were preserved. A transcript of these letters in the Serbian language was published in the journal *Bogoslovlje* in 1934 (Matić, 1934:5). Both letters were burned in the bombing of the Serbian National Library in Belgrade on 6 April 1941.

Lacko, the logothete of Hungarian king John Zápolya[12], wrote to Gavrilo a second time in 1534, on behalf of his king, mention-ing that Gavrilo's first letter, "instruction from Holy Scripture," was being kept in the King's treasury. In the introduction to the letter, it is

---

[11] Although Đorđe Radojčić claims that Gavrilo's surname was Mstislavić and that he was of Russian origin, Sima Ćirković cites the position of Gojko Subotić who investigated this matter and found no basis for such a claim. See Ćirković, 1997:476.

[12] Logothete Lacko probably ran the so-called Slavic Office, since there are previ-ously-known letters of his of Serbian editorship from the King's collection.

requested of Gavrilo that he respond "on the basis of Holy Scripture" regarding certain points of Luther's teaching and faith.

As Sima Ćirković says, what is surprising here is Zápolya's intention, in the event of discussions on the unification of the Churches, to obtain permission from the Sultan to allow the "Eastern patriarchs" to attend a council in his country. "What is surprising is the fact that Zápolya was ready to use his influence with the Sultan for the good of the Orthodox Church" (Ćirković, 1997:477).

The "humble priest" Gavrilo, in his reply to the logothete, offers his view as well as a fierce criticism of Luther's teaching, and replies in detail regarding relations with the "Roman church," but completely neglects to respond to the questions about the Orthodox Church. It is possible that Gavrilo's motives lay in his intention to bring the Orthodox Church as close as possible to the king and make it appealing to him, and hence the Catholics were described in negative terms and Luther even more so.

> ...and that there is also among you a philosopher by the name of Luther [Luftor in the original – author's note], and he errs in his teaching... And we say to him: that he is by no means a Christian, but rather a devilish Jew and a Turk by faith and is far from the Holy Orthodox Faith (Matić, 1934:8).

Printing press in Urach

A Glagolitic and Latin script printing press was founded in the town of Urach near Tübingen in Germany in 1561 in order to print books in Slovene, Croatian (in Glagolitic), and Italian, and in that same year a Cyrillic printing press was established too. Thus an institution came into being called the "Slovenačka, hrvatska i ćirilička štamparija" [Slovene, Croatian and Cyrillic Printing Press]. The press also housed a bindery. This was all thanks to Baron Hans von Ungnad, a Croat expelled to Germany for his Reformist views.

He established a printing press in the abandoned monastery of St. Amanda in order to spread the Protestant faith among the southern Slavs (Klaić, 1980:663). His work was primarily financed by the Bohemian King Maximilian, the great Duke Christoph of Württemberg and many other Protestant princes and free cities in Germany.

Cyrillic type was cast in 1561 and preparations were begun. For books intended for the Serbs, the most important thing was to find an educated man who would edit printed books in Cyrillic.

Primož Trubar, joined by former Catholic priest Stipan Konzul Istranin, following a recommendation, negotiated with a certain Serb, Dimitrije (Demeteros), who knew Cyrillic well, and also knew Greek, Romanian, Italian, and Turkish. He was said to have been the secretary and "levite" of the Patriarch in Constantinople for six years, and later secretary of the Moldavian Duke Alexander. Sources say that he was an upright and very educated man, and that he spent time in Wittenberg, Germany, where he joined the Reformation.

> This Dimitrije related that there were a number of Cyrillic translations of Scripture in Turkey and there was no need to translate it. They tried to persuade him to come to Germany and become a teacher of Greek but he gave up on the whole idea and went to the Despot of Moldavia, where he enjoyed great favor (Bučar, 1910).

The leaders of the Protestant movement thought that with the help of Cyrillic books, they could spread the Reformation among the Serbs, too. Because they did not have a single Serbian translation of the Bible, they printed Croatian translations in the Cyrillic script and called these versions "Illyrian" (Kilgar, 1939).

> These books, printed in the Glagolitic, Latin and Cyrillic scripts, in the common and Church languages, can be considered together due to the

fact that they were published within a few years of each other by this printing press in a foreign land, and that they contained Protestant religious writings, ranging from Bible translations to polemical articles (Ivić, 1971:58).

The Protestants had no recorded success among the Serbs with these Cyrillic books (Zbornik: Rukopisne..., 1952:33), and Protestantism gained relatively little popularity even in Croatia and Slovenia (Cambridge History..., 1963; also Južnoslovenski filolog, 1927).

The Protestants too wanted to make converts among the Serbs in the kingdom of Hungary and Croatia, but they did not succeed. In the second half of the sixteenth century, Protestants from Kranjska tried to use Cyrillic-printed Scriptures and other religious books in the Serbian language to plant Protestantism in the Sanjak of Pojega, i.e. Slavonia, and in the kingdom of Hungary too, but they did not succeed; one Protestant wrote from Hungary in 1562: Cyrillic books are not being accepted (Popović, 1992:579).

To help with the publication of Cyrillic books, Primož Trubar and Stipan Konzul Istranin called on Antun Dalmatin Aleksandrović, also a former Catholic priest, born in Sinj. Painter Jacob Salb cast the letters in Nuremberg based on their sketches.

In his search for suitable associates, Trubar succeeded in bringing two Orthodox priests to Urach – monk Matija Popović from Serbia and *uskok*[13] Jovan Maleševac from Bosnia. Maleševac is believed to be the renowned "Dijak Jovan Maleševac," who was a scribe at Trebinje between 1524 and 1546 and later worked in Montenegro at the monastery in Pljevlje. Maleševac had various ideas, and suggested

---

[13]   Irregular soldiers who fought the Ottomans (t/n).

that a book be printed for the Turkish sultan which would talk about "the real Gospel and against the Pope and Muhammad," that Cyrillic books be printed in Venice where everything needed to do this was already in place, etc.

In a quarrel that arose between Trubar and Stipan Istranin regarding the work in Urach there was later also discussion about the work of the Serbian priests. Thus in a letter to Baron Ungnad, Trubar writes: "…that they were of good service, with their books and their language…" (Medaković, 1958:233).

However, after the return of the priests to Bosnia, it was reported that Matija Popović had lost his life and that there was no trace of the other.

> And so the hopes of the reformers from Croatian and Kranj – who had had high expectations of the *uskok*, chief of which was that they would convert their fellow-countrymen, indeed the whole of Bosnia and Turkey, to the Reformation, accepting the Wittenberg "church order" – were dashed (Zbornik: Rukopisne…, 1952:66).

During the three years that this Protestant Cyrillic press was in existence, eight projects were completed. Of the Scriptures, only the New Testament was printed, and that in two parts, translated by Antun Dalmatinac and Stipan Istranin.

It is thought that they deliberately mixed dialects since the books contain synonyms printed in parallel – probably an attempt to ensure the broadest possible acceptance of the books. The strong influence of the Church Slavonic language can be felt in the Cyrillic texts.

In the second edition of the Catechesis, Trubar wrote extensively about the Orthodox liturgy, explaining how Communion was taken in both elements, emphasizing the role of the common language, and saying that there are no statues in churches, only icons and crucifixes with the image of Christ. Regarding books for the Serbs, Bulgarians, Bosnians and Croats, Trubar notes that Protestant books were needed because the earlier liturgical books had been poorly translated many years ago, so that many words found in the Gospels were incomprehensible even to the priests... (Rotar, 1983:503-525).

The Counter-Reformation which quickly followed had the aim of not only exterminating and persecuting the Protestants but also of destroying all their books by burning them. It is generally assumed that this was why these books never even reached the Serbs. Of the 10,800 Cyrillic books from Urach, less than forty copies have been preserved, amongst which there is not a single copy of *Drugi del novoga teštamenta* [Second part of the New Testament]. A single well-preserved copy of *Prvi del novoga teštamenta* [First part of the New Testament] is today kept in the library of the Serbian Orthodox Budim eparchy in Szentendre.

Count Petar Petrović[14]

In 1557, an assembly was held in Torda at which the disputing parties sought to present themselves in the best possible light before Empress Isabella in order to gain legislative backing for their theolog-

---

[14] As well as Petrović, some rare sources mention the Jakšić family of Serbian nobles, which received estates in the parish of Cluj and in Transylvania, as friends and protectors of the Protestants in their struggle against the Hungarian Catholic nobility, although this soon changed.

> All evidence points to the fact that these newcomers from Serbia initially found it hard to accustom themselves to the legal order and customs of the Hungarian nobles, who were rigidly organized into autonomous parishes. Thus in the early years, after the arrival of the Jakšić family in the kingdom of Hungary, there were frequent reports of conflicts and clashes with Hungarian nobles, towards whom the Jakšić's showed themselves remarkably bold and decisive. However, by the time of the second generation of the Jakšić family they had become accustomed to the circumstances and order of the kingdom of Hungary and had come to identify their interests with the interests of the Hungarian nobles.

ical standpoint. There is a positive note and a certain religious liberty evident in the concluding document of this council, though this was short-lived. Of particular interest to us are the activities, shortly prior to this, of the Calvinist leader Martin Kalmancsehi from Debrecen, who enjoyed the protection of the king's palatine[15] for Transylvania and his assistant Count Petar Petrović, governor of Transylvania and statesman and landowner from eastern Hungary. Kalmancsehi worked from Debrecen.

A dialog between the two Reformed camps (Lutherans and Calvinists) was held in Hungary as early as 1551, when Count Petrović was just a rich landowner from the east of the country; however, he never ceased to support Kalmancsehi. In 1558, Kalmancsehi succeeded in using his great influence to persuade the whole of Transylvania (Erdelj), excepting the Saxon Lutherans, to accept the Helvetic (Reformed) doctrine of the Lord's Supper, even though Petrović had died the previous year.

The historical records say that Count Petrović was a great friend of the Reformation. In 1554 he took over the function of protector of Transylvania on behalf of Zapolya's younger son. Since he held ultimate authority, he ensured that preachers were able to freely propagate the Reformation.

> Petrovich took away all the images from the churches, converted the monasteries into schools, removed the Popish priests from their parishes, coined the gold and silver vessels into money,[16] appropriated the Church property in the name of the State, and secured three-fourths of it for

---

For more information see Radonić, 1923:556.

[15] The palatines were the executive arm of royal rule from one annual assembly of the nobility to the next. It was their duty in the interim to implement both decisions of the assembly and royal decisions, and also to serve as mediators between the king and the nobility.

[16] The symbol of the cup featured on the flags of the Hussites and the Tavoricians in their battles with the Catholic armies. The cup represented the taking of communion under both aspects.

the salaries of the Protestant clergy. Thus was the whole of Transylvania, with the consent and co-operation of the people, freed from the jurisdiction of the Romish hierarchy, and the vast majority of its inhabitants passed over to the Protestant Confessions (Wylie, 1877:227).

Count Petar Petrović first appeared on the historical scene after the death of Jovan Nenad, on the side of Jovan Zapolya, with whom he had familial ties. In 1556, using Serbian troops, but also Turkish border vassals, he attacked the units of Emperor Ferdinand and succeeded in returning Queen Isabella to power (Ivić, 1914 and Ivić, 1929).

In October 1557, Petrović died and was replaced by Stefan Losonczy who banished many preachers including Stephen Kis from Szeged, Petrović's great friend, as well as Kis's colleagues.

The influence of Protestantism in Transylvania was felt even a century later. The Serbian Archbishop of Erdelj, Sava II (Branković), "resisted Calvinist proselytism most energetically," and because of this struggle even ended up in prison in 1680. Although he was quickly released, he died the next year (Sava, 1996:430).

Reports of Catholic Visitors

On the orders of the Congregation for the Propagation of the Faith, Catholic missionaries, led by the Jesuit Bartol Kašić, toured southern Vojvodina, Srem District and Turkish-occupied central Serbia.

The missionaries moved further towards the Drava and Baranja. They visited Calvinist settlements and had great trouble with this branch of the Protestants. Defiant and insolent, the Calvinists, with the help of the Turks, strove to hinder the work of the Catholic missionaries.

This can be seen from a later report from Don Šimun Matković, who even as a good speaker of Turkish, with much trouble and rich gifts, only just succeeded in foiling the intentions of the Calvinists (Arh. S. Congr. Scripta Varia. Decreta S. Congr. 162, p. 183-185) (Radonić, 1950:16).

In his report on the status of Catholics in this region in 1617, the Jesuit Marin de Bonis Dobrojević writes of the significant pressure exerted by the Turks on the Catholics, who were surrounded by heretics, Arians, Lutherans, Calvinists, Anabaptists, and other schismatics. Likewise, he says that Catholics, lacking in Catholic priests, would bring their children to be baptized by Protestant and Orthodox priests.

The papal visitor Petar Masarek (Draganović, 1938:1) sent a report in 1623 on his travels around the Balkans in which he noted the significant presence of Protestants in this region. Thus he says that in the south of the kingdom of Hungary, apart from the Serbian-speaking Orthodox, there were Calvinists, Lutherans, and Sabbatarians *(In Ungheria oltre li Schismatici, che parlano in Slauo, sono Caluini, Luterani et Sabbatini)*.

Masarek informs the Congregation that in the Drava Valley areas of Slavonija, a former Franciscan named Philip, is successfully at work, having cast off the cassock of his order, gotten married, and begun to spread the Calvinist doctrine. There is an interesting observation – that he was assisted in this work by a certain Đorđe Petrović, Licentiate (master of theology), who was actively at work in Sent Martin (Smicsiklasz). In the Drava Valley, there were another twenty "Illyrian villages" of the Calvinist faith. In the town of Tolna on the Danube, there were Calvinist Hungarians, as well as Serbs; as in Mohács, where there were schismatic Rascians, Calvinists, and Šokci. In the region around Baranyavár, Serbs lived alongside Turks; and in Darda, schismatic Serbs lived alongside Calvinists.

Information about Protestantism in Serbia in the Sixteenth through Eighteenth Centuries

Despite all this, there are few documents and sources dating from before the eighteenth century which talk about Protestantism in Serbia of today. German chronicler von Taube talks about this in brief terms. He writes that beginning in 1557, the Protestants crossed from Hungary (and Vojvodina) into Slavonia and that they gained so many adherents "that Reformed parishes numbered several hundred in the seventeenth century. But they disappeared again: apart from three Reformed villages in the area surrounding Osek [today Osijek in Croatia – author's note]" (Taube, 1777:59). The reasons for the crossing of Protestants into Slavonia can probably be found in the Turkish conquest of Vojvodina in the period between 1540 and 1560.

> In this period, the Turks occupied the Croatian lands from Zemun to Virovitica and Čazma... the Reformation spread, helped by the Turkish conquerors who were more tolerant towards Protestants than Catholics... (Jambrek, 1999:102).

In 1551, the Reformer Szegedi Kis István founded the oldest Reformist community in Zrenjanin, which is said to have been destroyed with the coming of the Turks (Sterlemann, 1988:38).

Vladimir Ćorović, in his *Istorija Srba* [*History of the Serbs*] comments that the Protestant movement did not, however, take root in the areas more densely populated by Serbs. "But among the people, the word 'lutor' came to denote a terrible heathen..." (Ćorović, 1999:438)

Nikola F. Pavković, speaking of the Turkish conquests and of religious shifts in the population says:

> ...and the Christians themselves were always in conflict amongst themselves: the Franciscans

against the Calvinists and Lutherans, whom
the Turks favored. In fact the Calvinists and
Lutherans were persecuted more by the Catholic
church than by the Muslims. The spread of
Protestantism, especially in Banat, was even
helped by the Turks, as well as by certain of the
Hungarian nobility who were opposed to the
Habsburg monarchy. (Pavković, 1998:230)

Other sources also talk of the tolerant attitude of the Turks
toward the Protestants in occupied territories. Thus Nikola Crnković
observes that the Turks favored the Calvinists, but that there is not
enough literature or data on how and to what extent Protestant communities survived in the wars of the sixteenth century, with all their
turmoil, mass-slaughter and exoduses. Crnković mentions that in the
regions of Bačka and Banat in the sixteenth and seventeenth centuries many congregations were "scattered" (Crnković, 1985:183).

Sterlemann merely hints at the fact that local Hungarian
Reformed fellowships east of the Tisa in Banat suffered greatly under
the persecution of the Counter-Reformation: those in Debeljača,
Novi Itebej, Velika Kikinda, Vršac, Vojlovica and another six, at the
beginning of the eighteenth century (Sterlemann, 1998:38).

In the latter half of the eighteenth century, the Serbian population in the kingdom of Hungary attended Protestant schools –
gymnasiums – in Germany and Hungary. One of those to do so was
Archimandrite Jovan Rajić.[17] The Lyceum in Pressburg (Bratislava)
enjoyed great popularity right up until the mid-nineteenth century[18].

---

[17] In Komoran he entered the Latin *gymnasium*, where the teachers were monks of
the Jesuit order, and there spent four years. In order to escape the Jesuits, who
wanted to convert him to Catholicism, he went to the Protestant *gymnasium* in
Sopron where in four years he graduated in the 'human sciences' (*čelovječlestva
nauke*). For more information see Skerlić, 1923:214.

[18] In addition to Jovan Rajić, the following were also educated at the Protestant
Lyceum in Bratislava (Pressburg, also known as Požun): Dositej Obradović,
educator and reformer; Jovan Muškatirović, the first Serbian attorney; Pavle
Kengelac, writer on world history and of the first Serbian writing in the natural
sciences; Atanasije Stojković, physicist, writer of the first book on physics in

Joakim Vujić, founder of the first Serbian theater, frequently spoke of the significance of his visit to this Lyceum (Pavlica, 2001:34). There is also a record of correspondence from that period, in 1728 and 1729, between Jovan Saski, rector of the Protestant school (the Evangelical Gymnasium) in Győr and Mojsije Petrović, Metropolitan of Belgrade. Saski wrote to the Metropolitan, informing him that he intended to write a history of the "kingdom of the Serbian lands" in Latin, and that he was seeking his assistance as he did not have the historical sources he needed. Saski established this connection via Jovan Čarnović, who was a student of metropolitan Mojsije Petrović and who went to school in Győr.

> ...he studied in Győr and at the wish of the Metropolitan, once he finished school, he was to go to the bishop's court, so that the bishops would not be compelled to take secretaries from other faiths and nationalities... But after the death of the Metropolitan Jovan shifted his interest to another area, that of the military. Whether it was at Saski's behest that he went to university in Germany, we do not know (Ruvarac, 1923:106).

---

the Serbian langage, lecturer at the University of Kharkiv; Milovan Vidaković, literary writer, author of the first novels in recent Serbian literature; Dimitrije Davidović, journalist and publicist; Teodor Pavlović, literary writer and publicist, first secretary of the Matica Srpska [the oldest cultural and academic institution in Serbia – t/n]; Jovan Sterija Popović, literary writer, lecturer at the Lyceum, founder of the Društvo Srbske Slovesnosti [Society of Serbian Letters]; Aleksa Janković, minister of education and justice in the Principality of Serbia; Đura Daničić, Serbian/Croatian philologist; Đorđe Natošević, great educational thinker; Svetozar Miletić, Serbian political leader under the Habsburg Monarchy; Jovan Đorđević, literary writer and publicist, founder of the Serbian National Theater in Novi Sad and teacher at the Belgrade High School (Velika Škola); Jovan Jovanović Zmaj, [Serbian poet]; Kosta Trifković, theater writer; Simo Popović, poet and publicist, Montenegrin duke and statesman; Jovan Grčić Milenko, poet and translator, and others. For more on this subject see Cerović, 1997.

Jovan Čarnović is later mentioned as the Oberstleutnant of the Pomoriška Krajna in 1749, and when he died in 1759 it was recorded that he had been a *"srbskog voinstva polkovnik"* [a colonel of the Serbian army].

In this period, Dositej Obradović[19] also took an interest in Protestantism and its principles relating to the use of the vernacular in church services. In 1784, in Leipzig, Germany, he translated a book by a Reformed preacher into the Serbian language and published it under the somewhat convoluted title *Slovo poučiteljno gospodina Georgija Joakima Colikofera pri reformatov obštestvu nemeckoga predikatora* [*The Instructive Word of Mr. George Joachim Zollikofer, German Preacher of the Reformed Community*] (Skerlić, 1923:274).

On the basis of the censuses of 1850 and 1857, we begin to get a better general picture of Protestant believers in the so-called Serbian Vojvodina at the beginning of the 1860s: in this region of the Austro-Hungarian Empire there were around 695,000 Catholics, 692,000 Orthodox Christians, 23,000 Jews, 27,500 Unitarians and around 60,000 Lutherans and 25,600 Calvinists.[20]

Lutherans and Evangelicals

Many Lutherans of varying nationalities in the Austro-Hungarian Empire belonged to a single church organization. However, after the First World War in the new kingdom of Serbs, Croats, and Slovenes, Lutherans became a minority that additionally faced the difficult task of uniting groups of differing origins and cultural backgrounds.

---

[19] Renowned Serbian educator and reformer.

[20] In this statistical report, published in *Stanovništvo Srbske Vojvodine...*, [Population of the Serbian Vojvodina...], 1863:104-140, the following data are given, by county: the county of Vršac - Lutherans (L) 84, Calvinists (C) 365; Lipovac L 20, C 27; Veliki Bečkerek [Zrenjanin] L 2,599, C 2,671; Novi Bečej L 60, C 14; Velika Kikinda L 129, C 21; Török Kanizsa L 33, C 88; Sombor L 3,402, C 20; Subotica L 34, C 7,380; Apatin L 42, C 8; the county of Senta had no Protestants; Kula L 15,732, C 7,312; Novi Sad L 20,187, C 3,461; Stari Bečej L 45; Palanka L 7,868, C 56; Ruma L 48, C 30; Ilok L 355, C 31.

Scattered across Vojvodina, Croatia, and northern Bosnia, Lutherans of Hungarian origin joined those of German nationality, while the Slovaks decided to continue working with them but to remain separate. For a full six years – until a law was passed officially recognizing the Lutherans – they were administrated through government decrees.

The Lutherans thus found themselves in a predominantly Slav state (which those of Slovak origin to this day call *Donja Zemlja*[21]) and since they had come from the German state church tradition, they were not interested in evangelizing. This was an obstacle to their growth in numbers. What is more, different language groups decided to remain in their own cultural surroundings, preserving their cultural and national identity. The Lutherans of these three nationalities ultimately showed a lack of interest in working together at a higher level.

The first German Protestants mostly settled in six areas of Banat – around 600 families. These colonists were established by way of Imperial Patent, of which one of the first was mentioned in a letter from Charles VI to the Count of Hessen-Darmstadt in April 1722 which lists Lutheran settlements founded by imperial decree.

German colonists continued to arrive in waves during the eighteenth and nineteenth centuries, at the invitation of multiple rulers. When the German prince Eugène of Savoy drove the Ottoman army and people out of Vojvodina and liberated Belgrade in 1717, large areas were left unpopulated. The Germans responded to the call of their prince and streamed in their thousands to the fertile plains of Vojvodina. There they raised settlements in the western areas, beside Slovaks, Serbs, and Romanians in Banat. Those who came to Banat were mostly Lutherans.[22] They built their churches and schools and developed their community life. Because they mostly came from Swabia, they earned the nickname *Švabe*[23]. According to one source,

---

[21] "the Lower Land" (t/n).
[22] Hutten, 1967:382-4. See also Vajta, 1977:70.
[23] A nickname still used pejoratively of Germans today (t/n).

the first church parish was established in 1793 in Franzfeld[24] (Saria, 1928:593). Parishes were established in Stara Pazova and Nova Pazova.

> The Danube Swabians were almost exclusively peasants. There were no real leaders among them. They played a significantly lesser role in history than, say, the Saxon Lutherans in Transylvania… These German peasants grew in the material sense for a time, but they were forgotten by their mother churches, and so they became bogged down in something we might call Christian fatalism, or to use more Christian terminology, passive submission to the will of God, coupled with the willingness to make compromises (Saria, 1928:593).

On October 13, 1781, Emperor Joseph II, son of Empress Maria Theresa, issued a decree titled the *Patent of Toleration*[25] (Britannica, 1971). As a result of this policy, Slovaks, Hungarians, Czechs and Germans emigrated to Vojvodina.

Thanks to the decisions of Joseph, as of 1787, Orthodox and Protestant believers were given the right to raise steeples and bell towers on their churches, and the following year funerals were allowed to be freely conducted according to the rites of each faith, and the doors of Orthodox and Protestant churches were permitted to face the main street.

One source says that the first church parishes were established alongside the settlements in Bojša, Bački Petrovac, and somewhat later in Srem and Banat districts, too.

In the newly established kingdom of SCS, a land ravaged by many years of war, the Lutherans sought assistance from abroad. In

---

[24] Later the town was renamed, first Banatsko Kraljićevo and then, as today, Kačarevo.

[25] Das Toleranzpatent Joseph II, see excerpt from text included here.

1919, the US National Lutheran Council began sending help, especially in the distribution of Scriptures, hymnbooks, and catechisms. In this new land the Lutherans lacked any rigid structure or contact with the earlier leadership.

> They tried initially to establish a kind of church union, which was meant to be joined, in addition to the Evangelicals of the Augsburg Confession (Lutherans), by Evangelicals of the Helvetic Confession (Calvinists or Reformers) and the Methodists. This attempt fell at the first hurdle, as it were, primarily due to language differences but also theological ones. Only Evangelicals of the Augsburg Confession (Lutherans) used four languages in their church services (Slovak, German, Slovene and Hungarian). The Reformers were Hungarian and German in nationality, while the Methodists were mostly Macedonians (Slovačka evangelička..., 1980:27).

Collaboration on the part of some German Lutherans with the Nazi regime during the Second World War, and the very fact of their German nationality, led to the halving of the membership of this church immediately after the Second World War.

According to the statistics of the Lutheran World Federation, there are around 48,500 members, including the family of baptized members. Viewed in historical terms, the Lutherans are the largest Protestant group ever to exist in the region of modern-day Serbia.

Reformers and Calvinists

There were members of Reformed churches among Germans and Hungarians who settled in Vojvodina following Joseph II's *Patent of Toleration*. During the reign of the Austro-Hungarian Empire in this region, they were members of the Hungarian Reformed Church, which was based in Budapest. One author, not naming any specific source, states that the first Lutheran parish existed as early as 1745 in Bački Petrovac and that Calvinism (Reformed Christianity) was observed among the Hungarians in the same period (Branković, 1996:117). This claim does not match the general facts known about the first Lutheran and other Protestant parishes in Vojvodina, of which the earliest is dated to 1793. Bogdan Saria, in the earlier-cited article on Protestant churches from the *Narodna enciklopedija*, mentions an even earlier date, 1733, but gives no further information than this.

In the early twentieth century, the kingdom of Serbia recognized the Calvinist (Reformed) Church in addition to the Orthodox, Roman Catholic and Lutheran.

Immediately after the first World War, the branch affiliated with the Hungarian church was forced to reorganize itself since it no longer belonged to the Budapest Seniorat. This was how the Reformed Church came about in the kingdom of SCS, comprised of Hungarians, Germans, and other immigrants to the new state. In 1930, the state published a law on relations with Protestant religious communities, which included the Reformed Church, and so ties were somewhat improved.

As of 1968, the so-called *Savez Protestantskih Crkava* [Union of Protestant Churches] became active in Yugoslavia, established in Novi Sad in the Slovak Evangelical Center. The only members were the Lutheran and the Calvinist churches, while the other smaller Protestant and Evangelical fellowships did not join this organization.

> The close collaboration between the Evangelical Lutheran and Reformed churches was sealed in 1968 with the establishment of the Union of Protestant Churches in Novi Sad, which was joined by these two Churches. The free Protestant churches did not enter this union, since to their way of thinking a Council of Protestant Churches would have been more suitable than a Union (Horak, 1970:131).

In 1999, the Reformed Church in Serbia had nineteen congregations with more than 16,000 members (although this figure probably includes both church members and their families). In the year 2001, figures indicate that the Reformed Church had 17,000 members in fifteen church fellowships, with thirteen priests and twenty-four preaching stations. There is also mention of the fact that this church is a member of the Ecumenical Council in Yugoslavia, and that the Hungarian, German, and Czech languages are used in its church services.

They published the magazine *Református Élet* and the annual *Reformatus Évkönyv*. The seat of the church – the bishopric – is currently in Feketić, and is determined according to the location of the chosen bishop; bishops are elected for a six-year term of office. Feketić is also home to the Leuenberger (ecumenical) Center for promoting better relations amongst Protestant churches. There are representatives of the Lutherans and of the Methodists on its board. The Reformers maintained international relations on many levels with fraternal churches in Germany and Hungary, as well as with the European Conference of Reformed Churches, the Basel Mission, and others.

Methodists

During the 1990s, the Methodist Church was involved in ecumenical prayers for peace held in Novi Sad throughout the years of armed conflict. In 1999, the Ecumenical Humanitarian Organization – EHO – was re-established after several years' break due to great opposition to their activities from the Serbian Orthodox Church in the mid-1990s.

In Vojvodina today, the Methodists have fourteen local churches with around 1,000 members (Miz, 2002:30). They trained their priests at the Baptist School (BBC Logos) in Novi Sad, in Austria, in Banjska Bistrica in Slovakia, and at the Hussite Theological Faculty in Prague. Today the Methodists publish a Slovak-language magazine *Put Života* [*Way of Life*], and a Serbian-language one called *Glas*

Jevandelja [*Voice of the Gospel*], which has been published since 1962, initially under the title *Crkvene Vesti* [*Church News*] and as of 1966 under the current name.

Methodists began their work in Serbia in 1898 among the German population. To begin with, their services were hindered or prohibited by the gendarmes. A 1904 report mentions seven mission stations, fifteen full-fledged members, sixty-one candidates and seventy-one new candidates. The first Methodist church was founded in Vrbas in 1904. The same year the Methodists also began work among the Hungarians.

In 1925, the Yugoslav government banned the Methodists from operating, but they were not in any case a recognized church. This situation gave cause for the Methodist Bishop for Europe, Nelsen, to appeal to the American government on behalf of the Yugoslav Methodists. The American government contacted that of Yugoslavia, alleviating the situation in Vojvodina, where local governments received instructions to take a more tolerant attitude towards the work of the American Methodist mission.

The Methodists were also instrumental in the distribution of Scriptures. In 1934, it was recorded that 34,000 Bibles were distributed across Yugoslavia in partnership with the Bible Society. There was cooperation with other denominations, too.

Before the second World War, the Methodists in Yugoslavia were known for their social involvement. In Novi Sad, they owned a hospital called Betanija (the maternity ward is still known by that name today), and there was a nursing home, too. Before the hospital was founded in 1924, the building housed a school and boarding facility for girls called the *Devojački Institut* [Girls' Institute]. It was owned and run by the Methodists (modeled on similar institutions in Macedonia). Teaching was structured according to the recommendations of the Ministry of Education, and the teachers were state employees and local officials. In Srbobran, the Methodists had an orphanage which the state expropriated after the Second World War.

In 1959, the Methodists had around forty preachers – laymen and priests, two deaconesses and eleven places of worship, although ministry was also conducted in mission stations. There were around

3,000 baptized members, with Sunday School attended by 400 children.

Baptists

The first Baptists in modern Serbia were probably a Hungarian husband and wife from Novi Sad, Franz Tabory and his wife Mária, who were baptized in Bucharest in 1862 by a German preacher.[26] In order to continue their missionary efforts, in 1869,[27] the Hamburg Baptists planned to send Heinrich Meyer, a German originating from the kingdom of Hungary, to serve as a pioneer of the Baptist work in Odessa, Ukraine. However, he somehow came into contact with Edward Millard of the Bible Society in Vienna, who offered him the job of Bible colporteur in Zagreb, which he accepted.

The next year, Meyer moved to Budapest where he successfully led the local Baptist church. One visitor to the church, who later returned to Novi Sad, was Adolf Hempt. He began holding meetings with a handful of former Nazarenes in Novi Sad, and in 1875 invited Meyer to come from Budapest and baptize a group of five people – or rather six, including him. Later another twenty people were baptized.

---

[26] At that time Scharschmidt was active in Bucharest, having moved there back in 1856. Ruben Knežević states that they were baptized by Heinrich Koch – see in Knežević, 2001:34.

[27] An anniversary was celebrated in relation to this year which, it seems, was held to mark the first Baptist baptism in the territory of then-Yugoslavia. At the end of January 1969, a meeting of preachers was held in Novi Sad to mark the occasion of the hundredth anniversary of the first baptism. Those present at the gathering submitted reports on their work and exchanged experiences, as reported on in a confidential report by the Provincial Committee for Relations with Religious Communities of 2 March 1969. The list of church parishes indicates that in 1969 the Baptists had 66 local fellowships in Vojvodina, and 27 pastors and preachers. According to the report in the document: Miloš Lisulov, "Babtistička crkva", Novi Sad, 3.2.1969, four pages, with annex "Popis crkvenih opština Saveza babtističkih crkava na teritoriji AP Vojvodine i odgovornih lica" [Census of church parishes of the Union of Baptist Churches in the territory of the Autonomous Province of Vojvodina, and responsible persons], on type-writer, Arhiv Vojvodine, F198 I kutija 880, arh. broj 26/1969.

This was how the first Baptist church in Serbia was established, initially as a mission station of the Budapest church.

At the first Baptist World Congress, held in 1905 in London, the report on the south of the kingdom of Hungary (Vojvodina) talks of nine Baptist churches with around a hundred believers, which meant a small number of believers in each church, and this is the first official mention of the Baptists in our region.

After the First World War ended, the Baptist movement was revitalized. In 1920, there were around seventy smaller Baptist groups with around 700 believers and around 400 Sunday School attendees, and another 100 members of youth groups (Klem, 1952:87) – this data refers to the whole of then-Yugoslavia. The work of the Baptists was reinforced by the arrival of the so-called Southern Baptists from the US and by the ongoing work of the German Baptist Mission.

The Vidovdan Constitution of June 1921 recognized the existence of the Baptists as a faith carried over from the former territories[28], and the Oktroisan Constitution (also known as the Imposed, or September Constitution) of 1931 formally allowed freedom of conscience and confession[29], but only to recognized and accepted religious communities.

In February 1991 in Belgrade, a meeting was held of the Executive Committee of the Baptist Union at which a decision was taken to dissolve the existing Yugoslav Union. The Baptists subsequently split internally, probably due to existing divisions that owing to current political, events rose to the surface again. However, this process was completed amicably. At the height of the painful events surrounding the disintegration of the former Yugoslavia, the leadership of the Union of Baptist Churches in Serbia called on its membership not to be drawn into the jingoist frenzy and to preserve multi-ethnicity, in which the Baptists in Serbia entirely succeeded during the war years.

---

[28] In Article 12, Ustav Kraljevine Srba…, 1921:4.
[29] In Article 11, Ustav Kraljevine Jugoslavije, 1931:5.

Adventists

The earliest reports from the Balkans talk of Adventist "witnesses" in the Turkish province (*vilayet*) of Monastir[30] in Macedonia as early as 1882.[31] However the first Seventh-Day Adventists (SDA) in the territory of modern Serbia (in Vojvodina) appeared around 1890.[32]

The first Adventist to preach in the Serbian language is thought to have been Petar Todor, in 1901. He gathered together a small group of believers in Kuman (eastern Vojvodina) and Lazar Eremić became elder of that church soon after. Eremić had been visited in 1900 by a missionary in response to letters Eremić had sent to Hamburg.

The rapid growth of the Adventist movement led in 1925 to the establishment of Conferences, the units into which the SDA churches were organized. This structure was extended with regions and mission fields in line with plans and with the geographical spread of missionary activity. In 1931, the Southern Division of the church was established, which covered central Serbia, Kosovo, and Macedonia. That year the headquarters of the Union were relocated from Novi Sad to Belgrade, as was the Preporod publishing house (Grulich, 1983:5). Another significant development at that time was the 1934 founding of the seminary in Belgrade, on Rankeova street, where candidates for the pastorate were trained, as well as future lay-preachers.

---

[30] Today this is Bitola, with surrounding area.

[31] Austrian Andres Zeefried (other sources say Seefried), colporteur of the British and Foreign Bible Society, was arrested and imprisoned in Skopje. There he witnessed to another prisoner, an Albanian, who after six weeks of Bible study accepted Christ and became the first Adventist disciple in the Balkans. For more details see Šušljić, 1980:12-19.

[32] Cvitković, 1989:214. This year, 1890, is also given by Šušljić in an earlier work, but only for the area of central Serbia, while for Vojvodina he gives the year 1893. See Šušljić, 1981:39-54.

In 1963, the Adventists had almost 3,000 believers in Vojvodina, and another 2,900 or so in central Serbia. The number of Adventists grew in the towns of Smederevo, Svilajnac, Paraćin, and other towns.[33]

The breakup of Yugoslavia required the Adventists in the Federal Republic of Yugoslavia to open a Theological Faculty in 1993, with boarding facilities, and the South-East European Union was founded, based in Belgrade and territorially covering the North Conference (Vojvodina), the South Conference in Niš, the South-West Conference (Banja Luka) and the Macedonian Mission. At the end of the 1990s, it numbered around 6,600 baptized believers. This administrative structure remains in place today, although it is believed the Adventists now number more than 10,000 members. If family members of baptized Adventists were included the number would probably be four times greater. Their official name today is *Hrišćanska Adventistička Crkva* [Christian Adventist Church].

Brethren Church and Church of Christ Brethren

Brethren churches[34] emerged in Serbia at the beginning of the twentieth century when missionaries from Great Britain and Slovakia came to Vojvodina and began missionary work in the Slovak ethnic community. Today the majority of Brethren church believers are Slovaks, and almost all are in Vojvodina, although they also have

---

[33] Bishop Hrizostom of the Serbian Orthodox Church said in 1965 that in his eparchy there were three hundred Adventists "but from their noise you would think there were thousands of them... Fortunately our soil is rather hard to teaching of that kind, and to the abstinence from drink and the avoidance of pork that the Adventists require of their members. Otherwise, considering their zeal, there is no telling what might happen," (cited in Žujović, 1990:98).

[34] Their official name today is Hristova Crkva Braće [Church of Christ Brethren], but until 1941 they were known as Slobodna Braća [Free Brethren]. The 1993 edition of *Operation World* calls them Christian Brethren, while Samardžić (1981:43) calls them the Church of Brethren in Christ. One document in the Federal Republic of Yugoslavia Archive (fond 14, fas. 3, jedinica 10) from May 1940 talks of the Hrišcanska Zajednica Slobodne Braće [Christian Fellowship of Free Brethren].

a small fellowship in Belgrade. According to figures, in 1999 there were 450 believers in around thirteen churches.[35]

The Brethren are a denomination in numerical decline in Serbia. From the very beginning, their work and their efforts have been oriented toward the Slovak ethnic minority in Serbia/Vojvodina. Their missionaries and representatives knew the language and manuals were already available in Slovak/Czech. Attempts to broaden its base among the Serb and Croat population in the 1930s in Novi Sad were interrupted by the outbreak of war.

Brethren fellowships did not grow at the same rate as other Protestant and Evangelical churches in the same region and in the same time period. One probable cause is the orientation toward only a single ethnic group, and a minority one in the province at that.[36] In 1992, a small mission station was established in Montenegro, in Podgorica ("among the Montenegrins").[37]

In the mid-1990s, the Brethren Church had a hand in the establishment of the Christian Evangelistic Center (KES) in Bački Petrovac, which was to play an important role towards the end of the twentieth century. It ran publishing activities and a one-year boarding Bible school, organized humanitarian work during the war years, held many conferences and youth meetings and housed a music

---

[35] Miroslav Čizmanski, email to author, Bački Petrovac, April 1999.

[36] There are insufficiently reliable data on the emergence and growth of the Hrišćanska Crkva Jevanđeoske Braće [Christian Evangelical Brethren Church] as a parallel Brethren church organization for non-Slovaks in the former Yugoslavia. They appear in sources relating to their membership of and subsequent withdrawal from the Pentecostal Union 1962-1964, but this was probably only the case with the church in Rijeka. However during the 1970s they had one fellowship in Pančevo with twenty-seven believers and were registered in Pančevo from 1972 until 1974, when they unregistered "until new premises were found." This group also had a fellowship in Belgrade.

[37] O.M.E.F.I. (the Italian Brethren Mission Agency), in its second news bulletin in fall of 1997, says that Vladimir and Marijana Čizmanski had begun a work in Podgorica, Montenegro, and that they had six believers at the time. More recent reports say that work has been established in Herceg Novi, Kamenari and other towns. Today the Christian Brethren Church in Podgorica numbers around thirty members.

recording studio. It also recorded radio programs in Serbian[38] and Slovak and broadcasted them on a local FM station and via TWR (formerly Trans World Radio) medium-wave transmitters, published Bible literature, and more besides.

According to available information from 2003, there are Brethren churches (fellowships) in the following towns and cities in Serbia: Bački Petrovac, Subotica, Novi Sad, Kisač, Kulpin, Stara Pazova, Beograd, Ilok, Jabuka, Kovačica, Padina, and Sremska Mitrovica.

Pentecostals

Several sources agree that the first meetings were held in Beška[39] around 1906[40], by members of the German Reformed church, and that the first preacher of the new faith to be appointed was Nikola Knizl, who brought the teaching from a trip around Germany.[41]

---

[38] Producer of many programs was Vladimir Čizmanski from Bački Petrovac, and one of the authors was Jarko Jurik, then pastor of the Yugoslav Church in Vienna. When the Ikonos Christian society was founded in Belgrade in 2000, the production of Serbian-language programs was relocated.

[39] Cvitković (1989:223) talks of Subotica as the place where they first gathered, but gives no other details.

[40] Although the exact year in which the first meetings of the *duhovnjaci* ["spirit believers"] began in Beška is not of fundamental importance, the range between 1905 and 1907 can be found in the literature. The most recent date (1907) is given by Dr. Stanko Jambrek in his article "Pentekostni pokret u Hrvatskoj 1907-2007" ["The Pentecostal Movement in Croatia 1907-2007"], *Kairos*, 2/2007, Zagreb, page 237. In the same issue of the journal *Kairos*, just a few pages earlier (226), Franc Kuzmić talks of 1906. Josip Sabo in his first *Okružnica* [*Circular*] of 1960 also gives 1906. Ullen in the interview mentioned a little later cites 1905 as the year, and so on. Since all the sources rely on oral tradition the discrepancies are understandable.

[41] Meetings were held sporadically and later registered with the authorities as meetings of the Blue Cross (Modri Križ), since it was at this time that Dr. Rohaček (from the Czech and Slovak lands of Austrohungary) began his visits and meetings of this organization, visiting regularly from Kisač where he had moved to. It is possible that members of both of these groups really did belong to both fellowships, at least at the beginning, although the connection between

Further evidence of this is found in the first circular letter of the Union of Christ's Churches from 1960. Here there is mention of a Benjamin Schilling and a Pastor Schell who visited from Germany. Ludwig Ullen, as the president of the Union of Pentecostal Churches in Yugoslavia, stated in 1968: "Actually, the first services were held in 1905. A brother by the name of Schell came from Germany to northern Serbia. Some people were saved and baptized in the Holy Spirit and the group increased…" (Williscroft, 1968:16).

The meetings held by the "Stundists"[42] were increasingly visited by evangelists coming from Germany, bringing the "new teaching." Josip Sabo states that this church in Beška, after the first World War, numbered around 400 members, and it was then that the first church building was constructed (Sabo, 1960:5). The teaching continued to spread, and Sabo says that after World War I, fellowships were established in Zemun, Belgrade, Vrdnik, Dobanovci, Brestač, and finally in 1936, Subotica. During the 1920s and 1930s, Beška was the center of the "*duhovne zajednice*" [spiritual congregations], as the Pentecostal churches were then referred to. Annual meetings were also held in Beška.

One of the earlier reports, which was published in the Swedish Pentecostal periodical *Evangelii Härold* in 1923, mentions that Georg Steen visited Yugoslavia – specifically Vojvodina and Belgrade. He tells of how he found some Pentecostal churches and says that the majority of believers were of German origin, although he also met Hungarians, Croats, and Serbs. Some of the fellowships were already fifteen years old (meaning that they had been established in 1907-1908). While they had had problems during the war, they had sta-

---

the German Reformers and the Slovak Lutherans is unclear, given that they spoke different languages, even if in the Austro-Hungarian Empire they were registered with the authorities within the same church union.

[42] The expression came from the German word *Stunde*, meaning "hour" or "lesson," and referred to the practice of meeting for prayer, Bible study or corporate singing, as spiritual disciplines which these believers practiced outside of and in addition to the activities organized by the local church. These "hours" were mostly organized in people's houses, independently.

bilized after 1918 and taken in new believers; but their fundamental problem was the lack of leaders.

The practice of only baptizing adults was established in the 1930s, which led to the further separation of several existing Pentecostal churches, which in any case lacked a hierarchical structure or a national leadership (at the Yugoslav level).

In the early 1990s, neo-Pentecostal (Charismatic) churches also began work in Serbia, the first among them probably the Golgota Christian Church[43] via missionaries in Subotica who first came in 1989, holding evangelistic events in town squares and parks. The beginning of their movement is formally taken to be 1993, when they bought a place of worship in Subotica. The Zajednica Vere[44] from Hungary, one of the largest churches in Europe, began its activities in Subotica and later Bačka Topola and the surrounding area in 1995. During the 1990s, the Raskršće [Crossroads] rehabilitation center for addicts[45] began its ministry, later founding a local church, *Crkva Hrista Spasitelja* [Church of Christ the Savior].

Hristove Pentekostne Crkve [Christ's Pentecostal Churches] in Serbia changed their name in 1998 to *Protestantske Evanđeoske Crkve* (PEC) [Protestant Evangelical Churches] having faced huge pressure in the form of denouncements by nationalist and threats and an organized media offensive[46]. The new name was convenient for the purposes of unification and consolidation, in view of the fact that different local churches had had various different names (Evangelical Church, HPC [Christ's Pentecostal Church], KDJC [Christ Spiritual Evangelical Church] and others).

---

[43] The Serbian name for Calvary Chapel.

[44] Hungarian: Hit Gyülekezete [Faith Church]. Up until 2005 they existed as *Udruženje građana za zaštitu zdravlja, porodice i omladine "Trezven život"* [The Sober Life Association for the Protection of Health, the Family and Youth].

[45] The Serbian affiliate of the Teen Challenge organization. It was founded by Saša and Svetlana Ivanović and more can be read about the beginnings of their ministry in the autobiography of Svetlana Ivanović, *Pierced* [Serbian title: *Transfixa*].

[46] For more on the media offensive against Evangelical Christians in the period 1995-2001 in Serbia, see the book *Udar na verske slobode* [Assault on Religious Freedoms].

Today it is estimated that there are more than a thousand believers in the Pentecostal congregations in Serbia following the "Only Jesus" doctrine and around 6,000-7,000 (Trinitarian) Pentecostal believers of all fellowships, unions and language groups[47].

In place of a conclusion

In the church and state archives of central Europe, in the Vatican archives, as well as in the published literature, one can still find unknown and/or little-known details and materials on the interesting subject of early Protestantism in this region. An academic and systematic approach to the materials could significantly contribute to the illumination of this little-researched subject and help to correct the entrenched understanding of the Reformation as a Western novelty in these parts.

Existing sources and materials can be divided into two groups: those shedding light on pre-Reformation events, and those that speak of the emergence, arrival, and settlement of Protestants from the sixteenth century onward. In the nineteenth century, other Protestant groups emerged, who began ministries with a greater or lesser degree of success; however, this was primarily among minority groups: the Podunavlje Germans, Slovaks, Hungarians, Romanians, etc.

It was in these circumstances, in the mid-nineteenth century, that the Nazarene movement arose, "the first new religious movement or sect to emerge in the kingdom of Hungary after the sixteenth century" (Aleksov, 2010:11).

---

[47] Serbian, Hungarian, Slovak, Romanian, Roma etc.

PATENT OF TOLERATION of Joseph II
13th October 1781
(portions)
To all Imperial and Royal Governments.

My dear Lieges!

Being convinced, on the one hand, that all violence to conscience is harmful, and, on the other, of the great benefit accruing
to religion and to the State from a true Christian tolerance, We have
found Ourselves moved to grant to the adherents of the Lutheran
and Calvinist religions, and also to the non-Uniate Greek religion,
everywhere, the appropriate private practice of their faith, regardless
of whether it had been previously customary or introduced, or not.

The Catholic religion alone shall continue to enjoy the prerog-
ative of the public practice of its faith... We allow:

Firstly, non-Catholic subjects, where there are one hundred
families, even if they are not all domiciled in the locality of the place
of worship or of the pastor, but part of them live as much as some
hours' distance away, to build a place of worship and school of their
own...to administer their sacraments and celebrate Divine service,
both in the place itself and conveyed to the sick in the Chapels of
Ease, and to conduct funerals with their pastor in attendance...but
may not, under pain of severest punishment, prevent a Catholic
priest from being called in, if any sick person wishes it.

In respect to the place of worship, We order expressly that it
shall not have any chimes, bells, or towers, unless such already exist,
or public entrance from the street signifying a church, but otherwise
they are free to build it of whatever material they will and shall be
completely free...

Where the father is a Catholic, all children, of either sex, are
to be brought up without question in the Catholic religion...where,
however, the father is Protestant and the mother Catholic, the sex of
the child shall decide.

The sole criteria in all choices or appointments to official posts
are — as has long been the case in Our army — to be the candidate's
integrity and competence. Priests are enjoined to conduct their offi-

cial duties faithfully, to entirely shun quarrels in their religious affairs, no matter the cause, and also always to conduct themselves with true forbearance, kindly and in love, towards those who have strayed, to refrain at all times from all unseemly words or curses directed against their religious opponents; what is more, they should endeavor, as indeed befits the duties of pious priests, to strengthen their parish with true faith, in which alone is salvation, or to bring back those who have strayed… (Srkulj, 1913:84) [48]

---

[48] It should be noted that Srkulj appears to have diverged from the original text. The source of the last paragraph in particular is uncertain. The full text of the Patent in German can be found here – http://germanhistorydocs.ghi-dc.org/ sub_document.cfm?document_id=3643.

THE CHRISTIAN NAZARENE COMMUNITY

Although Lutherans and Reformers were the first Protestant groups to emerge in the territory of what is today Serbia (for the most part as settlers back in the eighteenth century), ethnically they were largely German, Czech, Slovak, and Hungarian, with only occasional, individual adherents from among the South Slav peoples.

Nazarenes were the first Protestant group to amass a significant number of followers from among the Serbian population, as well as the Hungarian, Romanian, and German populations too, first in the southern kingdom of Hungary of the time and soon after in Central Serbia. Regarding the reasons for their arrival and spread, Aleksandar Birviš says the following,

> The railway brought new Roman Catholics to Obrenović-ruled Serbia, as well as the hitherto little-known Lutherans, somewhat fewer Calvinists and, later, members of free churches. Alongside the aforementioned influences grew – and also, over time, waned – the influence of the Nazarenes. They were a unique product of Vojvodina. Their emergence was aided by two factors: firstly the anti-feudal Hungarian revolt of 1848, when Serbian peasants in Vojvodina lost faith in their traditional church due to its loyalty to Vienna, and secondly the publication of Vuk's translation of the New Testament (in 1848), which made it possible for any literate Serb to

understand the teachings of Christ without an intermediary... (Birviš, 2001:101).

Nazarenes were among the most numerous users of the services and publications of the Bible Society in Central Serbia and Vojvodina. Dr. Peter Kuzmič has the following to say on this:

> A unique phenomenon connected with the activities of the Bible Society in our country comes in the shape of the Nazarenes. Reports written by the agents, depositaries and colporteurs of the Society show that of all the religious groups in this region they were most accepting, indeed supportive of the work of the Society. (Kuzmič, 1983:225).[49]

---

[49] Also of interest with regard to this claim is the observation of Dr. Slijepčević, who says that in the new Bible Society editions for 1902 there are visible changes "in view of the fact that the Holy Scriptures are usually to be found in the hands of Nazarenes." Thus, instead of the word *hram* [temple] the word *zbornica* [meeting-place] is used; instead of the word *sveštenik* [priest] *poglavica* [head/leader] is used; instead of *krštenje* [baptism/christening] *umivanje* [washing] is used, and so on (Slijepčević, 1943:56). Slijepčević was of the belief that the practice of "hawking" Scriptures, coupled with these changes to the text, was evidence that the Bible Society was actively promoting the Nazarene movement. This claim was not further investigated but is an interesting one. In his work on the Modri Križ (Blue Cross) abstinence movement, Methodist pastor Jano Sjanta writes of the positive influence colporteurs had on the development of the Blue Cross:

> A major contribution to the distribution of Bibles in Serbia and in the whole of the old Yugoslavia was made by colporteurs. Every colporteur was in touch with the Bible Society, which supplied him with Bibles. He would take these and sell them in all corners of the country... The colporteur would take a full load of books in a leather bag on his back, specially made for colporteurs, and another case of Bibles or other books in each hand. They traveled mostly on foot, from village to village, house to house... (Sjanta, 1987:47).

THE BELIEVERS IN CHRIST

In his study of the Nazarenes in Serbia, Dr. Slijepčević talks about the reasons for the emergence and rapid growth of the Nazarene movement in the princedom and subsequently kingdom of Serbia.

> The excessive bureaucratization of the Serbian Orthodox Church, which came about as a result of its fundamental disengagement from the people and transition into an institution which had its authentic religious passion and awareness of the need for spiritual missionary action stifled by administrative considerations, resulted in both the higher and lower ranks of the priesthood coming to resemble officials more than pastors. Overwhelmed with materialist and atheist propaganda, scandalized by the pastoral negligence of the priesthood and the harmful political wrangling that went on among the higher echelons of the Church hierarchy and the political representatives of the nation, ordinary people turned elsewhere for true spiritual comfort (Slijepčević, 1943:5).

In the late nineteenth century, the Nazarenes were a dominant, authentic, and autonomous Protestant movement, the reverberations of which were felt from the Russian steppe in the east to Alsace in France, even reaching the flatlands of the American Midwest. Today they are known as *Hrišćanska Nazarenska Zajednica* [Christian Nazarene Community], which is their official name in Serbia, although they are also popularly known by other names.[50] Several

---

[50] *Novoverci* ('the new believers'), *nazareni, nazarenci, "lazareni," pokajnici* ('the penitents'), *bugeri, novonazareni* ('new Nazarenes'), *verujući u Hrista* ('believers in Christ'), *sledbenici Hristovi* ('followers of Christ'), *Naslednici Hristovi* ('heirs of Christ'). It is thought that they got their name from the New Testament verse that says "He shall be called a Nazarene." Nazarenes should not be confused with the group from the United States called the Church of the Nazarene, which was established in 1895 in California as a branch of the Methodist Holiness

recently published books and articles have only guessed at their current numbers[51], which is partly due to their traditional policy of isolation, and partly due to the lack of a centralized administration that might collect and keep such data. This is also testament to the fundamental lack of interest on the part of the Serbian authorities (in all periods) in learning more about this religious community. And the story of the Nazarenes is essentially a story of persecution and of the government's fear of its own well-intentioned, humble, and peaceful

---

movement and belongs to the so-called Wesleyan denominations. This group later joined with at least two other movements and has gone by this name since 1919.

[51] David Steele (Steele, 1995:24-40), talks of there only being four Nazarene churches with around 440 members. John Lehn in his 1996 report, prepared as part of his master's thesis (manuscript in possession of this author), records the existence of only two Nazarene fellowships with not more than 200 members. Tomislav Branković, advisor in the Serbian Ministry of Religion, in his book *Sekte i Politika* [*Sects and Politics*], published in 2000, says there are no more than 500, although in the book *Protestantske Zajednice u Jugoslaviji* [*Protestant Churches in Yugoslavia*] published in 2006, he says that at the time of the breakup of Yugoslavia in the early 1990s, there were around 3,000. Dr. Zorica Kuburić in her article "*Konfesije*" ["Confessions"] in the journal *Context*, January-June issue, 2001, talks of 680 Nazarenes in five churches, and a wider community of 1,700 people. In a conversation with Pavle Božić, a member of the Nazarene community in Stari Banovci, conducted in Amsterdam 24 July 1999, I arrived at a figure of 1,500, possibly even 2,000 members. As of 1992, when alternative civilian service was introduced in lieu of military service, Nazarenes were no longer divided in terms of their acceptance or refusal of military service, which had been a major issue among them in previous times, and thus this reason ceased to have significance in terms of an individual's expression of affiliation to the community. Pavle Božić served multiple one-year prison sentences for his refusal to bear or use arms on the grounds of his religious convictions – the last time in 1998. In late 1999, I was told by Harold Otto that there were still two groups of Nazarenes in Vojvodina with around 2,000 members each (email, 13 July 1999). We can probably say with some certainty that there are at most 3,000 Nazarenes in Serbia today, in view of Pavle Božić's comment to me that there are still around 1,000 of the "tolerant" and around 1,500-2,000 of the "reactionaries" to which he belonged. Conversation with Pavle Božić 25 July 1999.

citizens.[52] It is increasingly becoming apparent that the Nazarenes were not persecuted primarily for their faith and their conscientious objection, but for their considerable early potential for expansion and growth, as they attracted a great many people with their ideas and their way of life.

In the mid-1990s in Hungary, there were around thirty-eight fellowships with some 2,100 members; in Romania there were also thirty-eight fellowships with 1,200 members and 200 friends; in Slovakia there were around 120 believers and in Ukraine there were around 500 believers in only two fellowships, although these were showing significant growth. In addition to Switzerland, the movement's followers have churches in the USA, the Apostolic Christian Churches.[53]

The Christian Nazarene religious community in Serbia is headquartered in Novi Sad at No. 12, Valentina Vodnika Street. Its legal agent is Karlo Hrubik the younger. In the 2002 population census, 1,426 people declared themselves as members of the Christian Nazarene community (Kuburić, 2011:196).

Beginnings in Switzerland

Samuel Heinrich Froehlich (or Fröhlich)[54] was born in Brugg in Switzerland and was a priest of the state Swiss Reformed Church in his canton. When he opposed the practice of infant baptism, he was ordered to resign and in 1830, was banned from serving as a minister[55]. Froehlich believed that a person had to believe before being

---

[52] Fear tends to overstatement: Politika, 18 February 1925, wrote that entire Serbian villages were joining the Nazarenes and Adventists and that their total number had already reached 150,000 people (Aleksov, 1999:3).

[53] According to data given in the introductory and concluding notes of Karoly Eotvos's book (Eotvos, 1997). For more on the ACC see Mead (1988:30), Mayer (1958:339) and Clark (1949:70).

[54] He lived from 1803 to 1857.

[55] For more information see Cvitković (1989:222).

baptized, and so opposed the practice of the state Protestant church, which baptized children, too.

He arrived at this stance after his conversion in 1828 under the influence of the Hernhutters, that is the Brethren, although he mentions a similar event from 1825 in his autobiography. Similar doctrine was also held to in Switzerland by the Anabaptists, the Heimberg Brethren, the Exclusive Brethren also known as Darbists, and others. Beginning in 1832, Froelich worked with the British Continental Baptist mission, having been baptized in 1831 as an adult, now fully convinced of the rightness of the doctrine of solely adult baptism.[56] However he was forced to end this association after a few years as the mission got into financial difficulties. Despite this, the 1836 annual mission report spoke of fourteen churches founded and 427 members. Other believers who took his teaching on board mostly remained in their old fellowships but were accorded the prefix "new" – and the state soon began to pay closer attention to this new movement.

In the period following 1835, the movement began to grow and amass numbers in the hundreds. Local sources say that Froehlich was very successful as a preacher, that healings occurred by faith and that the prayers were "mighty" (Bächtold, 1970:31). Froehlich later published a book which later became of great value to his movement, not only in Switzerland but later in Hungary, too, titled *On the Relationship between the Believer and the State Church*. The year 1837 saw the publication of the first issue of *Zions-Harfe* [*Zion's Harp*], the immensely popular Nazarene hymnbook, which he compiled from selected songs used by the Baptists, the Reformed Church, and even the Lutherans. Froehlich it seems continued his contacts with the Baptists, since from notes in his diary for 1840-1841, he talks about how he met back in 1839 with Gerhard Oncken, an acquaintance from his days in the Continental mission.

---

[56] Njistor has this to say:

> He abandoned the Calvinist faith...he quickly gathered a number of believers to himself and re-baptized them collectively, but not by immersion. However, when he later met Baptists from Germany he received baptism by total immersion from them... (Njistor, 1940:10).

State Investigation into the New Baptists in 1843

In late 1843, the Church Council of Zurich Canton sent an extensive questionnaire out to all local church bodies in an attempt to determine the scope, presence, and significance of the new movement, then referred to as the New Baptists. The responses collected give us a clearer insight into the Nazarenes of the period in Switzerland.

It was determined that the New Baptists had gained their popularity thanks to Froehlich's activities in the region, especially in the higher regions of the canton, in the districts of Uster and Pfäffikon, as well as around Lake Zurich. The report talks of 540 members in the larger towns and of "many places with a few believers in each" (Ruegger, 1985:63-70). The report further talks of the existence of at least two dozen Baptist churches in which New Baptists comprised the majority of the members, and of how they were for the most part the poorest and most modest members. It was further determined that the New Baptists had no sacred writings, religious, or confessional, other than Holy Scripture. They met together in municipal council chambers on weekday evenings and on Sundays, and at their meetings used the hymnbook *Christliche Harmonika* [*The Christian Harmonica*], which was published in Kassel, Germany, in 1838, as well as *Zion's Harp* – and sometimes both. Local members, and sometimes guests from other fellowships, ministered "from the Word" (the Scriptures) and prayers were spoken "from the heart." According to one of the reports, some groups had contacts with the Anabaptists in Alsace, France. Guest preachers would visit from other Swiss cantons.

Interestingly, mention is also made in the documents of a shared missions budget. The state church pastors who sent these reports noted that New Baptist children would attend confirmation classes right up to the actual act of confirmation, which they would then fail to attend. Almost all reported that they were very obedient in regard to civil laws and regulations, with the exception of military service, but that they were willing to perform civilian service in place of it. One comment read: "The New Baptists are conscientious, honest and peace-loving." Pastor Bemm from Dietikon wrote on January 10,

1844, that it was a matter of honor for the New Baptists to strictly adhere to the Gospel of Matthew 5:10-12 in the event that they were persecuted: "Blessed are they which are persecuted for righteousness' sake: for theirs is the kingdom of heaven…" (KJV).

Offer of Unification with the Baptists

On several occasions, Samuel Froehlich was invited to "reconcile" and "unite" with all Baptists and those who only baptized adults. In one of his responses, he declined to attend a planned gathering of Baptist preachers between the first part of September 1856 in Zurich. Froelich said:

> First and in general, I have a poor opinion of the benefit and results of such conferences, especially as they concern the truth and the kingdom of God. They remind me too much of the erstwhile church synods and councils where men desired to replace the missing truth by means of human inventions and wisdom, to great harm of the truth and the church of God. For just as there is only one truth, so also is the true church in itself just one, and this oneness (unity) has not to first be discovered or established by means of conferences. Here the words of the prayer of the Lord (John 17:21) do not at all apply, for Jesus did not pray the Father that many existing organizations, each resting on its own foundation, might be merged into one, for under none of these organizations could another foundation be laid than that on which it already rests… I maintain therefore, that every organization which teaches and believes that the man in Christ is a sinner also, like the man in Adam (I John 3), stands on a false foundation. And if they, under the circum-

stances, constitute a church ordained according to the Word and will of the Lord, then I must deny this. No apostle of the Lord would acknowledge them as such, inasmuch as they say that the various organizations, regardless of the difference of their views, should work together for the kingdom of God. In a true church of God, one permits no difference of views to arise or to obtain. Unity and agreement must exist even on points of minor importance... Division is better than the union of unlike elements. Finally, we would have to unite with such organizations that have accepted those who departed from us or who were expelled, whereby they prove sufficiently that we do not belong to one church, for the one church of Jesus Christ has not many entrances but only one... (*Writings of S.H. Froelich*, 1985:76-77).

On multiple occasions Froehlich expressed the view that real Christianity was only attainable within "his" religious community and by adhering to its understanding of the matters of forgiveness, sin, and repentance, while baptism had the power of salvation/renewal, and so significant ties were not maintained with any group of "separatists."

Meeting with Oncken

After Froehlich was expelled from all Swiss cantons in 1847 for his preaching and theology, he went to live in Strasburg. There he met Johann Gerhard Oncken, one of the pioneers of the Baptist movement in Europe and formerly an associate in the same Baptist mission. In his diary, Oncken noted his sadness at Froehlich's theological views on baptismal regeneration, and later visited the churches of the "Froehlichites" in Switzerland where he met many former Mennonites who had been baptized as adults by "sprinkling" and who believed that anybody who had not been baptized as they had was not saved. As Oncken observes, this was the origin of the connection between Froehlich's disciples and the objection to the bearing of arms – in these early Mennonite contacts he had, especially in the congregation of around 200 people in Langnau, Switzerland, which had earlier been majority Mennonite. These, even though they followed Froehlich, called their churches Baptist. Oncken notes in his diary:

> The damage done to the Baptists who join in this way because of the "believer's baptism" is inestimable. Froehlich and his disciples have declared war on all other Christians – indeed they do not consider a person a Christian or a brother if they have not been baptized and born again through baptism in this way.[57]

Oncken says he failed in Langnau but that he managed to leave the German Baptist articles of faith with them.[58]

---

[57] Interestingly, Oncken's journal bears testament to his efforts to visit the meetings of Nazarenes and turn them from their beliefs, teaching them about the Baptist understanding of the questions of salvation, baptism, sanctification etc. This practice was also continued by the Baptists in Southern Hungary of the time (Vojvodina), in several cases where new churches were being founded and where believers were drawn from Nazarene groups, as in the case of the Novi Sad church when it was founded. More on Oncken's travelog from Switzerland in Bächtold, 1970:54-6.

[58] The practice of the Nazarenes in Serbia with regard to baptism differs to that described, since it is conducted by immersion, i.e. submersion in water, and this has been so since the beginning. A description of a Nazarene baptism from 1887 says this:

> The Nazarenes baptize their believers out in the open, wherever they find water. There, [the candidate] having confessed his faith before a number of witnesses, with no prior blessing of the water, having changed his clothes, both the one baptizing and the one being baptized wade a little from the bank, to around their waists; with a hand

Froehlich remained in Strasburg, where he died in 1857.

Beginnings in Hungary

Karoly Eotvos in his book (Eotvos, 1997) on the Nazarenes of the early twentieth century mentions a John Denkel and a John Kropatschek, traveling apprentice key cutters, who encountered Froehlich and his teachings in Zurich in early 1839. On their return to Budapest the same year, the first meetings began. Lajos Hensey was the first to accept the new faith by baptism on May 8, 1840, witnessed by Lajos' brother Imre and Jozef Bela. Hensey[59] witnessed to a husband and wife, Jozef and Ana Nip Kovàcz in Nemes and the work of witness gradually spread. The next year, in February, another

---

on the head of the candidate, and having said the words: in the name of the Father and the Son and the Holy Spirit, the one baptizing submerges the one being baptized without taking his hand off his head. The act of baptism is thereby complete. After this, all present return to the meeting-place, as we mentioned earlier, break bread and drink the cup.

This is in the words of Jovan Malušev in his article "*O Nazarenima*" ["On the Nazarenes"], *Glas Istine*, No. 24, dated 31 December 1887. However just a few years later, Vladimir Dimitrijević in an article negates his own report on baptism given in his book *Nazarenstvo, Njegova Istorija i Suština* [*Nazareanism, Its History and Principles*] and corrects himself saying that the Nazarenes conduct baptism saying the following words: I baptize you with water for the forgiveness of sins, and notes that this is taken from the Gospel of Matthew 3:11. See in Dimitrijević: 1894/2:754. There may have been Nazarenes coming from Protestant denominations who did practice infant baptism. Since there was, at least at first, no firm structure to the Nazarene movement, nor any written articles of faith, it is possible that in the cases under consideration there was infant baptism; however this is not a recognized practice of the Nazarene movement as far as the available sources tell us.

[59] Dimitrijević, who refers to Hensey as Hemšej, believes that it was none other than he who brought the Nazarene faith to Vojvodina, having been expelled from Pest to his birthplace Pačir, from where the Nazarene faith later spread further. For more information see Dimitrijević, 1894/1: 101.

three people were baptized, and in May another sixteen. Although Hensey died at age twenty-four in Zurich during a visit to Froehlich, the movement continued to spread. In 1850 in Pest, while in prison, Bela witnessed to the warden, his wife, and her sister, and also witnessed in other prisons around Hungary. Prisons were the first evangelistic meeting places for the Nazarenes, and this practice continued well into the twentieth century.

The first recorded election of elders in a Nazarene fellowship was March 28, 1851 in Pest. In 1855, the authorities sent Bela to the US in order to rid themselves of this troublesome preacher of the new faith; however, he travelled back every other year to tend to the movement. Eotvos says that by the early 1860s, there were already several thousand Nazarenes in the then kingdom of Hungary, and that there was considerable persecution since the authorities were Austrian (Dimitrijević: 1894/1:208). There are sporadic reports that as early as 1857, three Hungarian Nazarenes from the Bačka district were "processed" for their refusal to take the oath.

The first recorded prison sentence for a Nazarene in the Austrian part of the dual monarchy was a three-month term handed down in Vienna in 1865 to a "Nazarene, Sager." Reports of the trial were published in the daily newspapers of the capital[60]. By the following year, there were reports that some Nazarenes were condemned to death for their refusal to bear arms in the Austro-Prussian War which broke out that year[61]. In 1872, two members of the Quaker movement in Britain published a short report on the Nazarenes in Hungary: "They are decidedly on the increase...Their reverence for Holy Scripture is

---

[60] In their articles of faith, Nazarenes teach that one should not swear oaths, nor bear arms that are intended to take life. On the Nazarene articles of faith, see later in this book.

[61] In fact, some authors mention earlier incidences of the execution of Nazarenes, during the war in Austria and Italy in 1859, as well as during the occupation of Bosnia and Herzegovina in 1878. Especially singled out for punishment were Serb Nazarenes, since they mostly belonged to the border units – the *freikorps* – who had been given a favorable position due to their role in defending the Empire in previous military conflicts. Since the Nazarene faith opposed violence and the bearing of arms, Nazarene Serbs were particularly persecuted. For more information see Brock, 1991:176 onwards.

striking. They bear a faithful testimony against Oaths and War."[62] A. P. Bier writes that in 1875 in Bačka, during recruitment, there were three young Nazarenes: one was shot and the other two died of a beating with clubs, but that they remained true to their faith to the end. Two more shootings were recorded during the annexation of Bosnia and Herzegovina, when two individuals declared that they would not shoot their brothers, that all men were brothers. They were tried on the spot, condemned and immediately shot (Oljhovski, 1905:52).[63] In 1889, the public were informed that nineteen Nazarenes had been arrested and tried in Budapest for proselytizing and for urging citizens to refuse the call to military service.

The authorities tried to stop them by prohibiting inter-faith marriage and forbidding conversion from one faith to another in 1868 and in 1875, but without success. Since the regulations applied to recognized religions, it did not apply to the Nazarenes and the Baptists who were also growing by then.[64] In 1892, one Budapest newspaper reported that amongst the recruits that year, there had been 210 Nazarenes who had refused to take up arms, all of them Serbs from Bačka district, while in 1891 in Serbia, a further eighty recruits did the same.[65] Joća Radovanov, a Serb from Bačka, who

---

[62] A letter from 22 September 1872, published by Bevan Braithwaite, A Friend of the Nineteenth Century, London: Hodder Stoughton, 1909, 205, as cited in Brock 1980:50-59. *The London Monthly Reporter* in February 1881 published a letter from a certain Ziemann of Belgrade in which the latter informs Braithwaite of a visit to the Belgrade fortress in which there were imprisoned Nazarenes. On this occasion, he talked to the prison warden who according to Makaji (n.d.:23) gave him a "favorable report on the Nazarenes." Bevan Braithwaite the elder was a well-known evangelically-oriented English Quaker of the 19th century who lived in London.

[63] This book was first published in abbreviated form in 1904 in the series "Obrazovanie" ["Education]", also under the name V. Oljhovski, which was in fact a pseudonym for Vladimir Dmitriyevich Bonch-Bruyevich, a Russian Socialist and Marxist who also wrote about the Nazarenes in 1922 in the book *Iz mira sektantov: Sbornik statei [From the World of the Sects: A Collection of Articles]*.

[64] Regulations no. 12.548 of 13 August 1868 and no. 563 of 13 January 1875.

[65] Oljhovski, 1905:21. Makovicky mentions, but only briefly, that there are Nazarenes in Bosnia too, and that in 1891 (he is not sure on this point)

refused arms in Budapest in the Sixth Regiment, Sixth Company was first sentenced to six hours of imprisonment, then to four days, then was held on remand for three months and then sentenced to two years. His elder brother had already served seven years in prison (from 1885). The newspapers gave a similar account in 1897 when 217 young Serbs "from the parts where the Tisza flows into the Danube" were called up to military service and refused to bear arms. Makovicky also wrote about Sava Nićetin from Bačka who in 1890 was sentenced to multiple terms – a total of fifteen years of imprisonment. To begin with, he was placed alone in a very small cell with a rifle, but he never touched it even though this would have ended the ordeal (Makovicky, 1896:21). When Makovicky learned of this, Nićetin had already served five years of his sentence.

In 1895, the authorities finally got around to addressing the issue of registries for the Nazarenes and Baptists, affirming that both communities were not recognized religions and were not permitted to perform weddings. It is interesting to note that this regulation referred to the Nazarenes as *sledbenici vere u Isusa* [followers of the faith in Jesus], *Jovanova braća* [John's Brothers] and *novoverci* [the New Believers]. However, in the Pančevo city archive there is a birth register of Nazarenes in nearby Vojlovica covering 1875-1895, meaning that the authorities had noted their existence and their beliefs twenty years previously.[66]

In 1897, the Czech newspapers wrote that the Nazarenes were spreading very rapidly among the Serbian population, giving the example of Bavanište, near Kovin in Banat district, where 117 people joined the Nazarene community on a single occasion. Reformed priest Aleksandar Nađ from Stara Beča (possibly Stari Bečej) reported that fifty-five families had left the local church and joined the Nazarenes.

---

there were around eighty Nazarene recruits who were sent to jail (Makovicky, 1896:15). There is no other information in the literature consulted.

[66] According to documents found in the Pančevo Archive, microfilms, roll 13b, Nazarene births register (Protokol Rođenih) 1875-1895, marriages register (Protokol Venčanih) 1896 and deaths register (Protokol Umrlih) 1876-1893, all from Vojlovica (today a suburb of Pančevo). Copies in possession of author. See Figure 1 at the end of this chapter.

That year, Nazarenes from the south of the kingdom of Hungary (Vojvodina) even gained an audience with the prime minister of the Hungarian government, Baron Bánffy, seeking freedom of assembly for their religious meetings. However, he refused their request, founding his arguments on their attitude towards the bearing and use of arms.[67] Around the same time, they also sought assistance from the League of Peace, then a well-known and influential international organization, and were received by the president of the Hungarian office Mavro Jokaj. The latter also turned them away, albeit extremely politely with a great deal of understanding and kind words.[68] Interestingly, in the Budapest military hospitals, most of the orderlies were by now Nazarenes – more than half – some of whom had already served prison terms (Brock, 1983:64-72).

By comparing sources, we can estimate that in the kingdom of Hungary in 1905, there were around 25,000 Nazarenes (although other sources mention 30,000 Nazarenes and Baptists together, of all ethnic groups).

In Vojvodina

The sources currently available testify that Jozsef Toth was probably the first Nazarene convert on the territory of modern-day Serbia. He became a believer in Subotica in the 1860s and later worked as a missionary based in the town of Vasahely in Hungary. In those years there were believers in Pačir (missionary Hahel) and Omorovica (Stefan Molnar), where there was also a certain Stevan Rab, a former librarian from Vienna.

Čedomilj Mijatović, in his *Memoari* [*Memoirs*] mentions a certain Serb who supposedly spent several years in the United States and who in the mid-nineteenth century returned to then-Southern Hungary (today Vojvodina) and there began to organize the Serbs into the Nazarene movement. He called on people to stay out of the

---

[67] Budapesti Hirlap, 11 August 1897.
[68] Magyar Hirlap, 4 November 1897.

official Orthodox Church, telling them that there was no need for priests between men and God, that they should not pray to saints and the Virgin Mary, that they should read the Holy Scriptures and continually pray to God, they should live in the way that Jesus taught his disciples to, and should do all those things as the Holy Spirit prompted them (Mijatovich, 1917:203). Since Mijatovich gives no details, we can assume that this was one version of the story of the emergence of the Nazarene movement, or one piece in a larger mosaic.

Bojan Aleksov, however, has uncovered information on a József Horváth Kiss, whom the Subotica district authorities report as being a dangerous Nazarene missionary, a convert from Calvinism who has been active among the Serbs of Novi Sad since 1860 (Aleksov, 2006:62). József Horváth Kiss wrote an epistle to the Hungarian Nazarenes of Pačir in 1861 informing them that in Novi Sad, their meetings were being held unhindered, greeting them on behalf of the believers in Piros [Rumenka], and then asking them to obtain a New Testament in the Serbian language from Pest or Baja "no matter the cost." Horváth Kiss evidently had plans to preach the Nazarene faith to the Serbs in those parts.[69] We have no account of any response to this plan or what became of it.

Orthodox writers, however, focus on reports of how the Nazarene faith came to Serbia across the river Sava, and mention a trail that leads to Karlovci.

> This Protestant sect emerged among the Serbs in 1865 in Sremski Karlovci and like an epidemic spread quickly despite the efforts of both church and state authorities to prevent this. They first appeared in southern Serbia in 1872 in Obrenovac. They benefited from both the material aid and diplomatic protection of the English

---

[69] It is interesting to note that this report was translated into Serbian by a young Jovan Jovanović Zmaj [a much-loved Serbian poet – t/n], then a police clerk in Subotica, and that this was later found and published by Vasa Stajić [prominent Serbian writer and philosopher – t/n] (Stajić, 1936:456).

> and the Germans... A wine-grower of Sremski
> Karlovci, Mata Rebrić[70], and a certain Jelić, both
> Roman Catholics, accepted the Nazarene faith
> and also infected many Serbs with it, and this
> sect spread rapidly among the Serbs of Vojvodina
> (Nikolaj & Milin, 1997).

The new faith came from Sremski Karlovci to the village of Sasa, and onwards into southern Srem, from where it reached central Serbia. Hungarians and Romanians talked about the new faith to their Serb neighbors in Omoljica, Bavanište, and Pančevo. It is thought that the Nazarene faith was brought to Banat by a watchmaker Harvanek from Timişoara as early as 1867. Dušan Makovický uncovered a source in the archive of the regimental court in Franzfeld (Kačarevo) recording the questioning of a Nazarene on April 8, 1869.

There is a source indicating that an Orthodox priest from Gračanica in Bosnia became a Nazarene during a visit to Novi Sad in 1870. When the movement began to spread among the Serbs and Croats in Karlovci, the authorities intervened and arrested the leaders, but the Nazarenes continue to spread, reaching Krčedin, Surduk, Banovci, Golubinci, Surčin, Boljevci, and other places (Dimitrijević, 1894/1:103). They usually met in people's houses and witnessed to one another, sharing from the Scriptures and singing from the *Zion's Harp*.

The British and Foreign Bible Society reported in 1868 on the distribution of Bibles among the Serbs in Vojvodina, and in that report, there is mention of a large number of Nazarene believers among the Serbs. The same report says that officers in the hospitals in Vojvodina and Slavonia forbade the distribution of Bibles to soldiers of Serbian origin (wounded during the Austro-Italian war of 1866):

> I discovered it, in the course of last summer,
> after I had got possession of the original docu-

---

[70] Mata Rebrić lived in Novi Slankamen.

ment, addressed to all the commanding officers in Slavonia. I was told that very frequently after the people began to read the Bible they went to the Nazarenes and soon after there generally sprang up some difficulty about serving in the army. Austria, it was said, could not exist without soldiers. In "the military frontiers" in particular everything: man, woman and child, school and church, is under military control (Servia, 1868:704).

In 1870, at the *Sabor Srpskog Naroda* [Assembly of the Serbian People] in Sremski, Karlovci, the question was even raised as to what the Orthodox Church planned to do about the new faith that had appeared in the Srem Archdiocese, referred to as *Naslednici Hristovi* [Heirs of Christ].

Đuro Daničić[71] gave an interesting response, also back in 1870, when asked by Ilarion Ruvarac[72] whether Vuk[73] had aided the Nazarenes in publishing a New Testament in the common language:

> I do not think one can say that Vuk forged a path for the Nazarenes: if that were so then the whole of Europe would long since be Nazarene. I do not think even the Nazarenes can help our people – they arrived too late for us and for others.[74]

In 1870, qualified Orthodox theologian and later priest, Paja Dimić from Oroslamoš (now Banatsko Aranđelovo) published a number of articles in installments on the Nazarenes, calling them *Nazirei*, which were actually translated from a booklet in Hungarian

---

[71] Prominent Serbian and Croatian philologist (t/n).

[72] Orthodox priest and historian (t/n).

[73] Referring to Vuk Stefan Karadžić, renowned reformer of the Serbian language and bible translator (t/n).

[74] Letter dated 12 May 1870 cited in *Karakter i rad Đure Daničića* [*The Character and Work of Đuro Daničić*], 1923:114-5.

published by the Nazarenes themselves a year earlier in Szeged, and which in Serbian translation were titled *Kratki pregled nazireiske ispovesti* [*A Short Overview of the Nazarene Faith*]. Dimić published the translation and then discussed the Nazarene faith in regard to matters of adult-only baptism, communion, marriage, funerals, church structure, Sunday as a holy day, the Nazarene question of holiness (sinlessness), and other matters (Dimić, 1870:335-403). This interesting source reveals early Nazarene beliefs as viewed by an Orthodox theologian.

Orthodox priest from Nadalj, Dušan Petrović, records how as early as 1874, one infant had remained unbaptized: "Ilija, son of Aleksa and Saveta Mašić, born 15 September 1874"; it is stated that this was a Nazarene child. The next year, three births of Nazarene infants were recorded: Luka, son of Pavle and Leksa Bekvalac, Miloš, son of Gavra and Kruna Jelikić and Sofija, daughter of Marko and Jana Ivanić. However, the Nazarene faith had reached Nadalj before then, in 1870 or 1871, "brought with him from Novi Sad by Novak Vesić, a mason, who soon after converted his brother Joca Vesić, a tailor and a local here, to the Nazarenes" (Petrović, 1880:6-7). By the 1880s, that Nazarene fellowship had grown to more than 150 souls. This is indirect evidence that there were Nazarenes in Novi Sad among the Serbian population even prior to 1870.

Rudolf Horvat says that there were Nazarenes registered in some places in Srem at the time a census was taken, in 1880: five Nazarenes in Erdevik, four in Neštin and one in Molovin. In 1890, they also surfaced in Adaševci, Trgovište, and Ljuba, and in a 1900 census there were Nazarenes in Ilinci, Sot, and Mala Vašica (Horvat, 2000). According to the Nazarenes' own tradition, the fellowship in Novi Sad was established a few years prior to 1890, having come from Sremski Karlovci.[75] An old house was soon purchased, which was demolished and rebuilt in 1921. Apparently, the first elder was a certain Mađar, who was succeeded by Milan Dunđerov.

---

[75] Although there are sources indicating that a Serbian Nazarene congregation existed before that time in Novi Sad, and that there may have been another, a Hungarian-speaking one.

Makovicki in 1896 comments on the distribution and number of Nazarenes in Vojvodina as follows:

> The largest number of Nazarenes are on the left bank of the Tisa, in Bačka, and in Srem. In the former Vojna Krajina [military frontier] there is not a Lutheran nor a Reformed church in which the Nazarenes do not have their meetings. As far as the nationalities living there are concerned, there are quite a number: Hungarians, Germans, Romanians, Serbs – of whom there are around three quarters of a million in this region – around 100 thousand Slovaks, as well as Bulgarians, Gypsies, Austrians, Rusyns and Jews. There are most Nazarenes among the Hungarians, Slovaks and Serbs, less among the Romanians and still less among the Germans. (Makovicky, 1896:14).

A newspaper article from *Srpski Sion* in 1897 tells of twelve Serbian families in Srpska Crnja that went over to the Nazarene faith in 1888. It says that this happened when a certain Englishman from Constantinople and "a local, Miša Markov" appeared in the village and first converted Markov's parents and then his three brothers and two brothers-in-law after them. Then Nazarenes began coming from Kikinda to continue working with those who were interested.[76]

The Nazarenes had so spread throughout Vojvodina, among the whole population and all ethnic communities, that the traditional churches called multiple times during this period for a common front against the Nazarenes. A conference was held along these lines in the village of Crepaja near Pančevo in June 1887. Fourteen Orthodox priests were in attendance, one Roman Catholic parish priest, six Lutheran pastors and two Reformed (Calvinist) priests. The sole

---

[76] "Nazarenstvo odnosno bezverje u Srp. Crnji u Temišvarskoj eparhiji" [Nazarean apostasy in Srpska Crnja in the Timişoara eparchy], *Srpski Sion*, godina 7, br. 13, 1897, p. 202.

topic of discussion was how to halt the spread of the Nazarene "sect." They agreed to write a letter of protest to the Minister of Religions and call on the authorities to enforce the regulations from 1868 and 1875. A similar conference was held later, in 1893, in Stara Pazova, again convened by the Orthodox parish priest.

Leo Tolstoy and the Nazarenes

A letter from October 1894 sent by Leo Tolstoy to his acquaintance Eugen Heinrich Schmitt[77] shows that he was interested in and knowledgeable about their existence and activity in Serbia and Austria:

> Salvation, I believe, will come neither from the workmen who are socialistically inclined nor from their leaders, but only from people who will accept religion as their only guide in life, as the Nazarenes in Serbia and others in certain places in Austria do – namely, that hundreds of them refuse to take the oath and do military service and are condemned for this to spend years in prisons and fortresses.

Leo Tolstoy mentions the Serbian Nazarenes in two more books: *The Kingdom of God is Within You* (published in 1893 in French and English) and *A Confession and Other Religious Writings* (published in Russian in 1884 and in English in 1887):

> And cases of refusing to comply with the demands of government when they are opposed to Christianity, and especially cases of refusing to serve in the army, are occurring of late not in Russia only, but everywhere. Thus, I happen to

---

[77] "Letters from Tolstoi," *The Nation*, 122/3162, probably from 1894.

know that in Serbia men of the so-called sect of
Nazarenes steadily refuse to serve in the army,
and the Austrian Government has been carrying
on a fruitless contest with them for years, punishing them with imprisonment. In the year 1885,
there were 130 such cases (Tolstoy, 2006:118).

Tolstoy's personal physician and follower Dušan Makovický
wrote an extensive report on the Nazarenes for Tolstoy, who was
closely watching events in Vojvodina. Makovický collected accounts
through correspondence with others, from newspaper reports, by
visiting far-flung areas and by talking to Nazarenes, recording their
beliefs and practices, and also corresponding with local priests who
provided him with considerable material. The Dušan Makovický
archive is kept in the literary archive of the Prague National Museum
and probably contains a great deal of source material on the Nazarene
movement up to the year 1896, when his book, *Nazarénové v Uhrách,*
was published in Prague (Královské Vinohrady).[78] When Dr. Jovan
Maksimović, well-known Russian-Serbian translator, visited Tolstoy
in 1909, Tolstoy was still very much interested in the Nazarenes in
Serbia and asked Maksimović for news.[79] At one point, persecution

---

[78] Brock, 2006:150. The author particularly emphasizes the use of the common
language in church services and compares the Nazarenes favorably to other
churches.

[79] From Maksimović, 1912:283-4:

I told him that I was personally acquainted with many of
our Nazarenes and that they left the impression on me of
spiritually very mature, sincerely religious, bold people.
There are some shortcomings in their understanding of
Christianity of a purely external, formal nature, but they
have a complete understanding of the essence of Christ's
teaching – God's law of love, nonresistance to evil, forgiveness, serenity, nonparticipation in the courts and the
military – and their lives are in harmony with Christ's
great commandments. Tolstoy listened with pleasure and
a happy smile to my account of a Belgrade Nazarene, a
poor street greengrocer, Uncle Todor Grujić, who at the

even led Tolstoy to consider moving to Serbia – Belgrade specifically – but the idea never came to fruition.[80]

Publishing

The Nazarenes primarily used the 1867 first edition Karadžić-Daničić translation of the Bible. The Bible Society recounts how new believers would bring Bibles to meetings with Orthodox priests in order to debate matters that concerned them. These were meetings organized by local priests with the intention of persuading the

---

insistence of the Belgrade clergy was arrested and tried by the state authorities for being more concerned with the law of God than the anti-Christian decrees of man (courts, the army…), which the modern state church has made compromise with. When on one occasion during his trial a judge began to threaten and intimidate him with severe punishment, including forced labor, Uncle Todor looked at the judge with his small, wise, twinkling eyes, smiled benignly at him and said,

"Do you really think you will scare me with that? Not only am I not afraid of your torture and forced labor, I welcome them gladly. What you threaten to do to me, you already did 1,900 years ago to my Christ – what better thing could I wish for myself? The greater the torture, the greater the honor for me!

Tolstoy listened to my story of the brave stand taken by Uncle Todor before the judges of this world with triumphant satisfaction…

[80] Interestingly, Tolstoy's descendants came to Serbia as Russian refugees from the Soviet Union, and further descendants of his were born here: great-grandson Ilija in Novi Bečej, Oleg in Tetovo – then old Serbia – and Nikita – later a Russian academic – in Vršac. Some of them later attended the Cadet Corps in Bela Crkva. Ilija's son Vladimir returned to Russia where he is today director of the museum-estate in Yasnaya Polyana. Leo Tolstoy was also conferred with honorary membership of the Serbian Royal Academy in 1903. Tolstoy's ideas on peaceful, non-violent resistance, so like the lives and deeds of the Nazarenes, later served as the basis for Mahatma Gandhi's guiding principles. See Erofeyev, 2010:8.

Nazarenes to return to the bosom of the Church (A Voice from Servia, 1880:654).

Although it is generally thought that the Nazarenes did not and still do not engage in publishing, with the exception of the *Zion's Harp* hymnbook, there are individual examples to the contrary. We have already mentioned the booklet in Hungarian published in 1869 in Szeged discussing the Nazarene articles of faith. In 1893, a certain Sima Stanojević took it upon himself to translate from the German and print a little booklet titled *Srce čovečije hram Božiji ili radionica sotone, predstavljeno u 10 slika* [*The Heart of Man – the Temple of God or the Workshop of Satan, A Representation in 10 Pictures*] and was intended for the "revival and spread of Christian teaching."

In 1903, the believers in Christ (the Nazarenes) printed *The Letters of Adina*, under the title *The Prince of the House of David: or, Three Years in the Holy City*. This was a collection of thirty-nine letters that talked about the life of Christ, written by the Rev. J. H. Ingraham.[81] Later the books *Quo Vadis* by Nobel laureate Henryk Sienkiewicz and Igraham's *Ben Hur* were also popular among the Nazarenes.

Later, in 1910, the Bela Kuna press in Bela Crkva printed a book titled *Dolazak Gospodnji, jedan vrlo radostan događaj za svo čovečanstvo* [*The Coming of the Lord, a Most Joyful Event for all Mankind*], apparently written by a local Nazarene elder[82]. They also continued to use *The Pilgrim's Progress* a great deal. It did not go unnoticed by the public at large that the Nazarenes very much enjoyed and appreciated Bunyan's book, translated by Čedomilj Mijatović and first published in 1879, later reprinted by the Nazarenes for their own edition in 1911.

---

[81] It is interesting to note that the screenplay for the Hollywood blockbuster *The Ten Commandments*, filmed in 1956, was partly based on Ingraham's book *Pillar of Fire*. When Ingraham published his novella *The Prince of the House of David*, it sold a full 250,000 copies within a short space of time, a huge achievement at the time in America, and in doing so secured the future of the novella as a literary form, which until then had not been greatly valued.

[82] Additionally, Nazarene elder for Srem, Grulović, who lived in Beška in the late nineteenth century, wrote a treatise on moral living that was never printed (Conversation with Goran Grulović, 23 December 2011).

Vladimir Dimitrijević, in his book published 1894, gives some interesting statistical data on the number of Nazarenes in Vojvodina. He says that in 1891, there were 6,891 Nazarenes in Vojvodina, of whom around 1,000 were Romanians, around 2,000 Hungarians and around 4,000 Serbs. The journal *Srpski Sion* estimated in 1893 that there were more than 4,400 Serb Nazarenes in Vojvodina. The next publication from 1898, speaks of 10,000 Nazarenes in Vojvodina and says that 4,460 of them were of Serb ethnicity (Milin, 1974:60). However, the 1912 Nazarene hymnbook had a print run of 12,000 copies in the Serbian language[83], which points to rapid growth among the Serb population in Vojvodina, as well as in central Serbia, then the kingdom of Serbia (Slijepčević, 1966:242).

Report of the British and Foreign Bible Society on the Nazarenes

In the annual report on its work and on the distribution and sales of Scriptures, the British and Foreign Bible Society (BFBS) for 1870, in the section about Slavonia, said that there were major obstacles to the work of the Society in the shape of the national churches, but that there were "indeed, groups of Nazarenes who appear like oases in the desert, and exercise a very healthy influence wherever they exist." The report goes on to talk about certain Serbs among whom "life is beginning to manifest itself as a result of their examination of the Scriptures…" (Annual Report, 1870).

In the report from Belgrade in 1871 a report was published on a conversion that happened in central Serbia:

> G. had served in the military, and had availed himself of his spare time to learn the art of painting. After he had left the army he devoted

---

[83] This hymnbook was also used for many years by the Adventists for their meetings, so they contributed to the total print run. One source says that the hymn book was printed in German, Hungarian, Serbian, Romanian, and Slovene (Alder, 1976:228).

the time he was not engaged in his farming to painting the pictures of saints for churches and monasteries, and to repairing old copies. By this means he earned a goodly sum of money. One day a wagon stopped at his door, and the two men who rode therein begged for a draught of water. G. gladly gave them what they wished, and asked whence they came. 'From Slankamen, the centre of the Nazarene movement,' was the reply. Could they not tell him about the 'new religion' that was making such a stir in that place? Oh, yes, but it was not a 'new religion,' but what had been from the beginning, the simple Gospel of Jesus Christ. Stimulated by this to hear more, G. pressed the strangers to enter his house, and they, being themselves Nazarenes, explained to him from the New Testament, which they had with them, the ground of their hope. On their departure, they left their New Testament in his hands. G. read and examined; saw the error in which he had been entangled, and resolved at once to start afresh. The saint's pictures, both those already ordered and those on sale, were at once removed, and the walls thus far decorated with them were cleaned down. This soon brought upon him the anger of his wife. The meekness and patience of the good man, however, prevailed at last, and so powerfully persuaded his wife of the superiority of his religion, that she has herself adopted it, and has sat down at the feet of Jesus. In the house of this man one of the largest meetings of the Nazarenes is now being regularly held (Annual Report, 1871).[84]

---

[84] This may be an account of the first Nazarene convert in central Serbia, Pavle Rosić from Obrenovac, of whom it is said in one report that he "buried his

There is a little on the Nazarenes in the report on Vojvodina from 1877. It is said that the Nazarene community continued to enjoy stable growth and that they became more energetic and earnest in proclaiming the Gospel. For years they had waited for the new Testament to be published in the Serbian language and now they had it.

"In the primitive simplicity of their worship, and anxious clinging to the very words of Scripture there is an element of strength, which fills our hearts with hope, however they may be despised by the 'wise, the mighty, and the noble.'" The report also talks about the testimony of one Nazarene who during the previous summer had brought fifteen people to the truth, and these had joined local Nazarene churches (Annual Report, 1877).

In the report for 1889, the BFBS reported that it has heard that the Nazarenes in Serbia faced great problems and that a considerable number of them — both men and women — had been arrested at a prayer meeting and sentenced in Belgrade to prison sentences of several months (Annual Report, 1889).

The report for 1898 stated that nobody in the town of A. (possibly Aranđelovac – author's note) wanted to buy Bibles, on account of these being "Nazarene books." There is an interesting account of an officer coming to a colporteur at night to buy a Bible, as the report puts it, "Nicodemus-like" (Annual report, 1898).

Peter Kuzmič also writes on the activities of the Bible Society among the Nazarenes:

> Reports written by the agents, depositaries and colporteurs of the Society show that of all the religious groups in this region they were most accepting, indeed supportive of the work of the Society… Since the Nazarenes primarily drew followers from the ranks of the Orthodox Church, and because of the distinctness of the Nazarene teaching concerning the Bible, the Orthodox

icons in the garden." See more in the section on the Nazarenes in central Serbia.

Church retaliated fiercely, not just against the
Nazarenes but also against the work of the Bible
Society and even against the translators them-
selves (Kuzmič, 1983:226).

Jaša Tomić and the Nazarenes

Well-known radical leader and later editor of the Novi Sad
newspaper *Zastava*, Jaša Tomić (1856-1922) in his writings from
the late nineteenth century, had much to say on the matter of the
Nazarenes, whom he considered harmful, especially owing to their
denial of the Serbian national identity and the connection to the
traditional church. In 1896, he wrote the novel *Nazareni* [*The
Nazarenes*] which from a literary point of view was not received in a
favorable critical light[85], but which sold out of its first edition immediately and was reprinted the same year (the Church parishes of Novi
Sad and Čurug ordered numerous copies in order to "distribute them
among the people"). The next year he wrote a book/treatise *Pametno
Nazarenstvo* [*Intelligent Nazareanism*], and in later works persisted
with this subject. At that time, many authors were seeking to understand the Nazarene movement, and one article gave social issues as
a fundamental reason for their emergence: "What is the immedi-
ate cause of Nazareanism? The poverty and misery of the people.
But there has always been poverty, while there has not always been
Nazareanism... We will recognize the features of this poverty if we
identify the economic conditions that have created it..."[86]

In *Intelligent Nazareanism*, Tomić praises the constancy of the
Nazarenes and their commitment to their religious convictions, and

---

[85] There was criticism of the literary kind in Prague too – a feuilleton in the
Narodne Novine by author Josef Holeček, who declared that the Nazarene sect
was very reminiscent of the Moravian Brethren and the Mennonites, as cited in
Ol'hovski, 1905:4.

[86] Bast, "Nazarenstvo sa gledišta moderne društvene nauke" [*Nazareanism From
the Perspective of the Modern Social Sciences*], *Zastava*, 9 April 1896. Bast was a
pseudonym of Vasilije (Basileus) Stajić.

particularly notes their socio-economic solidarity, their thriftiness, their work ethic, and their rejection of various vices (in particular the gambling and drunkenness that were wreaking havoc in families and entire villages). He recommended this same behavior to the members of farming cooperatives (those modeled on the Raiffeisen cooperatives[87]), referring to it as "intelligent Nazareanism." Tomić looked at every problem from the point of view of economics and he believed that the farming cooperatives would ultimately signal the end of the Nazarene movement. Additionally, from the Radical[88] political point of view, the Nazarenes could not be relied on for any national or political movement, and since their proliferation was greatest in those social classes in which the Radicals had a strong base, they were also considered harmful in terms of both national and political interests. This attitude toward them remains to this day, regardless of changes in the political system. The Nazarenes and other minority Protestant faith communities have always been accused of harming the national sensibility for their supposed service to "foreign political influences" and for "compromising the battle readiness and warrior spirit of the Serbian people."

"If the truth be known, Nazareanism also has its good side. They require honesty and diligence from every member; they counsel and help one another. And if anyone does not do as he should, he is expelled from the group..." wrote Tomić, whilst continuing to promote his idea of "intelligent Nazareanism," that is of farming cooperatives as a model for common labor and economic prosperity (Tomić, 1898:51).

In the journal *Žena* [*Woman*], in 1911, an anonymous short story was published (possibly by Jaša Tomić[89]) called "*Kako je Veljko Simeonov postao nazaren*" ["How Veljko Simeonov became a

---

[87] Friedrich Wilhelm Raiffeisen, 1818-1888 was the chairman of a local municipality in Austria who organized the distribution of flour and bread to hungry peasants and established the idea of cooperatives. For more see Gnjatović, 2010:16.

[88] Referring to the Serbian People's Radical Party of the late nineteenth and early twentieth century (t/n).

[89] Prominent Serbian politician and writer (t/n).

Nazarene"], with a sequel promised at the end for a future issue. The editor was Milica, wife of Jaša Tomić, hence the likelihood that this text was connected with his thinking about the Nazarenes, whom he first encountered as a high-school student, one of his neighbors (Milutin) being a Nazarene (Rakić, 1986:196).

The Nazarenes and the Socialist Movement in Vojvodina

In 1870-1871, Podgradski[90] in his *Otvorena Knjiga...* had described the Nazarenes as follows:

> Among the Nazarenes, true communism prevails – whoever has not, those who have give to him. They strive in life to be pious and moral in conduct. On certain days, they gather in a particular house, some of them read and interpret the Holy Gospels, each as he is able, afterwards they pray to God and go home. Each of them has a New Testament at home and reads it diligently... when someone says to them, "That little that you believe, you teach wisely and rightly, the Church teaches and believes the same," they reply: "We know this well; the difference is that in your Church there is much that is well-preached, but is not lived out in life; we however do so." (Podgradski, 1871:35).

The socialists in Vojvodina also addressed the matter of the Nazarene movement. In the early twentieth century, even the journal *Pravo Naroda* (March 1908) expressed the opinion that the Nazarenes could be considered socialists in political outlook since they, "strive towards the establishment of Christ's moral norms, who

[90] Later a friend of Leo Tolstoy, also known as the "Slovak from Belgrade."

was in terms of his views a forerunner of today's modern socialism"; nevertheless, the article concluded that faith is a personal matter for the individual.

Also in the late nineteenth century, it became evident that the main strongholds of the socialists were in the villages and towns in which there were large numbers of Nazarenes, which was probably a result of the socialist propaganda of equality and of sharing in common troubles. This propaganda, which gave clear voice to the aspirations of the poorest section of the population, began to also find adherents among the Nazarenes. In the south of the kingdom of Hungary, that is in modern-day Vojvodina, there was a law prohibiting public gatherings and decreeing how people were allowed to assemble, and thus Nazarene meetings were effectively outlawed. It was reported to the authorities that the Nazarenes were meeting in the evenings and discussing religious topics and their personal testimonies, as well as matters relating to property, expenditure, distribution and others. In Békéscsaba, the police arrested Nazarenes, placing them in custody, but failed to stop their evening meetings and gatherings, of which the Nazarenes said were "acts of conscience."

Also, from their beginnings, the Nazarenes upheld the principle of mutual aid, similar to the teachings of socialism (Hadži, 1896). In every difficulty the Nazarenes knew that they would not be abandoned and that their "brothers" would leap to their aid, even if only in prayer, which was a principle of solidarity that socialism recognized. One Nazarene village near Békéscsaba apparently even collected its possessions in one place, declaring it common property, and the believers there began living in a commune. Makovický said that the Nazarenes eagerly accepted the ideas of communism, asking, "What does a lord need a field for when he cannot till it?" and spoke of commerce as something founded on deceit. They greatly valued personal effort and the contribution of each individual (Makovický, 1896:10).

> However here, as in almost every sect community like it, we encounter communism of consumption but not collectivism of production. The Nazarenes are also celebrated for their fault-

less, constant and incorruptible honesty. In the
courts, when they are invited as witnesses, they
are not asked to swear the oath: "It doesn't matter, they will tell the truth anyway," the judges say
of them (Oljhovski, 1905:40).

Vasa Stajić criticized Jaša Tomić for his analysis of the Nazarene
movement and his suggestion that collectivism was the answer to this
movement. As a young high-school student, Stajić had tried to eval-
uate the extent to which the Nazarenes were themselves Marxists.[91]

There is an interesting episode recorded involving Nazarene
socialists in late 1903. Apparently a group of Nazarenes from
Bavanište came to Milan Stanković – socialist agitator and corre-
spondent of the *Narodna Reč* newspaper published in Budapest – and
said that they liked the socialist movement and wanted to "become
socialists" and subscribe to the newspaper. Stanković immediately
told his head office in Budapest about this, and wrote a few words for
the newspaper, since this was an interesting event that might encourage other Nazarenes to take a similar step.

Before long however, a "chief elder," Milan (possibly Dunđerov)
from Futog, appeared on the scene, "reprimanding" the Nazarene
socialists and ordering them to leave the socialist organization.

> The obedient Nazarenes came to me and timidly
> asked me to revoke their membership because
> their faith prohibited them from being social-
> ists even though the movement attracted them;
> but God who is good would set it all in order...
> (Stanković, 1952:31-32).

---

[91] Dr. Arpad Lebl comments on one of Stajić's early texts thus: "...Vasa Stajić
favors socialism, Jaša Tomić wants to halt the process of proletarianization
whilst also fighting socialism. J. Tomić sets out this view of his in the aforementioned brochure, but not in his novel, so only in 1897, after Vasa Stajić's
article. It seems to us that Vasa Stajić was the first writer to conduct a Marxist
analysis – albeit not entirely successfully – of the Nazarene movement...," (own
translation), see in Lebl, 1963:65.

Learning of this, the local social democratic chapter in Bavanište declared that in future it would boycott the Nazarenes in every way possible.[92]

Matavulj's "New Believers"

Simo Matavulj, Serbian writer and occasional intelligence agent, also took an interest in the Nazarenes. Based on an acquaintance in Stari Bečej, in the mid-1890s he described a Nazarene family in Belgrade and made a short story out of this titled *Novoverci* [*The New Believers*], published in the collection *Iz beogradskog života* [*From Belgrade Life*] for the first time in 1893 in Mostar. Although literary critics have analyzed the story, they have not been able to explain why Matavulj addressed this subject. Korać believes that the answer lies in the Nazarene dignity of Mita the cobbler and his philosophy of hope in "salvation from the filthy, impulsive, bestial world…hence there is no doubt that Matavulj's Mita the cobbler was true and real" (Korać, 1982:96). Kašanin believes that Matavulja was indignant at certain moral and social issues in the Belgrade of his day: "…not so much the lack of culture as the lack of morals. The Nazarenes are persecuted; why, when the New Believers are more righteous than the priests of the Orthodox Church?" (Kašanin, 1966:133).

There were other literary attempts to write about the Nazarenes, but it seems to us that almost all of those texts had an agenda of some kind; however, this subject has not been sufficiently researched. Much more recently a short story (Konstantinović, 1995:15-24)[93] was also published, about a Rusyn Nazarene. Very little is otherwise known about this group.

In the period immediately before the breakup of the Austro-Hungarian Empire, prior to the First World War, the figures talk of

---

[92] "Nazarenski bojkot" [The Nazarene boycott], *Narodna Reč*, no. 37 dated 11 December 1903.

[93] The story talks about a Janko Hromiš from Šid.

236 congregations and more than 86,000 members of all nationalities and languages in the Empire of the time (Klopfenstein, 1997:xi). With the collapse of the old Austro-Hungary and the division of its territories into the new states of Czechoslovakia, Hungary and the kingdom of Serbs, Croats and Slovenes, as well as Romania, the Nazarene movement became fragmented. Not long after the formation of the new kingdom of SCS, the great repression and persecution of the Nazarenes began.

The Nazarenes in Central Serbia

In December 1872, a local postman from Obrenovac, Ilija Marković, reported to the Serbian Orthodox Metropolitan of Belgrade, Mihajlo, the presence of some kind of sect in Obrenovac whose members "do not venerate icons and do not go to church..." (Slijepčević, 1943:13). This letter also mentions a certain Pavle Rosić as being a Nazarene missionary, very persistent in regard to the Nazarene faith, whom he had met in the village of Bogarica in Srem, where he frequently went. He had buried his icons in the garden and told his local priest that he did not care for holy water, but rather for God's Ten Commandments. Rosić got four month's jail time for organizing meetings for people who were interested. After serving his sentence, Rosić began organizing trips over to Srem and Progar where the Nazarenes were able to meet freely. Some of the Nazarenes from Srem came to Obrenovac, and Metropolitan Mihajlo even had to put pressure on the police to have them expelled; the police however replied that the people were "on the brink of rebellion" as a result of this kind of treatment by the authorities. Just a month later, the police reported that the Nazarenes had also spread around the surrounding villages, especially in Progar.

During the war with Turkey in 1876, Nazarenes were reported to be refusing to take up arms and some were sentenced to death, although Prince Milan subsequently commuted the sentences to life imprisonment.[94] Similarly, in the Bosnian uprising a year previously, the Nazarenes of Obrenovac had refused to bear arms. Initially they were punished, but later amnestied. The Orthodox priesthood judged these measures to have had a positive effect, and one priest proudly reported on June 13, 1877, that with the help of the police, he had succeeded in baptizing the children of one "sectarian." In the Belgrade suburb of Vračar in 1877, a group of twenty-two Nazarenes were arrested who had been meeting in secret for prayer. The Hungarian newspapers claimed that there had been some military deserters from the Austro-Hungarian Empire among their number.

Slijepčević says that the Nazarenes from Obrenovac came to Belgrade around 1881, primarily because they could move around and meet together more easily in the big city, although there is information indicating that there were Nazarenes held prisoner in the Belgrade fortress from 1877. By 1887, the number and the activity of the Nazarenes began to be noticed and reported by all local Belgrade priests. Each of them had previously been given the task of making a list of Nazarenes by name, as well as of their friends, and submitting those lists to the Metropolitan of Belgrade. First to be reported in Belgrade in this way was Rista Popović, a saddler, in whose home the Nazarenes began meeting in March that year and of whom "there was quite a number." The following year, fifteen people were arrested who had been praying in a private home.[95]

In *Srpska Nezavisnost*, in the issue of August 18,1888, someone under the pseudonym Teofan [Theophanes] describes the Nazarene movement in Belgrade as follows:

> In addition to the Latin snake, another serpent
> has coiled itself around the holy source of our
> Orthodox faith; it does not hiss so much, it is

---

[94] Some of them served their prison terms in Belgrade, but because they were so diligent and conscientious the prison regime was softened towards them over the years.

[95] Miša Mijučić, tailor, Damjan P., Krsto Opačić, farmer, Todor Grujić, greengrocer (whom Jovan Maksimović was to speak of to Leo Tolstoy) and Josif Grac, greengrocer.

true, but is dangerous nonetheless. This viper is Nazareanism, which has made its nest even in our capital. It takes advantage of the unfortunate state of our Church to spread its nets with impunity. Using money and deceit, it spreads its propaganda, especially amongst the poorest classes in Belgrade. The number of its adherents increases. It has already built its house of prayer – or we should rather say, house of blasphemy – in a respectable part of Belgrade. A foreigner[96] has been allowed to not only make a fool of the law, raising a whole new town on bought land, he has also been allowed to spread such a harmful sect as Nazareanism in this town...

The Nazarenes found a great friend in Belgrade in the shape of Francis Mackenzie[97], and in his friend, Serbian government minister Čedomilj Mijatović. It is estimated that in 1891 there were more than 100 Nazarenes[98], and in neighboring Pančevo and surrounding area, connected by steamboat to Belgrade, there were as many as 500. Mijatović frequently advocated for the rights of the Nazarenes. Mackenzie helped Nazarenes by visiting them in jail and even bring-

---

[96] See footnote 96.

[97] This was the "foreigner" referred to in the citation from Teofan above. Reports say that he visited the Nazarenes in Obrenovac a number of times in 1877, went to the prison to visit them and left money with their elder, tailor Dimitrije Mihailović to help the families. See the section **Francis Mackenzie - friend to the Nazarenes** (p. 65) for details.

[98] One report talks of how the Nazarenes in Belgrade "mostly live off the chicken trade, and whilst buying poultry from the peasants in the villages and selling it in the town they also spread their malevolent influence amongst the people using every possible form of pharisaical deceit" (own translation). From the report delivered by Velimir Marković, Belgrade priest, at the Board Meeting of the Association of Priests on his proposal for combating the Nazarene movement. For more details, see the minutes from the thirteenth regular Sveštenička Skupština [Assembly of Priests] published in *Vesnik Srpske Crkve*, godina XIII, sveska 10, dated October 1902, pages 866-883.

ing them home with him on Sundays. He also helped their families financially and in many other ways, especially when they had been deprived of their income while their husbands and fathers languished in jail. Mijatović also wrote about the Nazarenes in England, where he was the Serbian ambassador:

> That the Servians as a race are not incapable of religious fervour can be proved not only by their old history...but also by the religious fanaticism of the Servian Nazarenes. These are a Christian sect which, about the middle of the last century, originated in Hungary and spread rapidly among the Servians of that country and less rapidly among the people of the kingdom of Servia. They have several points of resemblance to the old Bogomili. They have no churches and no priests; they repudiate the worship of the Madonna and the Saints as idolatry, and they consider it as the greatest sin to kill a man, and therefore they refuse to bear arms and serve in the Army. In Servia some of them have been condemned to twenty years' imprisonment for having refused to comply with the lawful duty of every citizen to serve in the Army. They have cheerfully undergone that heavy sentence for conscience' sake, never murmuring a word of protest. They are absolutely honest and truth-loving people. I have been present at some of their prayer-meetings, and can testify to the earnestness and fervour of their improvised prayers. (Mijatovich, 1908:53).

Nazarenes were observed and reported in Aleksinac in 1887 (Kojić, 1906:740). Two years later, sixteen Nazarenes were arrested in Kragujevac and a letter dating from 1895, sent by the Metropolitan to the minister of education, talks of a Nazarene presence in Jagodina, Paraćin, and Zaječar. In the area around Topola, the first believers surfaced in the village of Gorovič. It was the family of Milan "Luka" Lukić, who became a believer in Belgrade in prison in around 1885, through a certain Deda Đura. Milan Lukić had served eight years in jail for an alleged murder, and was released under an amnesty by King Milan in 1885. However, he later went back to jail for his faith.

> My grandfather [Milan Lukić] was also jailed for his faith after the term he had served – a further four years and three months, and so he spent a total of 12 years and three months in jail, and of those 12 years, he spent four years with a ball and chain on his legs. This ball was a 5 or 6 kilogram weight on each leg, so he could not escape, and after four years they had to call a blacksmith to unfetter him. They could not be opened any more because his legs had thickened... (Lukić, 1984).

Around 1887, the Lukić family got in touch with believers in the Austro-Hungarian Empire and later continued to have close ties with them.

In Aranđelovac, the Nazarene faith spread through Aksentije Marković, a tailor who used to travel to work in Nadalj near Novi Sad with the Kojić family, who were also tailors and Nazarenes, probably during the late 1880s or early 1890s. He gave a New Testament to his brother-in-law Maksim Teofanović and told him to read it regularly. Teofanović later started going to Obrenovac having heard that Nazarenes were meeting there, and after he bought a house in Aranđelovac, services were held there. It was not unusual for the police to interrupt the meetings, and the believers would be given three to four months' jail time and frequent monetary fines. Baptisms were conducted secretly around midnight in the Kubršnica river, and services were held at four in the morning so that workers and servants could get to work in the morning.[99] The Nazarene faith spread from Aranđelovac to Natalinci, Kragujevac, Trstenik and even to Užice.

The state now officially began to take repressive measures. The minister of the army wrote in 1899 to the minister of education and religions that "for a number of years now" the military courts had been doing what they could, taking extremely strict measures against these "prodigals," but that more needed to be done "on the other, moral side, to repress this deadly and wicked falsehood which has taken many otherwise good and honest people and ruined so many a family" (O suzbijanju nazarenstva..., 1912:81). Even in this indirect sense, we see agreement by all parties that the Nazarene movement was flourishing in the period preceding the First World War, including in the kingdom of Serbia.

There are a number of occasions recorded of Nazarenes meeting in Belgrade, one in 1893 when the interior minister informed the Serbian Orthodox Church that Nazarene meetings were being held every week in the Terazije part of town at the house of the brothers Đorđević, attended by thirteen people: five women, seven men and one high school student, all of them of poor material status.

Hrišćanski Vesnik from 1910 says the following of the Nazarenes in central Serbia:

> The results the Nazarenes have achieved with their intensive efforts and systematic propa-
> ganda in the heart of Šumadija cannot remain
> unknown to the public. They are to be found
> here and there around Serbia [proper], but in
> smaller numbers and with less influence on their
> surroundings. In Aranđelovac, in the liveliest part
> of this provincial town, they have built a respect-
> able building as their house of prayer, where the
> 'true believers' from Aranđelovac and neighbor-

---

[99] From the recollections of Rada Nikolić, née Teofanović (1893-1983) and Zora Milovančev, née Teofanović, written down in *Odakle je u Aranđelovac (Srbija) došla nazarenska vera* [*Where the Nazarene Faith Came From in Aranđelovac (Serbia)*]. Transcript of manuscript in possession of author.

ing counties gather on Sundays, morning and afternoon. Their propaganda is very enthusiastic, and their membership is growing appreciably, especially amongst the youth of both sexes (B.A., 1910:903).

Zion's Harp and Jovan Jovanović Zmaj

The edition of the Nazarene hymnbook *Zion's Harp* from 1994 speaks of the 120-year history of this collection of spiritual songs: a collection of choruses and songs of praise for the Christ-believing congregations, as the subtitle says. The first Serbian-language edition was published in 1876, *Zbirka pjesama na hvalu Bogu po naredbi Božijoj, troškom sunasljednika Hristovi nazarena* [*Collection of Songs to the Praise of God at the Command of God, Published by the Co-Heirs with Christ, the Nazarenes*] in a print run of 800, then in 1886 in a run of 2,000 and again in 1896 in a run of another 8,600 copies together with the 103-page *Novi dodatak uza Harfu Siona* [*New Addition to the Zion's Harp*]. This edition was a translation of a hymnbook published in Zurich in 1855, titled *Neue Zionsharfe: Eine Sammlung von Liedern für die Gemeinde der Glaubenden in Christo* [*New Zion's Harp: A Collection of Songs for the Fellowship of the Believers in Christ*]. The next edition was published on the eve of the war, in 1913, and then reprinted in 1931. After the Second World War the hymnbook was reprinted in 1953, 1965, 1969, 1974, 1980, and finally in 1994, published by the Apostolic Christian Church[100] in Windsor, Ontario, Canada.

The translation of these songs for the first edition was mostly carried out by Đorđe Radojković (the first 250), and the remaining

---

[100] The name adopted by the Nazarene fellowships in the USA and Canada which as of the mid-1990s, numbered around 11,000 members in eighty congregations, of which seventy-seven were in the US, two in Japan and one in Canada. Figures from Mead, 1988:30.

fifty-six songs by Jovan Jovanović Zmaj[101]. Zmaj himself later denied his active interest in or any serious work on the hymnbook, writing a long letter to the Novi Sad daily *Zastava* which was published June 23, 1899. Zmaj describes how he merely translated a few songs for use by "some pious people who wanted to sing them within their own circles" (which is probably an accurate description and reflects the truth of the matter). Here Zmaj also addresses the harm caused to the Orthodox faith by the Nazarenes in recent times, another indirect testimony to the strength of this movement in the late nineteenth century. One statement of Zmaj's in particular sounds somewhat bitter, but is really a criticism of the existing state of affairs:

> Those few songs that I translated, I liked them, I am not ashamed of them even today. Every one of those songs could be sung in the Orthodox Church before our entire priesthood and no-one could say that they contradict pure Orthodoxy in the least.[102]

Criticism was everywhere. In Pančevo in 1897, Lutheran (Evangelical) priest Karl Bohus from Franzfeld (Kačarevo) published a booklet in German: *Čuvaj ono što imaš, pojašnjenje evangeličkim hrišćanima protiv zabluda nazarena* [*Guard What You Have, An Explanation for Evangelical Christians Against the Error of the Nazarenes*] (Bohus, 1897:6), in which he attempts to explain the "Nazarene error" to his parishioners. He briefly describes their history over the previous sixty years and addresses two topics in particular – the belief of the Nazarenes that one could be saved only within the Nazarene fellowship, which he certainly disputed, and the ques-

---

[101] Jovan "Jova" Jovanović, 24 November 1833 – 1 June 1904, nicknamed Zmaj, today a household name, one of the best-known and best-loved Serbian poets and writers of children's rhymes (t/n).

[102] In his writings back in 1862 (*Komarac*, no. 138), Zmaj mocked the Nazarenes and their strange "constitutions and reforms," their abstinence and so on. However a few decades later Zmaj was saying that *Zion's Harp* could be sung in Orthodox churches.

tion of the origins of the Nazarene hymnbook, the *Harfa Siona (nova sionska pesmarica)* [*Zion's Harp (a New Zion Hymnbook)*]:

> They boast of another's goods – in my research I discovered that of the 251 songs in their songbook, 72 were simply taken from various Lutheran songbooks and claimed to be original Nazarene songs... (Bohus, 1897:8)

Bohus systematically analyzed the songs and quoted the Lutheran originals, finding that around sixty songs were from the Württemberg Lutheran hymnal. He also talked about songs that the Nazarenes used that related to religious holidays (which the Nazarenes did not celebrate) and infant baptism (which the Nazarenes did not practice), citing this as proof that the songs had been taken wholesale. Bohus also talked about the Nazarene teaching that all other churches were "Babylon," that they erroneously considered themselves to be people without sin, and that they rejected priests because of their "wrong teaching." Bohus also devotes a little attention at the end to the question of oath-swearing and military service, both of which the Nazarenes rejected. The mere fact that this booklet was written at all, and that it was privately financed – seen from the fact that no publisher is named, only the *Braća Jovanović* [Brothers Jovanović] printing press in Pančevo – speaks to the influence and significance the Nazarenes had among the German-speaking population in Vojvodina.

Francis Mackenzie – Friend to the Nazarenes

Francis Harford Mackenzie, was born in 1833 on an estate in Gairloch, Ross-shire, Scotland, as the younger son of Baron Francis Mackenzie, a title later taken on by his eldest brother Kenneth. After the death of his parents, his upbringing was entrusted to his uncle on his father's side, Dr. John, and his stepmother Mary, who was a Quaker. The Mackenzie family belonged to the Free Church of Scotland – a Reformed denomination (Palaret, 1992:137), and Francis Mackenzie showed an interest in and inclination towards the activities of the Plymouth Brethren.[103] He spent his youth serving as a navy officer in the British fleet during the Crimean War, and after the peace treaty was signed, he lived as a young, rich London "lord-ling." After his religious conversion, he donated a large part of his inheritance to missionary work in France and the establishment of missionary schools for China and Africa. Prior to coming to Serbia, he spent two years in southern France, where he also distinguished himself with his humanitarian and charity work.

Mackenzie came to Serbia during the Serbian-Turkish war of 1876 with the intention of helping the wounded close to the front lines at Knjaževac and around Zaječar, having read reports in the English newspapers of the sufferings of the Serbian people in the Knjaževac district under the Turks. Mijatović tells of how he met a Serbian colonel there whom he zealously witnessed to about Jesus, having learned that the officer was an atheist, yet he was unsuccess-ful. Mackenzie was in poor health at the time (with pneumonia) and this officer and the military surgeons fought for his life and, as Mijatović puts it, "although he (the Colonel) did not believe in Jesus Christ as the Saviour, his conduct was that of a perfect Christian and, therefore, of a true gentleman" (Mijatovich, 1917:198).

He got involved in financing the construction of a public road near Užice, but had to quickly abandon this project as the workers demanded more gold sovereigns, that Queen Victoria had suppos-edly "sent…to be freely distributed" through him. On his return to Belgrade, he received the Cross of Knight Commander of the Takovo Order from King Milan, but refused to go before the king person-ally and so the medal was sent to him. Mijatović says he never wore it. Later, according to Palaret (1992:146), Mackenzie took a keen interest in the then-flourishing Nazarenes, with whom he shared an

---

[103] Known in Serbia as Crkva Braće [Church of the Brethren]. To be precise, in his memoirs, his friend of many decades Čedomilj Mijatović says that at one point, Mackenzie came to a personal faith in the Savior Jesus and that he believed and then became a member of the Plymouth Brothers, i.e. the Brethren (Mijatovich, 1917:200).

interest in the Gospel in the sense of opening people's eyes and turning them from light to darkness.

In 1877 in Belgrade, he met Čedomilj Mijatović, a minister in several governments of the late nineteenth century[104], whose wife Elodie Lawton was English, and a Methodist by confession (of the Wesleyan Church). She had spent some time in the US as an activist in the abolitionist movement, and was also an author and translator. Mackenzie and Mijatović maintained a continual friendship from 1877 to 1889, when the Mijatovićs went to England, although Mackenzie visited them later, too, and they remained very close. It

---

[104] In 1864 and 1865, with the help of his wife Elodie, Čedomilj translated Dickens' Christmas Stories. See Kabiljo-Šutić, 1989:19. Of Mijatović's translations we also read the following:

> Between 1868 and 1901, Čedomilj Mijatović translated some important works from the English language – travelogs, fictional works, memoirs and religious works, and sermons, bringing to Serbia those English modes of thinking that he thought might help bring about a more proper interpretation of the problem of the Eastern Question, the introduction of new conceptions of the historical sciences and a different understanding of religious issues…
>
> Realizing there was a lack of good religious literature in the Serbian language, Mijatović translated a classic work of seventeenth-century English literature: Bunyan's *Pilgrim's Progress*, which was reprinted in Serbia several times. Recognizing the poor standard of learning among Serbian priests, Mijatović also translated several sermons of the renowned – at the time – English preacher Spurgeon, who was already very popular with the Russians, with the intention of reviving the once well-developed but by then completely neglected preaching literature.

In 1878 Mijatović translated two sermons: "Be of Good Comfort, Rise; He Calls You" and "Come and Welcome," which were further reprinted. Elodie Mijatović translated religious stories from English for the journal *Vidovdan* and other publications in the capital. She is not a household name among the Serbian public despite also having written the following books in London in English between 1870-1878: *The History of Modern Serbia; Serbian Folklore; Battle of Kosovo, a Poem;* and others.

was very early on, as Čedomilj Mijatović testifies, that Mackenzie began helping persecuted Nazarene prisoners.

> I met him in Belgrade in spring 1877. He was brought to me by the famous friend of the Serbian people, Dr. Sandwith. We quickly became good friends, especially after the day I gladly agreed that he could meet some Nazarenes in my house, who had been warmly recommended to me by English friends, and who were serving jail sentences in the city of Belgrade; and also when one day I accompanied him to the city to visit those Nazarenes in the prison, who were not allowed to go out into the town (Mijatović, 1895:3).

It is thought that the first news of the persecution of the Nazarenes in Serbia was sent out into the world by British mining engineer Charles Bright[105], who forwarded the 1877 Nazarene petition to the British embassy in Belgrade. The report somehow reached Lord Radstock[106], who wrote to him about the persecution of the Nazarenes in Serbia. Dr. Ziemann traveled to Belgrade representing the Quakers and visited the Nazarenes. He took a petition for their release to Prince Milan, and in May wrote a report to Bevan Braithwaite in England, which helped spread the news about

---

[105] Charles Tilston Bright (1832-1888) was made a British life peer and knight of the French Legion of Honor. Together with his brother, he managed copper ore mining operations in Serbia between 1873 and 1877. He was known for patenting inventions that contributed to the development and laying of undersea transatlantic cables for sending telegraph messages between Great Britain and America. According to the Encyclopaedia Britannica, he was "successful" mining in Serbia.

[106] Granville Waldegrave (1833-1913), 3rd Baron Radstock, was a leading evangelical lay leader of the Anglican Church in the nineteenth century. He was friendly with the great missionary Hudson Taylor and financially supported missions in China, India and Tibet. He spent his whole life advocating for the rights of the poor, of refugees and of the oppressed, and so was not well-loved among the nobility (Trotter, 1914:9).

the Nazarenes. The letter was first published in *The Herald of Peace*, January 1, 1881, and then also reprinted in *Bible Society Monthly Newsletter* of February 1, 1881, (Prisoners for Peace…, 1881:679).

Mackenzie, having been told about the imprisoned Nazarenes, traveled to Obrenovac, visited the Nazarenes, and probably helped them financially since their homes had been vandalized. Makaji writes of how Mackenzie also visited Nazarenes imprisoned in Belgrade jails, "encouraging them not to lose heart but to persevere in their faith" (Makaji, 1975:12). Mackenzie and Mijatović then visited Valjevo where they found a few farmers who were Nazarenes and had been sentenced to twenty years hard labor for their refusal to bear arms (Mijatovich, 1917:202).

After the war ended, in 1877, Mackenzie bought a 120-hectare homestead from Đorđe Simić on what was then the southern outskirts of Belgrade, divided it into lots and leased a large portion out to the poor for them to live on. This part of town was quickly dubbed *Englezovac* – "Englishtown." There was just one condition: no shop selling alcoholic beverages was permitted in the settlement. Mackenzie was a believer in abstinence, especially having witnessed alcohol's destruction of poorer families and even those of more average means.

In 1878, he was back in the field in Užice, helping Serbian wounded, as well as *hajduks*[107] escaping from Bosnia. Mackenzie wanted to provide schooling to refugee children but the Ministry of Education would not support him, accusing him of being a Protestant and suggesting that he would sooner or later abandon the schools, burdening the state with their care.

Mackenzie was a humanitarian but was also an evangelist. Palairet believes that he was influenced by the (Plymouth) Brethren movement, as also testified by Mijatović in his memoirs, although he says that Mackenzie never adopted their theological exclusivism, maintaining his freedom of conscience.

In the early days of his time in Serbia, he patronized the *Hrišćanski Vesnik* journal, edited by Orthodox priest Aleksa Ilić, subscribing to

---

[107] Outlaws who fought against Ottoman and later Habsburg rule (t/n).

thirty copies. Later, even posthumously, he would also finance David Brown's *The Four Gospels: A Commentary*, translated by Čedomilj Mijatović; *Character* by Samuel Smiles, a book on the upbringing of children (as it was promoted in Serbia) that ran to three editions, as well as other projects. In February 1888, he did much to facilitate the visit to Belgrade by famous Scots preacher Alexander Somerville. His three sermons provoked some interest in Belgrade, leading the authorities to fear proselytization. In spite of King Milan's expression of dissatisfaction to Mackenzie, Čedomilj Mijatović succeeded in taking Somerville to Mihajlo, the Metropolitan of Belgrade, during which host and guest discussed the works of John Chrysostom. George Smith writes that Mackenzie helped Somerville greatly during his mission, and also that Mijatović interpreted for him. In fact, the Mijatović house was used for some of the meetings, attended by members of the Serbian elite. Later the meetings, moved to larger premises, saw as many as 300 attending, including officials, priests and teachers. The sermon, from Isaiah 60:8, was transcribed verbatim by the police, and the police commissaire on reading it declared it to be "very good" (see Smith, 1891:358).

Mackenzie was mindful of the opinions of the Orthodox Church but was also a great critic. This can be clearly seen in the description Mijatović gives in his book (see Appendix 2 at the end of this chapter). However he was careful to ensure that relations were never entirely soured. Although he supported the Nazarene movement in Serbia, he did not identify himself with it. His great friend Čedomilj Mijatović defended him in his foreword to *The Four Gospels* in 1897:

> But if I may I would say this much: that he was not a Nazarene, as he was suspected of being by certain people; nor did he belong to any English sect or church; nor did he ever, in any way, work in Serbia and among the Serbs in the interests of propaganda of any sort. He truly felt, with real pain in his soul, the paucity of religious life in Serbia, but he believed that God could nevertheless use the national Orthodox Serbian Church

as his means of reviving faith among the Serbs! He best and most clearly demonstrated his mood towards the Serbian Church in presenting the Serbian Metropolitan with land[108] for the construction of the Church of Saint Sava in Belgrade! (Mijatović, 1898:V).

The Peace Hall[109]

In order to promote religious life among the people, in 1890[110] Mackenzie built the so-called Hall of Peace on the land he had bought around what is now Slavija Square in Belgrade, intended as a place for lessons on faith to be held. To this end he translated several sermons and financed the publication of the *Kalendar Za Svakoga* [*Calendar for Everyone*], in which each date had a text from the Scriptures alongside it. Next to the hall he built a hotel that did not serve alcohol, but he soon had to give up on the work and the building was bought by the Mijatović family as their first house in

---

[108] In another place, Mijatović says that he received a letter from Mackenzie in which he told how he had gifted 7,000-8,000 square meters of land for the Church of Saint Sava in "Englezovac" and how Metropolitan Mihajlo had personally thanked him, visiting him and refusing to allow him to kiss his hands, instead kissing Mackenzie's face.

[109] For more on the Peace Hall, see the article by Nedić, 1995:123-132.

[110] Professor Ivanka Tipsarević-Lukić, in a comment published in the daily newspaper *Politika* on 29 November 2006, on page 11, claims that the Peace Hall was opened as early as May 1889. Professor Tipsarević-Lukić further says that the public had christened the street – previously called Oraška Street – "Makenzijeva" (Mackenzie Street), less than a year after his death in 1896, in memory of the great philanthropist. However the anonymous article by Teofan, mentioned in the section on the Nazarenes in central Serbia, published in *Srpska Nezavisnost* in Belgrade on 18 August 1888, mentions that the Nazarene movement, by this date, "…has already built its house of prayer – or better say, house of blasphemy – in a respectable part of Belgrade…" Later it transpired that the building was meant for all kinds of Bible and other teaching, and not as a place of worship, much less for a single religious group. Mackenzie had further-reaching plans.

Belgrade. The Hall was the venue for weekly meetings which ran between 1878 and 1889 – a full twelve years.

Mijatović testifies that the Serbian authorities knew the Nazarenes were exemplary citizens and Christians, pleasant people, willing to obey, sincere, harmonious, modest, and respectful of the law in all matters except in their refusal to bear arms as soldiers. In this last matter, respecting their principles of faith brought them into conflict with military laws, since they refused to do armed military service, which the law required of every male Serbian citizen. For this offense the courts handed down the severest possible sentences to Nazarenes. Mijatović says that the penalty was always twenty years of imprisonment with forced labor but that because the Nazarenes were sincere, good-natured and honest workers they would quickly win the trust of the prison wardens and frequently be released early.

When the meetings began at the Mijatovićs on Sunday afternoons, Mackenzie asked Mijatović to obtain the permission of the prison's administration in Belgrade for the two Nazarenes who were in jail but who had special prison privileges to go into town to carry out various jobs for the prison, to attend Scripture readings and prayers on Sunday afternoons. These meetings were also attended by foreigners who were staying in the city. Mackenzie organized the meetings and the Mijatović's were the hosts.

> It caused quite a sensation when it was rumoured that two Nazarene convicts came every Sunday to Minister Chedo's to pray with him. This not unnaturally led to my being suspected of being a Nazarene myself, although it was known that in the last war (in 1876 and 1877) I had served as major, and was...decorated...
>
> Later, the two Nazarene convicts took Mackenzie to the secret prayer-meetings of the Belgrade Nazarenes, and henceforth he went regularly to these meetings to pray. He was pleased when those simple but deeply religious men received

him as if he had been one of themselves. I say "simple," because they were mostly small artisans and labourers. After a few months, one Sunday evening, my friend came to me deeply perturbed, pale, sad and almost in tears. "What on earth is the matter?" "A great blow has been dealt at me this evening," he answered. "I went, as usual, to the prayer-meeting of the Nazarenes, but was met at the door by their leader, who told me, 'Some of us had our doubts about the propriety of admitting you, who are not a Nazarene, to our meetings, and asked for enlightenment from our bishop in Hungary. We have received a sharp rebuke for our foolish action, and an order not to admit you any more.'"

I sympathised with him the more sincerely as I know that two weeks earlier he had paid a distinguished Serbian lawyer a hundred and twenty pounds for a short but successful defence of a Nazarene who had refused to join the Army (Mijatovich, 1917:205).

In May 1891, Mackenzie sought permission to start a Sunday School. The opening of this day school was even advertized in the newspapers (see Appendix 1 at the end of this chapter), but was highly criticized from the beginning. The school eventually closed in 1892 despite the large number of students and lecturing Orthodox priests. There was even a debate in the Serbian parliament, and the elderly Metropolitan accused of supporting the activities of the Nazarenes.

Mackenzie defended himself in the newspapers stating that he was not personally a Nazarene but that he could see and understand their need for spirituality. He had a favorable opinion of the Nazarenes for two reasons. The first was that they read the Scriptures in their homes and met for prayer. The second was that since they were persecuted by the authorities for their meetings he felt it his duty to protect and encourage them – he was of the belief that the provisions of the Congress of Berlin granted each man the freedom to pray to God in the way he saw fit.

> Finding that these people, whose piety was to his mind never in any doubt, were being unjustly persecuted, he felt sympathy towards them, and when a Nazarene was arrested and taken before the courts merely for attending prayer meetings, he would procure attorneys for them, pay for their court costs and in several cases helped support the families of the convicted financially. But to the Nazarenes themselves he always said, giving proof with verses from Scripture, that they were wrong to refuse to bear arms... (Mijatović, 1895:3).

The Hall of Peace was later turned from a "Sunday school for Christian teaching" (Makenzi, 1892) into a "school for practical crafts for female children," which was its most successful venture. The teacher was a Ms. Kondić and the children were also taught Scripture. Before his death in 1895, he had plans to also open a children's nursery school, which he had already suggested in the early 1890s to the Lutherans and Reformed in Belgrade (the Belgrade Protestant Parish). Mijatović also talked about Mackenzie's opinions on the Nazarenes in the articles he wrote upon Mackenzie's death (see Appendix 4 at the end of this chapter).

Mackenzie was constantly involved in charity work. A tenth of his revenue from the lease of Englezovac and other income was paid to the Belgrade municipality to be used to help the poor, and he required his tenants to sign an undertaking that they would not sell alcoholic beverages. In 1886, Mackenzie wrote to the Municipal Committee of Belgrade concerning the boundaries of central Belgrade and his proposed urban plan for this neighborhood which he wanted to be included in Belgrade proper. In 1891, he wrote to Belgrade daily newspapers asking for the establishment of a society for the protection of animals, to which he was prepared to immediately remit a large sum so it could begin operating (see Appendix 3).

> Mackenzie – helper of the Nazarenes, of fallen women, of the wounded, of the spiritually backslidden, of beggars – was a true founding-father of the philanthropic movement in Serbia. Helping him in most of his endeavors was Mijatović. For this reason both of them deserve credit for disseminating the ideas of Christian charity and religious renewal... (Marković, 2006:65)

Francis Mackenzie died August 22, 1895, in Upper Norwood, England. Just seven hours before his death, he dictated a letter concerning the children's nursery in Belgrade and his involvement in that work. However, his will remained unchanged and funds intended for the work in Serbia ended up going to a missions college after all.

Marking Mackenzie's death, the British and Foreign Bible Society published an article looking back over their partnership with Mackenzie during his time in Serbia. The article was written by Edward Millard, who had overseen the work in the Balkans from the Society's Vienna depot. He noted that not long before that, Mackenzie had been very ill, practically at death's door, and that the Belgrade authorities had wanted to gift Mackenzie a grave as a mark of gratitude for his philanthropic work in the city. Mackenzie had subsequently made a recovery, but a few years later succumbed to illness (Millard, 1896:22).

Conclusion

The Nazarenes were the first Protestant group to amass a significant number of followers among the Serbian population in the kingdom of Hungary, today Vojvodina. The movement quickly spread to central Serbia, too. The primary reasons for their spread, according to Slijepčević, Birviš, and Kuzmič, can be found in the arrival of the railway and of industrialization in Serbia in the mid-to-latter half of the nineteenth century, and with them a large number of Protestants from the German lands and central Europe. Additional factors were Vuk Karadžić's translation of the New Testament into the common language, and the later translations of the whole Scriptures, as well as the state of affairs in the Serbian Orthodox Church, which was characterized by the neglect of believers on the part of the priesthood at the local level and political wrangling among the higher ranks.

We might add a fourth reason to these three: a spiritual need among the people for the unadulterated message of the Gospel, a deep-seated spiritual need of the time. This was something people could not appreciate until they accepted the teaching, and the light of salvation came into the lives of individuals. This was why the simplicity of the message, its communication from neighbor to neighbor, rather than along national/ethnic lines, and the hope in the Good News for the reasons given above, facilitated the spread of a movement full of self-confidence and heartfelt enthusiasm. Their conviction regarding the truth and their faith were such that many Nazarenes endured terrible punishment and years of penal labor, and some even gave their lives for their pacifist beliefs.

This firm stance required conviction of the deepest kind but also an understanding of the consequences. The Nazarenes held to biblical principles and their understanding of the commands of Jesus Christ. Their moral compass in that sense was exceptional.

From the moment that they crossed the banks of the River Sava, which denoted the border between the Austro-Hungarian empire and Serbia, and came to Obrenovac, the Nazarenes continued to quickly spread further, up to the borders of the new kingdom, only shortly before being recognized at the Congress of Berlin. Since the Serbian Orthodox Church in Serbia was a state church, attacks on and persecution of the Nazarenes became increasingly frequent.

Local priests kept the authorities informed about the situation at hand, with the help of local gendarmerie. The authorities, informed by the church hierarchy, would then use the state system to stop the Nazarenes' activities, usually employing the police and the education system.

Local priests occasionally used the police to forcibly baptize children from Nazarene families, having obtained information on them from the local schools in which they taught religious education. Some Nazarenes were sentenced to prison, a few were released under sporadic amnesties.

In the period leading up to the Balkan Wars, the Serbian authorities took the view that the influence of the Nazarenes in Serbia had been reduced to tolerable levels. A repressive state apparatus in league with the state Orthodox Church presented a major obstacle to the further spread of the movement. In the fifty years after the arrival of the Nazarene movement in Obrenovac, it succeeded in spreading to all corners of the princedom—later kingdom—but the years of effort invested in halting their spread did show results. Apart from strong local churches in Obrenovac, Belgrade and Aranđelovac, there were few places where they survived in greater numbers. On the eve of the First World War, the survival of the movement depended on developments on the Vojvodina side.

Appendix 1 – *Dnevni list,* February 21, 1891

Belgrade News – New evening school

In the building at Novo Selište, constructed next to the Slavija tavern, an evening school has been opened for all literate and illiterate orphans from this area who are unable to attend school during the day. Currently there are as many as forty pupils, with lessons held between 7:00 and 9:00 p.m. They are all taught by a single teacher, and subjects are reading, writing and arithmetic. The owner of the house – who founded the school and is concerned with its upkeep – also frequently visits.

Appendix 2 – Typical Serbian priest

My Scotch friend, the late Francis H. Mackenzie of Ross-shire – one of the most religious men I have ever met – expressed once to me the wish to be acquainted with a typical Servian clergyman of modern times. I have always though that my friend, the Archimandrite Nikanor Duchich, was an ideal Servian Churchman, and consequently I invited him to meet my Scotch friend at my house. They met, had a long, interesting and satisfactory talk, until Mr Mackenzie touched on the question of the efficacy of prayer and our duty to pray.

"I have travelled much about your country," my Scotch friend said to the Archimandrite, "and I was rejoiced to see on every side and on every occasion proofs of the great intelligence of your people. But I must add that I was saddened to see your churches empty and your people praying so rarely. You ought to teach your people to pray more!"

"I beg your pardon!" answered my ideal Servian clergyman. "I do not think our people should pray more, or even as much as they do now! Our people have been praying to God for more than four centuries to deliver them from the Turks, but God never answered their prayers! What we want nowadays is not prayer, but good education, good schools, good soldiers, good officers and good arms!"

Mr. Mackenzie turned to me with deeply saddened face, and *sotto voce* asked me: "Is this your ideal Servian clergyman?" I was myself astonished and saddened by the unexpected answer of my "mitre-bearing" friend but I had by a nod to confirm that he was so!

From the English book by Chedo Mijatovich, *Servia of the Servians*, New edition, London, Sir Isaac Pitman & Sons, 1911, page 37.

Appendix 3 – *Dnevni list,* issue 159 of 24 July 1891

To the editor of *Dnevni list,*

In a recent issue of your paper you wrote on the case of the cruel treatment of a horse here in Belgrade and ended with the statement that it was high time a society for the protection of animals were established in this country.

If I may say so, I have thought the same for a number of years, and would be willing to give 500 dinars to a society established with that objective.

In England there is a large society of this kind, with several policemen in its service, and the law against the cruel treatment of animals is so strictly enforced that where it is learned that a monetary fine would not be severely felt, rich offenders are usually sentenced to jail and the effect of some such examples has very much reduced the cruel treatment of cattle.

However, the conduct of charity amongst people using such funds is of no less importance than saving our necessary, good and dumb servants from mistreatment.

Belgrade, 19 July 1891
Francis H. Mackenzie

Appendix 4 – † Francis H. Mackenzie by Čedomilj Mijatović

Published in installments in the *Male Novine*, 3-7 September 1895, in Belgrade

We quickly became good friends, especially after the day I gladly agreed that he could meet some Nazarenes in my house, who had been warmly recommended to me by English friends, and who were serving jail sentences in the city of Belgrade; and also when one day I accompanied him to the city (1877) to visit those Nazarenes in the prison who were not allowed to go out into the town.

He took a considerable personal interest in the Nazarenes, for two reasons: firstly because they were the only people in Serbia to read the Scriptures in their homes in the Serbian language, and who met together to pray to God, again, in their everyday language; secondly, because to him as a man born and bred in the freedom of England, it seemed that the authorities were not right to imprison people merely for meeting together to pray to God! Finding that these people, whose piety was to his mind never in any doubt, were being unjustly persecuted, he felt sympathy towards them, and when a Nazarene was arrested and taken before the courts merely for attending prayer meetings he would provide attorneys for them, pay for their court costs and in several cases he helped financially support the families of the convicted...

What is more, at every opportunity he told the Nazarenes and others that the state was quite right to convict, through the courts, any citizen who would not fulfill their public duty to serve in the army and fight for their fatherland. To begin with, the Nazarenes, acknowledging his material assistance and sympathies for them, allowed him to attend their prayer meetings. However, after hearing directly from him on many occasions that, as regarded the question of arms, they had not the right in terms of Holy Scripture, they told some kind of bishop of theirs in the kingdom of Hungary and they received this order: not to allow him to attend their prayer meetings under any circumstances, and to take nothing from him! I remember – I can almost see it now before me – Mackenzie, despondent and deeply saddened, coming to me to bemoan the fact that he had gone to pray with the Nazarenes that day and that they had come to him and said that they had received an order from their elder to drive him away if he ever came to their meetings!

Figure 1 – Photocopy of the front cover and first page of the register of births of Nazarenes in the Pančevo Archive.

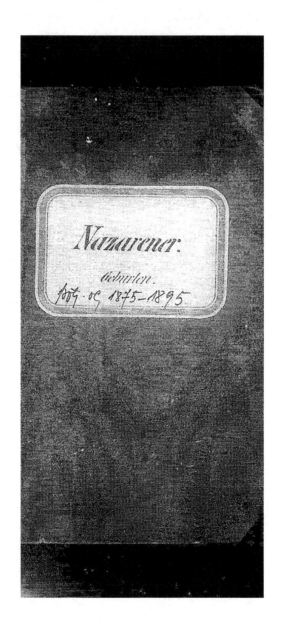

THE NAZARENES IN THE
NEW STATE (1918-1941)

Although some Nazarenes were willing to serve in the army during the war (both in the Austro-Hungarian and in the Serbian armies), mostly in noncombatant roles, they continued to be severely punished for their refusal to bear arms. The reports talk of some who were executed by firing squad and others who were thrown in dungeons. However, there were exceptions. like those who were allowed to serve in the army as cooks, couriers, grooms, and medics. The position of the Nazarenes was not fully clarified in either of the two world wars.[111]

John Graham talks about the very difficult situation the Nazarenes found themselves in during the First World War. While some young men served in noncombatant positions in the Austro-Hungarian army and were even decorated for their committed service, others languished in jail and some even died for their refusal to take up arms (Graham: 1992, 356).[112] After a large number of cases

---

[111] Hieromonk Irinej published a war story/report in 1927 about a Nazarene in the Serbian army who was shot because, when he was given a weapon and sent out on a scouting mission, on encountering the enemy he threw down his rifle and fled. Before receiving the weapon this Nazarene had been imprisoned and sentenced to death by shooting before the whole regiment as an example. Just before he was to be shot, when the officer asked him a third time to take up arms, the Nazarene had accepted a rifle (Stojanović, 1927:6).

[112] "Hadžija," an anonymous Nazarene from Belgrade, mentions the following cases in his book: having refused to take up arms, a Serb from Mramorak was killed with two shots from a revolver before assembled soldiers by an officer in the Austro-Hungarian army, somewhere around the beginning of hostilities. Because of this case the officer was brought before the military court (the ver-

had gone before the Austro-Hungarian military high court, a general decision was taken to allow Nazarenes to serve in hospitals, the medical corps, and in noncombatant roles. Graham mentions the case of Maxa Dilber, who as a Nazarene was initially drafted and made a civilian truck driver, but later transferred to the ranks and shot for insubordination when he refused to take up arms. Doctor Štern from Zagreb testified that after the high court decision came into effect, certain commanders saw fit to continue making life difficult for the Nazarenes. He gave the example of Nazarenes serving in a military hospital, where the order was given for the Nazarenes to only be tasked with the most serious cases. This concession only applied to those Nazarenes who were willing to swear the oath that the state required of them. After swearing, they were assigned their noncombatant duties. However many did not want to make this compromise with the military authorities. They ended up in jail, some were executed by hanging (even though they had the right to be shot) and the situation was not made easier for them in the least.

After hostilities ended and draftees returned to their homes, it might have been expected that the situation would become more relaxed, but in fact, hundreds of Nazarenes remained in jail. In September 1921, Graham reported that more than 200 Nazarenes were still in jails all over Hungary (in the newly-founded republic) as a result of convictions during the First World War, which had ended in 1918.

Horvat's sources from this time speak of Nazarenes recorded in Srem in the following places: Bačinci, Batrovci, Berkasovo, Erdevik, Ilinci, Adaševci, Ljuba, Molovin, Trgovište, and Privina Glava (Horvat, 2000:121).

---

dict is not known) and after that orders soon came from Vienna that Nazarenes were not to be punished for refusing to accept arms. The order said that such people should be sent to the front lines to "cut wire," presumably referring to barbed wire. It is then recorded that on August 11, 1914, two Nazarenes (and possibly a third) of Serbian nationality were shot with a revolver, together with other non-Nazarene Serbs and others. Before the order from Vienna came into force, a Nazarene in Srem and another near Srbobran were also shot (Hadžija, 1936:14-15).

Prohibition of Activity

In the new state that was established in 1918, the mood towards the Nazarenes and Adventists continued to worsen. Although the kingdom of SCS had in its new territory retained the laws and regulations relating to religious communities that had applied in the precursor states, specifically in Austria-Hungary, and affirmed these through subsidiary legislation, the situation continued to deteriorate. The law explicitly referred to existing legislation and religious communities:

> Article 2: Adherents also of religious movements that are not legally recognized shall be permitted to privately conduct religious ceremonies in the home and family.

> Article 3: All those religions are recognized in the Kingdom as a whole that have in any of its parts in which they are established already received legal recognition (Lanović, 1920).

Austria-Hungary had on December 12, 1895, passed an order of the Imperial Provincial Government, Department of Religions and Education, and Department of the Interior, under number 12,200 (Sbornik 1895, komad XX, broj 87) setting in order certain matters relating to the lives of Nazarenes and Baptists, which had until then been unrecognized as religious communities in its territory. Thereby these two religious communities were practically brought into the legal system, even though the order could freely be described as very restrictive.

The empire then passed a Law on Confessional Relations. In the order for the enactment of the law of April 15, 1907, in the commentary on Article One of this law, we read: "The regulations on corporate worship by the followers of the Nazarene and Baptist sects can be found in the previous Order of the Government," referring to that from 1895. This law thus rested on a previous legal enactment.

Although these enactments had legal force in the kingdom of SCS, after only a few years certain politicians began to act autocratically. Minister Janjić decided to "ban" the Nazarenes in 1924. The political situation in the country meant that coalition ministers probably did not interfere in the work of their colleagues from other parties and so it is possible, though unlikely, that Janjić launched this little crusade against the Nazarene religious community as well as the Adventists, on his own initiative.

The Ministry of Religions of the kingdom of SCS was established in late 1918 and had supreme supervisory and executive authority over all religious-political affairs "where they came into the sphere of state business" (Gardašević, 1971:40). The kingdom proclaimed the equality of all faiths, the announcement made in a statement by Prince Regent Alexander on Serbian Orthodox Christmas Eve which was January 6, 1919. From the establishment of the new state on December 1, 1918, until the enactment of the so-called Vidovdan Constitution, passed June 28, 1921, the legal status of religious communities remained as it had been at the time of the entry of the territory and the communities themselves into the new state[113]. The Vidovdan Constitution proclaimed full freedom of religion and conscience, but named only the Serbian Orthodox Church, the Catholic Church, the Greek Catholic Church and the Lutherans, together with the Reformed Church, and the Islamic and Mosaic faiths. Nazarenes, as well as other small Protestant religious communities, were not allowed.

---

[113] Under the 1919 Treaty of St. Germain, the Allied and Associated states (the kingdom of SCS was considered an associated power under this agreement) agreed to continue tolerating all Christian religious missions and organizations that had existed in Austrian territory and had been founded and financed by Austrian nationals at the time. The Allied and Associated Powers agreed to ensure the interests of these organizations were protected. See Article 376, Part XIV of the Treaty of Peace of St. Germain-en-Laye. The treaty was signed on behalf of the king and the state by then-Prime Minister Nikola Pašić and Foreign Minister Ante Trumbić.

A special law covered religious oaths in court, the
state services and the army. Marriage could only
be entered into by way of a religious ceremony.
Arbitration and marital disputes were under the
jurisdiction of the confessional communities. It
was they who maintained the registries of births,
deaths and marriages (Rakić, 2002, book 1:22).

In 1921, the authorities tried to take a stance on the major
religions, organizing a ten-day consultation in Belgrade titled *Verska
Anketa* [Survey on the Religions]. From November 15-22, and then
again at a number of later gatherings, representatives of the churches
and religious communities and of the state held plenary and group
consultations on a number of points: the legal status of all recognized religious communities, how to set interconfessional relations in
order, how to provide materially for priests and a proposed calendar
of religious holidays in the kingdom of SCS. One of the participants,
Dr. Rado Kušej, a university professor from Ljubljana and representative of the Catholic church, later published his own conclusions
and results of the survey, allowing us an insight into the atmosphere
at the gathering. The only Protestant group there was the Lutherans
who, having had a common synod with the Reformed church in
Austro-Hungary, also represented the Reformed church at the Survey
on the Religions. The situation then was by no means straightfor-
ward, as can be seen in the report by their group. When we see the
attitude that was taken by the new state towards the Lutherans and
Reformers, the hard stance toward the Nazarenes is no surprise, nor
is the change in state policy.

At the end of the proceedings, a whole list of
complaints was added relating to the behaviour
of the authorities towards Lutheran pastors and
schools. It is claimed that pastors were made to
hold worship services on the holy days of other
confessions (Saints Cyril and Methodius' Day,

zadušnice[114] and the *parastos*[115]). In one town the pastor was made to hold a memorial service for the Catholic bishop. Schools were expropriated from church parishes against their will and teachers dismissed without pensions. As well as schools, church property (buildings) were also confiscated, causing loss to the churches amounting to 52 million kruna in our money (Kušej, 1922:30).

In late 1923, changes came about in the government of the kingdom of SCS, and Dr. Vojislav Janjić[116] became the new Minister of Religions, who threw himself energetically into addressing the so-called "problem" of the Nazarenes and Adventists in the new state. In an article titled "*Verska pitanja u našoj zemlji*" ["Religious Issues in our Country"], published by *Politika* on January 5, 1924, he stated that he could not recognize the Adventists and Nazarenes. He added that their defeatist attitude had been brought in "from outside" and that they were a foreign influence aimed at destabilizing the state. Several months later, Janjić revoked the previous temporary orders granting a certain amount of freedom to individual religious communities in territories that had previously been part of other states, and issued a new decision that, as will later be seen, brought a great deal of misery and misfortune to these two religious communities, especially the Nazarenes. Here is cited in full the much-quoted and documented Order no. 8765/1924 of 1 May 1924.

Kingdom of SCS
Ministry of Religion, General Department

---

[114] A Serbian Orthodox holiday celebrated four times a year in remembrance of the dead, similar to All Souls' Day (t/n).

[115] A Serbian Orthodox memorial liturgy for the recently deceased (t/n).

[116] Professor Dr. Vojislav "Voja" Janjić was an Orthodox priest and member of the National Radical Party leadership. He was a minister in a number of royal governments. He was succeeded by Miša Trifunović, earlier an official in the same ministry, who was responsible for carrying out this order of Janjić's.

V. Br. 8765
5 May 1924
Belgrade

Article 12 of the Constitution of our Kingdom guarantees the freedom of public confession only of those faiths which have in any part of the Kingdom already been granted legal recognition. Not every faith may be preached, disseminated nor manifested until it is recognized by special Law. According to the Constitution the State has the right by Law and by all legal means to prohibit the dissemination of all faiths that act in opposition to the State and its interests, and to forbid the congregation of adherents of such unrecognized faiths where there is the belief that at these meetings are preached principles contrary to the interests of the State.

At the moment in our State, as you are no doubt aware, there are two Christian sects: Nazarenism and Adventism.

Neither of these two sects were recognized in any of our provinces before the 1921 Constitution, nor are they recognized by the Constitution. However it is known that both Nazarenism and Adventism act directly against the State and its interests, teaching their adherents not to comply with certain of their civil duties such as military service, swearing oaths etc. Where circumstances have nevertheless brought members of these sects into positions of public duty, they are unusually persistent in spreading and propagating the idea of strict refusal to carry out one's civil and state duties. They also have no compunction, everywhere and at all times in their meetings, speeches and sermons, in discrediting the State. Yet they are very well-practised in collecting funds from their adherents, which are then sent to their headquarters outside our State.

They also very adept at keeping secret their meetings and meeting-places.

The Adventists additionally have a well-developed popular publishing activity, and these are books in the form of large, traditional calendars and such-like, which they sell cunningly and aggressively.

It is obvious that the members of these sects are the victims of well thought-out plans, hatched elsewhere and brought into our country under the guise of faith, in order to achieve their objectives through the fragmentation of society and the weakening of the character of our people.

In notifying you of the foregoing, and as duty demands of me – to concern myself with the security of the land in this area – I recommend that you kindly investigate all matters in this regard with great care and learn if one or both of these sects are present anywhere, and if it is determined that they are, take strict and energetic measures in order to:

a) close these houses/meeting places in which they gather and permanently prohibit their access to these; and to take good care that they do not meet elsewhere;

b) dismantle their organizations and stop all activities of the administrative bodies of their associations, which cannot have the character of private/legal corporations; and

c) prohibit their preachers, and every Nazarene and Adventist individually, from spreading and propagating these sects.

And in order that my Ministry know locally exactly where any of these sects are present and where they are active, please be so kind as to submit your detailed report to me, as well as a report on the measures taken against them and the results achieved.

MINISTER OF RELIGIONS,
Voj. Janjić

During 1923 there had been an effort to shut down Adventist and Nazarene places of worship, but judging by complaints from the Archdiocesan Consistory held in Sremski Karlovci in 1931 it seems that this order was not carried out:

> According to the memorandum of the Holy Synod of Bishops of 6/19 October 1925, Syn. no. 1700, the Minister of Religions, by his decision in principle dated 25 September 1923, no. 11622, forbade the preaching of the Adventist and Nazarene sects and the spread and dissemination of these sects, and decreed that the premises in which these two sects meet should be closed down and their organizations broken up...[117]

Minister Janjić's 1924 order was quick to be put into effect, however. Trifunović, an official in the Ministry of Religions, in his own circular no. 22562/1924 ordered the prohibition and prevention of "the spread of propaganda" of the Nazarenes and Adventists. This circular was a result of the earlier-cited order 8765/1924 by Minister Janjić and was sent out to everyone. Local authorities received clear instructions on what to do and how to do it. Nazarene meetings were to be prohibited, books confiscated, buildings and places of worship

---

[117] Archive of Serbia and Montenegro, fond 63, fascikla 144, Broj K. 32/zap. – 1931 of 4/17 February 1931. Copy of document in possession of author.

placed under lock and key, and members made note of. The police and gendarmerie were to play the leading role in this. The state apparatus of repression rolled into action.

However this sudden and, in our opinion, legally baseless decision, lead to some unexpected problems. Although the authorities had possession of the ownership and land registry books, they were not ready for the changes that had taken place in previous years in regard to property owned by Nazarenes. Acting on the minister's order, the Novi Sad Captaincy (the local police) shut down the Nazarene house of prayer in 1924 and dissolved the organization, "individually forbidding each member from further spreading and disseminating" their faith. But they also informed the Ministry in Belgrade that the Nazarenes had, back in 1923, purchased a plot of land and a building with contributions collected from members and entered them in the land registry where they were recorded as the "*Nazarensko bogomoljsko udruženje u Vršcu*" [The Nazarene Prayer Association in Vršac] The authorities did not know what to do since this was now a matter of private ownership. In any case, these measures proved inadequate to prevent the activities of the Nazarenes and Adventists at the local level.

Број пи. 229. предс. 1926.

Господину

В е л и к о м Ж у п а н у
Бачке Области

С О М Б О Р

На допис бр. 6808 част ми је известити Вас, да је напред
речена богомоља у Новом Саду затворена и запечаћена.

Кључ исте се налази код род. вел. запечаћен на чувању
до даљег наређења.

У Новом Саду - 10/XII. 1926. год.

градски начелник,

Translation:

To the esteemed,

Great Prefect
of the Bačka District

SOMBOR

In response to letter ref. no. 6802, it is my pleasure to inform you that the Nazarene place of worship in Novi Sad has been closed and sealed.

Its key is with the High Captaincy for safekeeping until further orders.

Novi Sad, 10 December 1925
City Chief

Report from the Novi Sad city police chief to the Bačka district prefect on the closure of a place of worship

The Minister of Religions then sent a new memorandum to the Minister of the Interior, Božidar Maksimović on June 22, 1925, warning him that neither the measures being taken by district prefects nor those taken by the governor of the city of Belgrade were producing sufficient results.[118] The minister was unhappy with the work of the police as "it had come to his attention" that local state authorities were not devoting sufficient attention to these "sects" since the Nazarenes had in many town reopened their houses of worship and "were conducting their meetings in them unhindered." He commented:

---

[118] Archive of Serbia and Montenegro, fond/fascikla 63/144, Ministry of Religions pov. br. 104/1925 dated 22 June 1925. Copy of document in possession of author.

Were it not for their religious aspect, these sects might be considered a part of the communist movement, to whom they are closest in the method and purpose of their propaganda. In fact though, they are some kind of faith founded on a literal, layman's interpretation of the Holy Scripture, which unites people in religious feeling but actually has a political tendency, which is disseminated by agents from outside our state who have the task of introducing confusion in the souls of our weak-faithed, easily-led peasants and politically irresolute folk in the newly-liberated regions. And it is precisely this religious aspect which makes these sects all the more dangerous, and a serious threat to the well-being of our state and nation and to the establishment of political order in our country. Having all of this in mind we must not allow the state authorities to take an entirely ambivalent attitude towards these sects, or to encourage them.

Concluding this sharply-worded letter, the minister of religions requests that the minister of the interior write to the district prefects and the governor of Belgrade at the earliest opportunity, reinforcing the order of the Ministry of Religions from 1924. Ever-diligent, Police Minister Maksimović reported on August 30, 1925, that a Nazarene place of worship had been discovered in Vršac that had been "entered in the land registry in the name of a legal subject (the Nazarene Prayer Association) which could not legally exist..." and sought advice as to what to do with the confiscated property of the sect and how to liquidate it.[119] The Nazarenes it seems had made use of a registered organization in Vršac to purchase and register two

---

[119] Archive of Serbia and Montenegro, fond/fascikla broj 63/144, Ministry of Religions Pov. Br. 380/1925 of 30 August 1925. Copy of document in possession of author.

pieces of land and two buildings, one in Vršac and the other in Novi Sad.[120] The executive authorities did not know how to deal with private property that had been given to an unrecognized religious community for them to use.

Another interesting case is that of Panta Jovina, president of the Nazarene house of prayer in Obrovac, who in 1925 applied to the county court in Bačka Palanka for entry of "immovables" in Obrovac listed under br. 9, top. br. 571 with ownership rights registered to the "*Nazarenska Bogomolja*" [Nazarene House of Prayer], but was refused. In Bačka Palanka they had already been warned regarding the case in Vršac. The Nazarene movement was recognized neither as a religious community, nor as a tolerated community, nor as a legal subject, and the authorities repressed them in every way they could.[121] In the case in question, Judge Mandić referred back to an

---

[120] Archive of Serbia and Montenegro, fond/fascikla broj 63/144, br. 39684 dated 16/04/1925.

[121] In a written report by the Autonomous Province of Vojvodina Commission for Religious Affairs concerning the visit by Dušan Tubić, representative of the Nazarene religious community in Novi Sad, dated 25 October 1966, there is, indicatively, mention of the initiative on the part of the Nazarenes regarding the problem of ownership of buildings in which Nazarene places of worship are housed. This document shows us how the Nazarenes tackled the problem of ownership of their houses of prayer during the 1920s:

> ...Since before the war the Nazarenes were hindered in their activities, they resorted to purchasing property – the houses in which their places of worship were located, under the name of individual believers. Now the problem arises that the inheritors of these buildings in some places want to take ownership of them, even though they are themselves aware that they are the *de facto* property of the Nazarene religious community. I advised him (Kosta Gucunja, Chair of the Commission, advised Tubić – author's note) to take this matter up with the relevant government authorities or with the courts in order to resolve these property ownership issues. Tubić proposed an attempt to resolve this issue with a circular letter, at which I replied to him that in my opinion such an approach could not achieve anything,

earlier government document that forbade the Nazarenes from exercising property ownership rights.

Persecution Orchestrated by the Authorities

In early February 1920, a twenty-one-year-old Nazarene, Paja Tordaj, was called up to military service. During the First World War, he had been drafted into the Austro-Hungarian army but had been allowed to serve without swearing the oath or taking up arms.[122]

Refusing once again to take up arms, but this time in the army of the kingdom of SCS, he served his first two months in the Engineer Battalion in Senta and was then deployed to Kumanovo. It seems that the local officers sympathized with him and sent him to serve in the transportation department. Paja was in the army in Serbia for a year-and-a-half, and a further six months on the border with Albania. Having completed his military service, plus a month more than was required by law, he was reported by his superior officer to the military court for his refusal to take up arms, and he was sentenced to five years and eight months imprisonment. He served his term in Sremska Mitrovica and was released on July 18, 1926. He was immediately sent to a military unit, the Twenty-Second Infantry Regiment, Fifth Company, stationed in Kriva Palanka. There, commander Ljubomir Tošić ordered him to take up arms, and when he refused to do so he was first struck in the face, and then the duty guard and the officer aimed loaded guns at his face to try to force him to accept the weapon. When this failed, Lieutenant Anton Milekić had him held in a storeroom, tied up with ten rifles hanging round his neck, so that he nearly died of strangulation on three separate occasions.

The next few days officers took turns, two at a time, to tie Paja to a light machine gun six times before noon and another six times

---

and that each individual case would need to be resolved in court proceedings. Tubić agreed with this...

[122] In 1886 the Austro-Hungarian Empire had allowed Nazarenes to give a "pledge" rather than swear an oath.

during the afternoon. Every day the officers would try to make him swear, and when he refused to do so he would be beaten until he was bleeding or he lost consciousness. Officer Dragoljub Carić took his New Testament away and spat on it and tore it.

Hoping to weaken his resolve, they made Tordaj a bed with spikes hammered in from underneath so that he could not even move and could only lie on his side for several nights. The battalion commander, visiting on an inspection, forbade this practice and ordered that he be sent to the military court. However this never happened, and the officers continued to beat and mistreat him.[123]

In September 1924, all men aged between twenty and fifty living in the territory of Vojvodina were called up for military exercises and to swear an oath to the new state. At that time around 1,400 Nazarenes refused to take the oath and all were first sent before a military court and then to prison. The greatest number of them were in Petrovaradin. Some of them were led through the villages, their legs in chains, to serve as an example. One officer is alleged to have said, "Kill them, take everything they own, burn their houses…nothing will happen to you" (Stäubli, 1928).

The newspapers reported on these events. "In a camp where the Nazarenes are held there is perfect order, peace, and love, it looks like a church. When they speak, the discussion is about Jesus, when they read, the literature is the Bible and when they sing, they sing the Psalms" (Czako, 1925:61).

As it happened, though, the authorities entered into some kind of agreement with the elders, which happened to coincide with election time, and a solution was found for the "oaths problem."[124] The Nazarenes were allowed to go home, and the Radicals received more votes in the election than previously. Supposedly the Nazarenes promised certain Radicals, members of parliament, that they would vote for them at the next election, which helped secure the release of the Nazarenes.

---

[123] The further fate of Paja Tordaj is not known to us. The case is presented here from a petition by his mother dated 22 July 1927, three months after he was sent to the Kriva Palanka barracks. See Stäubli, 1928:10.

[124] It is possible that this is the "pledge" referred to in Appendix 2.

> At some point in history we voted. King Alexander
> made it possible for us to not have to take the
> oath, only to make a pledge, but in return we
> would vote, and would do so for the option that
> suited the authorities. This practice continued
> until the communists came to power.[125]

However in 1925, the police again began prohibiting Nazarene
meetings and closing down their places of worship, and regularly
reporting back on this to their superiors.[126] The *Politika* daily
reported that all the "associations" of the Nazarenes and Adventists
were being closed down, that there were a significant number of
Nazarenes in Obrenovac and that they even had their own church
(meaning a building) in Aranđelovac.[127] Journalists from the daily
newspapers learned that the Ministry of Religions had sent a new
order to the police authorities to forbid the activities of all Nazarene
(and Adventist) associations, to close down their meeting places and
to have their preachers and missionary workers arrested and brought
before the court. The media witch-hunt began with the claim that
there were more than 150,000 sect members and that their numbers
had been on the increase in recent years. With this kind of reporting—of course fabricated to achieve maximum effect—the public
expected the authorities to act.

The authorities made their next move, informing the county
prefects that they no longer needed to keep registries of births, marriages, and deaths for members of the Nazarene community (which

---

[125] From a conversation between Karlo Hrubik, elder of the Novi Sad Nazarene fellowship and Sanja Stanković. For more information see Stanković, 2007:40-57.

[126] Order of the Ministry of the Interior for Banat, Bačka and Baranja br.
25320/1924 on the dissolution of the Adventist and Nazarene sects. See also
the Archive of Serbia and Montenegro, fond/fascikla 63/144, pov. br. 528/1925
dated 14 September 1925 – High Captaincy of the City of Novi Sad, in which
the High Captain informs the Ministry of Religions that after the closure of
Adventist and Nazarene places of worship in Novi Sad there are no further signs
of activity.

[127] "Borba protiv novoveraca" [The fight against the new believers], *Politika*, 18
February 1925, page 5.

had been the practice since 1895). It was the opinion of the authorities that the decision of the Ministry of Religions of 1924 had voided the decision from 1895 and that the county and town authorities "no longer had to keep registries of the births, deaths and marriages of Nazarenes."[128]

However, in practice not everything went as planned. Memorandum number 4859 from 1925 reminds the Ministry of the Interior of the 1924 order and says that the regional authorities in Vojvodina "are to continue their further operations in accordance with the order of the Minister of Religions." In the same memorandum, the instruction is given that the orders of the Ministry are not to be revoked at the local level except under the direct order of the Ministry of Faith.[129]

In April 1925, there was a new turn of events. The Ministry of the Interior approved the reopening of Nazarene places of worship, issuing enactment no. 3779, dated April 10, 1925. Learning of these developments, on June 16 that same year, the Ministry of Religions responded with the demand that this decision be immediately made void. However, this was delayed, probably due to personnel changes.[130]

In a 1929 memorandum from the Bačka District Prefect – in which the facts surrounding the closure, then reopening, then subsequent reclosure of places of worship are set out in chronological order – we see why the Ministry of the Interior acted in this way in 1925, as well as the questions raised after the enactment of the so-called January Sixth Dictatorship of King Alexander:

---

[128] Vojvodina Archive, F 126 II D.Z.Br. 7976. dated 1 October 1926.

[129] Archive of Serbia and Montenegro, fond br. 63, fascikla 144. Dopis Ministarstva Vera br. 4859/25 dated 25 April 1925. Copy of document in possession of author.

[130] The Ministry of Religions, by way of Memorandum no. 11797 dated 27 August 1925, informed its Catholic department of the steps taken to declare this decision void, and said that as yet no response had been received from the Ministry of the Interior. Copy of document in possession of author.

...to date no resolution has been received from the Ministry of Religions in response to this memorandum and report from the Captaincy, but prior to the previous elections to the National Assembly places of worship and bookshops were reopened after verbal intervention by members of the Assembly...Since the newly-established organization of the state has effected the suspension of the Constitution, and therefore all constitutional regulations relating to religion, we request your urgent instruction as to the position that the local police here are to take in regard to the Adventists and Nazarenes.[131]

SOC in the campaign against the Nazarenes

From the very beginnings of the Nazarene movement, documents and printed publications talk of the common struggle of the state and the SOC (Serbian Orthodox Church) against the Nazarenes, mostly initiated by the SOC. When the district governor reported the presence of Nazarenes in Kragujevac on July 24, 1889, the minister of police wrote that same day to the Minister of Education asking him to make enquiries with Metropolitan Mihailo. The response came back that the Church had already issued instructions as to what was to be done with this "virulent disease of the corrupt Nazarene minds." The Church asked for schoolteachers and the police to get involved. Thus the Minister of Education instructed the principal of the Kragujevac Gymnasium to "render entirely impossible the harmful influence of the Nazarenes on the school youth." The minister of police, for his part, gave instructions for the arrest of Nazarenes in

---

[131] Archive of Serbia and Montenegro, fond 63, fascikla 144, br. 157-B dated 20 March 1929 – Bačka District Prefect. Copy of document in possession of author. A response to the District Prefect's question arrived from the Ministry of Justice, br. 8898/29, dated 27 April 1929, in which it was briefly stated that the order of 5 May 1924 remained in force.

Belgrade, Valjevo, and Kragujevac, and for the police to pay strict attention to and report back on the movements of the agents of the British and Foreign Bible Society.

> Metropolitan Mihailo was of the opinion that the priests alone could not stand in the way of this evil: the help of the state authorities was needed, who had more facilities at their disposal for the repression of this "virulent disease of the corrupt Nazarene minds." In view of the fact that the Nazarene sect had put down considerable roots among school pupils, Metropolitan Mihailo thought that in addition to priests, schoolteachers should also become involved in weeding out this sect... In addition to the priesthood and the schools, Metropolitan Mihailo thought that the police authorities could also provide considerable assistance in suppressing Nazareanism, prosecuting them, preventing them from holding their meetings or becoming Assembly members or serfs, bringing them before the civil courts for their teaching, which was false and harmful to the state, and also to pay special attention to persons who "hawk and sell books of the Holy Scripture and the Old and New Testament to the people, and in the course of selling see fit to offer their own interpretation of Holy Scripture and to preach sayings from it, turning aside Orthodox teaching of the faith. Where these are foreign subjects, do not give them shelter in our country but send them to their native country and fatherland. This would of course be a final and extreme measure, if it did not come into collision with the state order" (Puzović, 1997:286).

For his part, the Metropolitan wrote to the priesthood of all districts, telling them to help prevent the spread of the Nazarene faith through suitable sermons and religious teaching. When Bible Society representative Wilhelm Lichtenberger requested an extension to his permit to distribute books in 1890, the minister asked the Metropolitan of the SOC what to do and the latter asked the Holy Synod of Bishops. The response came back "not to allow the hawking of religious law books," but that they could be sold in bookshops. Permits and prohibitions were issued to the Bible Society for another two years after that, but after 1893 there is no record that this practice was continued. One explanation for this can be found in the fact that Belgrade Metropolitan Mihailo, a major leader in the fight against the Nazarenes, died in 1898.

In 1891, the SOC Synod debated the Nazarenes, and the minister of police asked the Minister of Education and Religions to ensure that teachers and priests continued to work on suppressing this sect since "the civil authorities alone cannot do everything that is needed." The close cooperation between the SOC and the state authorities reached the point in 1895 where police and agents were recording Nazarenes and their supporters in order to ensure they were constantly monitored and "every undertaking of theirs in that regard" suppressed.[132]

In a letter to the Ministry of Education and Church Affairs in January 1895, Metropolitan Mihailo[133] continued his crusade against

---

[132] Archive of Serbia, Ministarstvo prosvete i crkvenih dela, B-3227, br. 83, 23 February 1895. Copy of document in possession of author.

[133] Puzović concludes in relation to Metropolitan Mihailo and his efforts to suppress the Nazarenes:

> Metropolitan Mihailo, together with the priesthood and state authorities, did everything he could until the end of his days to stand in the way of this sect. It must be admitted that the results were not significant, because the sectarians went into hiding and when favourable conditions were re-established they continued with their activities. Thus there are records of this sect, albeit fewer, even in the time of Metropolitan Mihailo's successors.

the Nazarenes, giving information on their growth, obtained from reports by local priests. The Nazarene movement in the then-kingdom of Serbia had spread via Obrenovac and Aranđelovac to Kragujevac, Jagodina, Paraćin, Belgrade and in the surrounding villages, and after that in Zaječar and surrounding area.

The preoccupation of the church and state authorities in Serbia was such that the Russian ambassador to Belgrade reported to Moscow on the matter in 1892. The SOC Synod frequently discussed them too, and in 1906, ordered that a certain Paja Janjatović of Sombor must continue to pay the *parohijal* (the church/school tax), since although he had become a Nazarene, his children continued to attend school (Rakić, 1986:197). The situation was so alarming that some priests even proposed a subject be introduced at seminary against the Nazarenes.

The editors of *Vesnik srpske crkve* in 1902 reported that they had gone to Obrenovac to a Nazarene meeting where there was "a significant number" of them. There they talked to the Nazarene elders, referred to as Čika Steva and Čika Đura, and reported that Čika Steva was in 1876 sentenced to twenty years of imprisonment after refusing to take up arms, but that he was later released thanks to the mediation of English "friends of the Nazarenes" after hostilities had ceased.[134] At the Thirteenth Assembly of Priests, held at the Belgrade

---

Here we must emphasize that the lack of reports from the field are not a valid basis for Puzović's conclusion that the Nazarene movement had diminished – it may only have meant that priests were not reporting back, or thought that they had done their job in acting on instructions from the Church leadership. By consulting other sources we can conclude that the Nazarenes were in fact very active in Vojvodina and Serbia precisely in the final decade of the nineteenth century and first decade of the twentieth century, one indication of this being the number of printed copies of the Zion's Harp hymnbook.

[134] *Nazarenstvo u Obrenovcu [Nazareanism in Obrenovac]*, *Vesnik srpske crkve*, sveska 10, godina XIII, p. 933. These English friends were probably Quaker groups who were monitoring the situation with the Nazarenes in Serbia and keeping the public informed about this. This may also refer to Mackenzie, who had taken an interest in the fate of imprisoned Nazarenes.

High School, the topic of the Nazarenes and how to suppress them sparked a lengthy debate, and resulted in two resolutions.[135]

In 1903, there were reports on Nazarenes in Smederevo, which said that the Nazarenes had well-established fellowships in Obrenovac, Zvečka, the villages of Subotinac near Aleksinac and Radljevo in the Tamnava district. Two missionary families – those of Samuilo Vitid and Lazar Sremac – had come there from Austro-Hungary, the report notes (Popović, 1903:25-35). In Belgrade another group was arrested a year later.[136] It is interesting to note that in 1906 they further report on Subotinac, saying that the new religion arrived "a quarter of a century ago"—so as early as 1880—that the new believers were well-off in material terms and that they comprised three families, and that one of them was "some sort of elder," together with a cobbler from Kruševac. The report mentions meetings in Niš, Leskovac, Knjaževac, and another report mentions Soko Banja (Soko Banjska). This document, like the last one, ended with the expressed wish of the local parish priest for a full priest's wage which, he deemed, would be of key importance in the struggle against the Nazarenes! (Kojić, 1906:730-742)

It is probable that from Serbia the Nazarenes spread into Bulgaria. Around 1910, Nazarene meeting-places were registered in Sofia, Gabrovo, Samokov, Rustchuk (Ruse) and Varna.

---

[135] Transcript of introductory speech and discussion on this topic at the Assembly in *Vesnik srpske crkve,* sveska 10, godina XIII, October 1902, pp. 866-883.

[136] "In Đušina street, Belgrade, number 10, in the apartment of Antonije Bogdanović, a builder, it was noted that various persons had been gathering in recent times. This seemed suspicious to the police, and 10 May this year, at 10:00 a.m., the police duty clerk entered Antonije's apartment along with two citizens. In the room, in which, apart from four benches, set in rows like school benches, and one table, there was no furniture, sat: Aleksije Milićević, Todor Grcić greengrocer, Avram Glišić worker from the Monopol company, and Trivun Savić day laborer, with several working-class women, reading books which they held in front of them. One of them sat at the table and read out loud from the Holy Scriptures to those present. When the clerk entered the room, the one reading from Scripture said quite calmly: 'Let us finish and fall before the face of the Lord.'" From the article "Nazareni u Beogradu i timočkoj eparhiji" ["The Nazarenes in Belgrade and the Timok Parish"], *Hrišćanski vesnik,* godina 21, broj 6-7, June-July 1904, p. 355.

That year, and the year after, 1911, the Nazarenes in Serbia were persecuted and prohibited for holding their meetings, but also for proselytism, as stated by Grujić in his article on them, published in the Narodna Enciklopedija in 1928. In the article "*Nazareni pred sudom*" ["The Nazarenes Before the Court"] in *Glasnik pravoslavne crkve*[137] there is mention of fourteen men and women from Žarkovo near Belgrade who were brought before the court in 1910 accused of proselytism.

Belgrade priest Ljubomir "Miroljub" Mitrović took an active interest in the new Nazarene and Adventist believers in the parishes in which he served, and several times even moved home in response to the emergence of Adventist and Nazarene groups in a particular part of town. Not without a certain amount of pride, in his book published in 1929, he talks of his efforts during 1910 and 1911 to bring the Adventists back to the "true path." He compares the Adventists with the Nazarenes:

> In terms of their external religious life they especially resemble the Nazarenes. At certain times on the Sabbath (the Nazarenes on Sunday), in the morning and afternoon, they gather together in their so-called "assemblies" [*skupštine*]... They are also similar to the Nazarenes in the fact that they have no Holy Sacraments, only rites in their most primitive form: the rite of the Lord's Supper, the rite of repentance, the rite of baptism, the rite of foot-washing, the rite of priesthood and the rite of marriage. Because of this great similarity with the Nazarenes, many of them are going over to the Adventists. Both the Adventists and Nazarenes look upon the order of the Orthodox, Catholic and Protestant churches as unchristian

---

[137] An Orthodox Church journal (t/n)

and heathen; they especially war against icons
and the Holy Cross (Mitrović, 1929:8).[138]

One academic article analyzed judgments pronounced against
Nazarenes and determined that the courts were actually interpreting
Article 102 of the 1910 Penal Code incorrectly. One court characterized the Nazarenes as people who had "hidden their existence, their
objectives, and their structure from the established authority in the
land," although there was no basis for such an assertion since the
Nazarenes had never concealed their religious sentiment and beliefs
from the state. Sentences of three months imprisonment apiece were
confirmed by the Court of Appeal and later the Court of Cassation.[139]
However, although these judgments were unlawful, as this academic
article showed, nothing was done to have the sentences commuted
or overturned.

Essays and letters from readers and priests, published in the
1920s in *Vesnik*, are indicative of the attitudes of the Church and
its priesthood towards people of the Nazarene faith among the people.[140] So, for example, a SOC parish priest from Kladovo, in an arti-

---

[138] Towards the end of his book Mitrović concludes: Our state authorities are not
yet aware of the danger presented to the state and the people from the religious
sects, especially the Adventists and Nazarenes (who are in Vojvodina officially
regarded as a faithless group and not as a form of proselytism and are thus protected!). (Mitrović, 1929:64)

[139] "Nazarenstvo je kažljivo po čl. 102 kazn. zak" [Nazareanism is punishable pursuant to Article 102 of the Penal Code], *Arhiv za pravne i društvene nauke*, sv. 1,
knj. XVII.

[140] The attitude of the SOC towards the Nazarenes may also be seen in documents not directly relating to this issue. In a memorandum from the Orthodox
Metropolitanate of Skopje in 1923 to the Minister of Religions, in a long document, the SOC considers the reports of local priests on the spread of Adventism
and Methodism. At one point, underlining the negative aspects of the Adventist
movement and explaining that the Order of 1922 (permitting the activities of
the Adventists) had been extremely harmful, we read:

> Ultimately its teaching is directed both against the
> Christian faith and against the State. It absolutely denies
> the Sunday, considering Saturday the seventh day, denies

cle published in October 1925, talks about the Nazarenes rejecting the Orthodox Church and therefore renouncing their faith, and in turn their nation, and refusing arms and therefore renouncing their state (Ilić, 1925:2-3). Describing them in negative terms and giving the example of Serb Nazarenes from who had moved from Čurug and were meeting under the leadership of a certain "Nazarene Deda [Grandpa] Čekić," the priest gives his view that they are "God's creatures with a soul yet without a soul," ready to commit the worst of criminal acts and betray their country in the event of the outbreak of war. The Prota [priest] happily reports that the police have burst in on their meeting, confiscated books, determined that they were disseminating "immorality of the worst kind" with certain young female persons and that they have been "dealt with in accordance with law." In Kladovo the Nazarenes were thus arrested, their religious literature confiscated and the aforementioned Deda Čekić was expelled from the region. At the end of his article, Prota Ilić calls on the SOC Holy Synod of Bishops to issue a "circular or instructions informing the priesthood how to act towards these sects[141] and what to do."

---

the significance, holiness and veneration of the Mother of God, saints and icons, denies the obligation of oath-taking before the courts and the authorities...does not give honor to the Ruler and of course is opposed to the army. Accordingly, the Seventh Day Adventists are nothing more than a form of the Nazarenes...

Arhiv SCG, fond br. 63, fascikla 144. Dopis Ministru vera Pravoslavne mitropolije skopljanske, Pov. M. Br. 8 dated 25 January 1923. Copy of document in possession of author.

[141] In one place, Prota Ilić lists the following religious communities that are active among the Serbs, "dividing them into different faiths, and especially sects: Nazareanism, Calvinism and Adventism." Speaking of Nazareanism and Adventism, the Prota is referring to known but unrecognized religious communities in the period in question. When he mentions Calvinism as a religious community that is spreading among the Serbian population, it is not sure whom he is referring to, since this term was normally used as a short form for believers of the Reformed church, widespread both then and now, mostly

The next issue of *Vesnik* contained an article by a certain Mr. Tornjanski who saw the primary reason for the spread of the Nazarene faith as being the fact that in Bačka, where the author is from, priests "spend six days lazing around, and not working the seventh, that they are despised, that they are anything but Christ's disciples and that they each receive a 10,000 dinar monthly wage," which for that time was a significant sum. In the next issue of *Vesnik*, responding to the accusations that the SOC bore the greater part of the responsibility for the spread of the Nazarene faith, Vladimir Aleksić, parish priest from Šajkaš St. Ivan speaks out in opposition to "mudslinging" against the profession, but also makes an interesting statement:

> For the sake of Mr. Tornjanski's peace of mind I must say that our Church is closely watching the life and growth of this sect, and also that our Episcopate, as well as the priesthood, is making every effort to remove this sore from the body of the Church... I will not provide him with evidence, which is both of a private and official nature (Aleksić, 1926:3).

The Serbian Orthodox Church continued its campaign against the Nazarenes in the period under consideration, although to a lesser extent, since the state had taken upon itself to implement significant repressive measures, using both military and police resources to do so, of which there will be further discussion in this chapter. Nevertheless, Church attacks on the Nazarenes did not cease.

In 1939, the SOC Calendar contained a list of four dangerous "sects," with brief descriptions of the nature of their error. The groups listed were the Nazarenes, Adventists, Baptists, and Salvation Army. The Nazarenes were particularly criticized for rejecting Sacred Tradition, for observing only two Sacraments (Baptism and Communion according to the Calvinist rite), for not honoring the

---

among the Hungarian population in Vojvodina. It is possible that this is a reference to the Baptists, but the author of this book lacks evidence for this.

Holy Cross and its symbols, for conducting baptism outdoors and not in church, for not recognizing priests, icons and intercession for the dead before God and for not praying for their deceased. They would not recognize the obligation to swear the oath and would not bear arms. The Nazarenes were also criticized for rejecting national-ism and preaching internationalism (E.S, 1939:108).

In 1940, the book *Nazareni* by Zoltán Nyisztor (Njistor, 1940) was translated from the Hungarian and published with a note that it was "in the spirit of the Orthodox Church." On the inside cover there was an additional note: "This translation has been approved by the Holy Synod of Bishops..." The book looked at the primary features of the Nazarene faith—oath-swearing, the bearing of arms, the need for a church (building), prayer (the Lord's Prayer etc.)—and criticized the practices of the Nazarenes.

It is interesting to note here that the emergence of the Bogomoljci[142] in the Serbian Orthodox Church, which reached its zenith in the 1920s, was at least in part a result of the existence and activities of the Nazarenes among the Serbs. In the second half of the nineteenth century, when the Nazarene movement began to spread through Vojvodina, some believers in the SOC began organizing themselves into informal prayer groups and meeting on Sundays and holidays, first in people's homes and later in churches and monaster-ies. On occasion, meetings were also held as part of matins services in monasteries.

Dr Slijepčević believes that the Nazarene movement, with its emphasis on reading the Scriptures and its religious zeal, was the cat-alyst for the Bogomoljci movement. He felt that the Nazarene move-ment was one form of protest by the common man against irreligious living, just as the Bogomoljci movement was a kind of protest against stagnation in the Church (Slijepčević, 1943:61-62).

Dimitrijević believed that Nazareanism represented a very serious indictment of the state of affairs in the Serbian Orthodox Church, joined also by the Bogomoljci, who in their own way were a "...protest against our indifference to and negligence of religion...

---

[142] Lit. "those who pray to God" (t/n).

[O]ur souls are indolent and our hearts cold to faith, like icy rocks" (Dimitrijević, 1903/1:5-6).

Bishop Hrizostom describes the emergence of the Bogomoljci as a moral and religious revival of "purely Orthodox provenance," initiated by the people.

After the First World War, the Bogomoljci movement spread to Šumadija, Mačva, Stig, Pomoravlje and Vojvodina. One report explains the reasons: "A time came, after the horrors of war, when the souls of men began to thirst after something better, more exalted and more spiritual. A time came that was very much like that promised to the prophet Amos 8:11, and many folk preachers arose in Serbia in those days." Another report, from Čurug, said: "If anyone is sick, gifts are taken to him, and all offer him aid. The new mother is watched over after the birth, they visit her and help her with her household tasks. At the funeral of a deceased member, all attend and sing graveside songs, and others crowd closer to hear... When they are read the Holy Gospel or a prayer in the Serbian language, then their soul is all the more satisfied at understanding it" (Hrizostom, 1991:229-253).

Comparing the customs and practices of the Bogomoljci movement and the Nazarenes, we can see considerable similarities, the basic difference being that the Bogomoljci movement also emerged partially as a reaction to Nazarene resistance to priestly inertia, tradition, and liturgy through personal piety and the search for spirituality. In these respects, these two movements have more in common than has previously been realized.

The Question of Religious Education

The extent of state "concern" for the Nazarenes can also be seen in the order by the Ministry of Education from March 1926 on how to treat pupils whose parents are Nazarenes. The principal of the State Gymnasium in Veliki Bečkerek (Zrenjanin) wrote to the ministry with the following questions:

Do the children of parents who practice one of the unrecognized religions have to participate in all religious obligations (Communion, Confession, church attendance etc.) or only need to attend Religious Education classes? Since Nazareanism is not a recognized faith, it is not taught in school and therefore such children have no grades in Religious Education… [H]ow will Nazarene pupils be treated in high schools who do not take Religious Education, nor perform other religious duties such as attending their confessional church, who do not take Communion, and on top of all that are not even baptized?[143]

---

[143] Archive of Serbia and Montenegro, fond 63, fascikla 144, broj 19207/II dated 6 March 1926. Copy of document in possession of author.

Broj: 195.
1.927.

Uprava muške osnovne škole
u Sr. Mitrovici, 5. VII. 1.927.

Predmet: Nazareni – upis u školu.

Gradskomu poglavarstvu

Sr. Mitrovici

Umoljava se naslov, da izvoli obavijestiti ovu školu, da li se mogu upisivati u školu i ona djeca, koja nisu krštena, a roditelji su im pripadnici Nazarenske sekte, koja po državi nije priznata kao vjeroispovijest.

Upravitelj škole:

Ivo Nikolić

Translation:

Ref. no. 195/1927
Administration of the Primary School for Boys in Sremska Mitrovica,
5 July 1927

Re: The Nazarenes – enrollment in school

To the city government of Sremska Mitrovica

We kindly request the above-titled, at its convenience, to inform this
school as to whether those children who have not been baptized,
and whose parents are members of the Nazarene sect, which is not
recognized by the state as a religious confession, may also be enrolled
in school.

School Principal,
Ivo Nikolić

Correspondence from administration of primary school for boys to the city authorities in Sremska Mitrovica

The question of attendance of Religious Education classes in
schools in some areas was addressed by force, but this led to other
complications. In Plavna, the local Roman Catholic parish priest registered the children of Nazarenes for religious education in his class
on the basis of an 1895 Hungarian law which required children to
attend religious education classes for the religion which their parents
had belonged to prior to leaving their faith and going over to the
Nazarene faith. From the report we can see that the school inspec-
tors breathed a sigh of relief and quickly reported back to headquarters that such problems were a thing of the past in some places in
Vojvodina – the problem had seemingly been resolved.

However the parish priest once again asked the school authorities to organize baptisms for such children at the beginning of the
school year, and for the school management to respond positively

to this request by the Catholic Church, which the school refused since it "went beyond its educational purview." The school's inspector expressed satisfaction that children were now attending religious education after all, but also said that "there was no order in place giving school authorities the right to force parents to have their children baptized into one confession or another," expressing the hope that the matter was thereby resolved. However, a few months later, the Ministry of Religions reversed this and ordered that this "well-grounded" principle be put into effect and the baptism of children into the Roman Catholic faith carried out at the beginning of the next school year. The rationale for this was that the parents of the children had not opted for any other legally recognized confession and so the children were to be sent to attend Roman Catholic religious instruction and baptized into that faith against their will, "but without denying them the legal right to either remain in it or change it upon reaching the age of religious independence."[144] The persecution continued.

In 1928, the Ministry of Religions, in a memorandum dated March 9, addressed to the District Prefect in Vukovar, ordered the following in connection with unbaptized Nazarene children:

> ...the authorities must first discuss the religious affiliation of that child...and then take a final decision...and order the parents, and/or the tutor, that the child be baptized according to the rite of the confession to which it legally belongs...under threat of penalty.[145]

In the event that the parents refused to go along with this order – and such cases were more frequent than those where the parents acquiesced – the authorities had several legal remedies at their dis-

---

[144] Ministry of Religions, Katoličko Odeljenje, broj 6460/236 dated 18 February 1927. Copy of document in possession of author.

[145] Archive of Serbia and Montenegro, fond 63, fascikla 144, Ministry of Religions broj 3236 dated 9 March 1928. Copy of document in possession of author.

posal, including the Law on the Protection of State Security and the Order of August 2, 1921.

In 1931, the Ministry of Justice issued very similar instructions. In a memorandum relating to proceedings brought against Nazarenes who "forbid their children from performing their religious duties," the Minister of Justice explained that children born "either before or after" their parents' move to the Nazarenes were considered members of the legally recognized religious community to which their parents had previously belonged, until the age of eighteen. The Minister of Justice further explained that these children must be baptized, must attend church, go to religious classes, go to confession and communion and be buried according to the same rite.[146]

Military Exercises and Penalties for Failure to Respond

As a result of the earlier mentioned meeting of Nazarene elders and the authorities in late December 1924, all Nazarenes were released to their homes, but only after meetings were held in the prisons at which the Nazarenes pledged their loyalty to king and homeland. For several months, it seemed that the agreement was being kept to by both sides.

Veliki Bečkerek

However, on August 1, 1926, the Veliki Bečkerek (today Zrenjanin) military district called up all Nazarenes for military exercises. The call was answered by fifty-six. The officers ordered them to take up arms and swear an oath to the king, even though most of them had already made a "pledge" in 1924. The newspapers covered this quite extensively, in particular *Zastava* and *Rad*.[147]

---

[146] Archive of Serbia and Montenegro, fond 63, fascikla 144, broj 21616/31-XV, undated. Copy of document in possession of author.

[147] *Zastava* issues 9/18/1926; 9/21/1926; 9/25/1926; *Rad* 11/16/1926 and 1/2/1927. We quote from the latter: "What do you say to this? Three hundred

The mistreatment had resumed. Because of their refusal to swear the oath, they were all arrested for "insubordination" (i.e., refusal to act on orders). For this reason, and because of their membership of a sect not recognized by the state, harsh sentences were meted out to fifty of them in Belgrade, some of them to as long as ten years of imprisonment. Some of these Nazarenes, already in their fifties, had served prison time back in Austro-Hungary.

The Belgrade daily *Politika*, in the October 3, 1926 issue, reported on the court proceedings against nine Nazarenes from this group. On August 3 that year in Veliki Bečkerek, they had refused to take up arms in the barrracks. They were brought to trial in a prison truck before the military court of the Danube Division. They were escorted by soldiers with loaded rifles and drawn bayonets. All were tried and found guilty on two counts: refusal to bear arms and belonging to the Nazarenes. Spira Matić (a Nazarene since 1907), Panta Nedeljkov (since 1906), Steva Popadić, Nikola Rasić (father of seven), Živa Jevremović (also convicted by the Austrians), Stefan Uliki and Stefan Popadić, and others. The trial was brief. All were sentenced to ten years apiece, nine years on the first count and one year on the second. They signed the rulings and were led back to jail.

Stari Bečej

The persecutions continued. In the Stari Bečej military district, military exercises for reservists were scheduled for September 10, 1926, and 176 Nazarenes from this region were arrested. In Stari Bečej, just as in Zrenjanin, call-ups were received only by Nazarenes. Nobody else was required to attend the "military exercise." This group met the same fate as the Nazarenes in Zrenjanin. Another six

---

people have now been languishing [in prison] for eight months in Petrovaradin. They are not recruits, they are former Austro-Hungarian soldiers aged between 30 and 50 who are being told to swear again. Some have been sentenced, to ten years each at that… They are to vote for the Radicals in the local election so as to be released, like in 1924…".

Nazarenes from Bečkerek [Zrenjanin] were called up in December and they met the same fate as the previous two groups mentioned.

Punishments were again meted out. However in this case, there was a reaction from churches in Switzerland and the US to the news from Yugoslavia, and in January 1927, the Swiss confirmed the truth of the reports from Yugoslavia after a visit by a four-man delegation. An international outcry followed, and a protest was lodged with the Yugoslav delegates to the international Minorities Commission in Brussels that same year. One report[148] states that on their return, the visiting delegates had informed King Alexander of this matter and he had released a number of Nazarenes from prison (more than 200 people were released March 7, 1927 – see Stäubli, 1928:8) who gave their "pledge" of loyalty; however a large number remained imprisoned.

However, many Nazarenes who were released in March were called up for military exercises again in June, and the same thing happened to them. These pardoned Nazarenes had been released from prison but had also had their civil rights reinstated, which included the right to serve in the army reserves. The call-ups began again. The Nazarenes responded to the call-ups but refused arms and were thrown in prison.

Those who had been pardoned in March were now convicted of "repeat offenses," with an additional year-and-a-half for belonging to the "Nazarene sect." For its part, the army had been regularly reporting to central command since 1926 on the Nazarenes in their areas, making lists and laying plans for this "harmful sect" to be systematically rooted out and destroyed. Special effort was invested in compiling lists of Nazarene families with young men who were close to military age so that the authorities would know ahead of time where there were likely to be "problems."

However the public did not remain ambivalent and the newspapers reported on individual cases where this treatment was protested.

---

[148] "War resisters in Jugo-slavia: 72 Nazarenes sentenced to 10 years' imprisonment," The War Resisters' International, Enfield, England, UK, October 1928. Copy of document in possession of author. International Institute of Social History, War Resisters' International Archive, binder 420.

Some of the notable headlines were in the newspapers *Politika* in February of 1925; *Rad* in September of 1926; *Vidovdan* and *Zastava* also in September of 1926. *Politika's* October 3 edition in 1926 published a transcript of a Nazarene trial. At this trial, the judge told the punished Nazarenes that they should recant, and promised that their convictions would be revised if they did so. Further articles on this trial were published by *Rad* in February 1927.

Tisa Division

Stäubli says that in 1926, in the territory of the Tisa Division, all Nazarenes who had not been called up to the army (reserves) in 1924 were now called up. The newspapers reported on this, too. *Zastava* in the September 18 issue from 1926 says the following:

> The military authorities have a great deal of trouble with their conscripts who, misled or bewitched by their "peace-loving" preachers and "apostles," refuse to undergo military training and will not take up arms... On the orders of the minister of the military, in recent days all new believers of more mature age have been called up to state their position on this matter; proceedings will be brought against those who will not take up arms.

Around 300 hundred answered the call-up and all of them were sent before the military court. Only a few recanted the Nazarene teaching and accepted arms, while the others were tried in Belgrade and sentenced to ten years in prison. In March 1927, a certain number were released, on condition that they pledge their loyalty like their predecessors two years before. However 109 of them remained in prison (Stäubli, 1927:21).

A tragic story, recorded in the Belgrade daily *Politika*, tells of three Nazarenes who in 1921 were sentenced to five years and eight months' imprisonment each, followed by loss of all civil rights on release.[149] They served their full prison terms. In March 1927, they were included in the royal amnesty and their civil rights restored. Since one of those rights was military service, they were again called up and again ended up in court and then prison.

On November 16, 1926, *Rad* reported that 175 Nazarenes from the Stari Bečej district were locked up in the Petrovaradin military prison, with another fifty prisoners in Veliki Bečkerek.

---

[149] *Politika* on 5 November 1927 reported on a trial before the military court of persons who were "reoffending" Nazarenes: Milorad Zorić, a tailor from Belgrade; Milorad Paščan, a farmer and Kuzman Pavlović, a farm laborer, both of the latter from Senta. The next to be convicted was the youthful Ljuba Doroslovac, son of Nazarene elder Milan Doroslovac from Beodra (now Novo Miloševo). Zorić and Kuzman were sentenced to eleven-and-a-half years each; ten years each for refusing to bear arms and another year and a half for being of the Nazarene faith. Paščan was sentenced to ten and Doroslovac to six years' imprisonment. The judges were: Dušan Besarabić, infantry colonel, Dragoljub Veličković, cavalry colonel and Stjepo Korlajet, court Major:

> The trial of the first three is interesting, and differs from the previous trials in that all three had already been sentenced for the same crime. This had been in 1921, when as recruits they had been sentenced to five years and eight months each. They had served their sentences and returned home with loss of civil and military honors, but convinced that they had finished with the army once and for all.
>
> However on 1 April this year they were called by the military command and told that they had been pardoned of the guilt for which they had already served their sentences, their civil and military status had been restored, and therefore it was as if they had never been convicted. Hence they were required to swear the oath and take up arms... They were led out before assembled troops on 4 April and offered guns. When they refused to take them they were locked up. Their trial was yesterday...

Subotica

The case of Jovo Đukić of Gospođinci is particularly interesting in terms of gaining a better understanding of the simple and sincere attitude of the Nazarenes towards the military and state authorities. He, along with a group of Nazarenes, received the call to report to the military authorities in Subotica. There were sixty-nine Nazarenes in this group, including Đukić, who was already gray-haired, having passed the age of forty-nine. In fact, he was only three days short of his fiftieth birthday (military service and the reserves were not required after one reached the age of fifty). Instead of going into hiding for a few days, Jovo answered the call as required and only three days before his obligation as an active army reservist came to an end, he refused to take up arms. He was sent to court.

Politika on Augst 3, 1927, had an extensive article on the trials and sentences in Subotica in the Thirty-Fourth Regiment of the Yugoslav army against the following Nazarenes: Jovo Đukić of Gospođinci, wealthy trader Stepanović of Subotica, Dušan Gruić one-time volunteer in Dobruja, the wealthy Stevan Ivanić of Nadalj, Konstantin Naumović, Paja Alarčić, Branko Purać, Stevo Stelović, Peter Husoš an ethnic Rusyn, Paja Opra, Milan Naumov, Petar Svicav, Miloš Bakalski, Danilo Stojkov, Aleksandar Popov, Vlada Kocanti, Miloš Antić, Zdravko Tutin, Danilo Alardžić, and others. The reporter commented: "All the Nazarenes showed themselves to be true Nazarenes."[150]

---

[150] Excerpt from the article "Robiju da, pušku ne" [Prison yes, gun no], *Politika* 3 August 1927, page 6:

> "Steva Čelović!" an officer called a particularly large and strong Nazarene, who also shrugged his shoulders:
> "I cannot."
> "You at least shouldn't have any trouble carrying it," the commander said to him, "look at the size of you!"
> "I can carry ten of those," he replied, "but my faith does not allow me."
> Ivanić, a landowner, was [then] brought before the troops.
> "Come on, Steva, old man!" the commander said to him.

Talks With the Authorities

All this went on even though the Nazarene elders had on more than one occasion made it clear to the military and state authorities that they were prepared to serve in the military in those units that did not bear arms: the medical corps, in stores, in transport etc. Since that was evidently not enough, Stäubli says that the Nazarenes offered to serve a longer period than was usual if their request were met.

Zastava in September of 1926 reported that a Nazarene delegation, headed by farmer Laza Stojšić from Nadalj, had been to Belgrade to visit and have talks with the authorities.[151] The Nazarenes had previously met amongst themselves and agreed to present an organized front to the military authorities. The delegation visited the Army Ministry and filed a petition for the Nazarenes to be allowed to make a "pledge." Journalists of *Zastava* on September 25, 1926,

---

"I cannot," he smiled. "I was born in this faith, I did time under the Hungarians and I'll do time now. I've been through it all before – but whoever fights the battle to the last is the winner. What can I do! Christ said: Love your enemies and those who hate you. Christ also said this: if anyone strikes you on one cheek, offer him the other…that's how it is, Sir, the old-timer smiled again, and returned to the ranks."

A good-looking young blond man stepped out, Petar Husoš.

"You are a Hungarian?" the commander asked him.

"No, I am a Rusyn."

"Come on, take the gun Petar!" the commander encouraged him in a friendly tone. "You're young, it would be a shame."

"I cannot."

"Since when have you been of that faith?"

"Since I was fifteen."

"How old are you now?"

"Twenty and two. Last year I was released, as the breadwinner…"

[151] "Among the new believers themselves, this action on the part of the government was a source of some consternation, since they decisively rejected the accusation that they were not good Serbs and patriots," *Zastava* 9/21/1926, page 3. Just a few days later, in the 9/25/1926 edition, *Zastava* reported that the Army Ministry had "laid down a procedure to be followed when the oath is being taken by military conscripts who are new believers," which is an obvious reference to the direct intention of the authorities to take action against the Nazarenes.

reported that they had contacted General Dušan Trifunović,[152] and that although the Nazarenes had not really been in favor of leveraging public criticism and international pressure, they nevertheless decided to seek help abroad. Individuals and organizations from abroad also tried to help the situation on their own initiative.

But despite this, besides the cases mentioned earlier, there were more than fifty young men in various prisons around Yugoslavia serving sentences of between four and eight years. Some were even sentenced to solitary confinement and mostly served their sentences alongside criminals. There is a recorded case of a young man from Sremska Mitrovica who was relieved of military duties by army doctors four times, only for this decision to be annulled every time by the local commander and the young man drafted again. Finally the commander personally removed his file and medical reports and had him conducted to the unit under guard.

Visits from Switzerland

During 1927, on three occasions, delegations from Switzerland visited Belgrade and tried to reach a solution with the authorities. Although there were around 17,000 Nazarenes at the time, only around forty recruits reached military age every year, which ought not to have been a problem at all for the Royal Army, as they could be sent to work in medical units, on farmland and in administrative posts. A more significant problem was that of reservists, of whom there were some three thousand aged between eighteen and fifty.

The first delegation of representatives from foreign churches came in 1927. Four representatives from Switzerland came to the kingdom and quickly confirmed the truth of the Nazarene reports of persecution.

The second attempt at assistance came in February the same year when Professor Bovet, on behalf of the Swiss Nazarenes, appealed to the

---

[152] Later commander of the Seventh Army, died in captivity in 1942. At the time under consideration he was the Army Minister.

delegation of the kingdom of SCS for the situation with the Nazarenes to change. As mentioned previously, under the royal amnesty of March 7, 1927, more than two hundred Nazarenes were released. However at least fifty individual (young) believers remained in various prisons.

A third attempt to intervene, naive though it may seem, was nevertheless a further step in the effort to find the best possible solution to the "Nazarene question." Having learned that King Alexander was traveling to Bled in Slovenia, the three Swiss representatives set off to Bled in 1927 with the intention of meeting the king. However they gave up after three days waiting for an audience.

The authorities finally agreed to talk to the international delegates who were seeking a meeting. At a meeting held October 22, 1927, in Belgrade, attended by believers from Switzerland on one side and Generals Mihajlović and Jovanović on the other, no agreement was reached. The generals advised the Swiss to persuade the Nazarenes to give up and accept arms, which was the only acceptable scenario for the army. For their part, the Swiss delegation lodged a complaint regarding the police surveillance and the prohibition of meetings in the towns of those Nazarenes who had foreign contacts (Stäubli, 1927:37). The authorities continued as before. A memorandum from late 1927 to the court in Varaždin emphasizes that order 8765/1924 is still in force regarding the prohibition on the activities of the Adventists and the Nazarenes.[153]

Some Nazarene families (usually those with a large number of children—eight or more) tried to resolve this situation with the authorities by seeking the necessary permission and documents to emigrate, mostly to Canada, and a smaller number to Argentina. Unfortunately only a small number of requests was granted. Again the Nazarene elders tried to appeal to the Yugoslav authorities – to follow the example of the solutions implemented in the legal systems of Germany and Switzerland of the day in regard to the Nazarene question, but to no avail.

---

[153] Archive of Serbia and Montenegro, fond br. 63, fascikla 144, Ministry of Religions memorandum to the Royal Court Table in Varaždin under br. 16919, 30 December 1927. Copy of document in possession of author.

Three representatives of the Nazarenes from Switzerland managed to attend the conference of the League of Nations in Brussels in 1928. They clashed with the Yugoslav delegates there, who publicly stated that there was no religious persecution in the kingdom of SCS. The Nazarene delegates then presented a document comprising a secret order by the army from June 1926, and this resulted in broad denunciation of the Yugoslav delegates by those present. But to no effect. Plans were laid to propose to the army that Nazarenes, upon conscription, be deployed directly to hospital units, to attempt to approach the king again, to try with the council of ministers – but none of these approaches succeeded. In October 1928, seventy-two convictions were handed down whereby Nazarenes who had already served five years each were sentenced to a further ten years in jail. Some of them had not yet even been released, some spent the rest of their days in prison.

The Nazarenes and the Adventists

In mid-1929, the Courts Section of the Ministry of the army and navy sent a memorandum to the Chief of General Staff expressing their opinions on the matter of the confusion between the Nazarenes and the Adventists. In this document, sent on June 1 that year, there was an analysis of some reports that had come in from the field in which these two religious communities were being equated with one another in connection with the questions of military service, swearing the oath and bearing arms. In view of the fact that in the meantime Močnik's book *Adventizam* had been published, in which there were a number of testimonies from Adventists in the military, the Courts Section asked for an investigation, and for the facts to be determined.[154]

It is interesting to note from the historical aspect that the Ministry of the Interior, State Protection Department, more than a year before this June 1929 memorandum from the Ministry of Religions, had

---

[154] Archive of Serbia and Montenegro, fond/fascikla 63/144, S. Br. 10238 dated 1 June 1929 – Ministry of the Army and Navy. Copy of document in possession of author.

sought concrete information on whether the Adventists were to be considered together with the Nazarenes in regard to oath-swearing and the refusal to bear arms:

> In regard to this claim by said Ministry concerning Adventism, which to this Ministry is very much news according to the reports of the relevant authorities, that is, something unknown until now, and on the assumption that this Ministry issued its order solely on the basis of specific facts…with all these ends in mind, the Ministry of the Interior cordially requests that this Ministry most urgently supply [information on] all specific acts committed to date against the legal order by Adventist adherents…[155]

The Ministry of Religions, in its fanatical crusade against citizens of non-Orthodox faith, especially those of Serbian nationality, for years conveniently ignored the significant differences between the two religious communities, which were entirely evident and transparent from the outset. The Ministry of Justice, responding to inquiries from the field, maintained existing conditions in accordance with the 1924 order.[156]

---

[155] Archive of Serbia and Montenegro, fond/fascikla 63/144, D.Z. Broj 1150 dated 10 February 1928 – Ministry of the Interior, State Protection Department. Copy of document in possession of author.

[156] Archive of Serbia and Montenegro, fond 63, fascikla 144, memorandum from the Ministry of Justice to the Ministry of the Interior, V. Br. 14451/29-XV, 7 November 1929 says the following:

> Since to date the Ministry of Justice has not yet received any response from the Ministry of the Army and Navy regarding the enactment of that Ministry of 2 May this year, without which response we cannot give this Ministry our considered opinion…we hereby give cordial notice that until further orders, the memorandum of the Ministry of Religions of 5 May 1924 is to be acted on…

Since the facts indicated that Adventists did respond to military and court summonses and that they did swear the oath and do their military service, the army continued to focus close attention only on the Nazarene cases. Thus in 1929 military and gendarme units all over the country were issued the task of analyzing the situation in their respective territories and continuing to report in advance on existing Nazarene families that had sons close to service age, since these were problems waiting to happen. For example, on August 16, 1929, the Niš gendarmerie reported that there were six Nazarenes in their district, of whom two had served in the war and discharged their military obligations before becoming Nazarenes, while a further four men had been convicted.

Other local military and gendarmerie units filed similar reports:

- July 11, 1929, the Kumanovo military district[157] and the Veles military district;[158]
- July 12, 1929, central command of the Kosovo divisional military district;[159]
- July 13, 1929, central command of the Bregalnica divisional district;[160]
- July 14, 1929, Kosovska Mitrovica military district;[161]
- July 15, 1929, central command of the fifth army district in Niš;[162]
- July 16, 1929, Gendarmerie Regiment in Novi Sad;[163]
- July 17, 1929, Courts Section of the Third Command of the Skoplje army district;[164]

Copy of transcription of document in possession of author.

[157] All footnotes numbered 156-171 are from the Archive of Serbia and Montenegro, fond 63, fascikla 144. Copies of all documents in possession of author. This document is Broj 8850, 11 July 1929.

[158] Broj 6261, 11 July 1929.

[159] Broj 11296, 12 July 1929.

[160] S. Br. 869 of 13 July 1929.

[161] Pov. Br. 1215 of 14 July 1929.

[162] S. Br. 272 of 15 July 1929.

[163] J.B. Br. 1283 of 16 July 1929.

[164] S. Br. 991 of 17 July 1929.

- July 18, 1929, central command of the second army district, based in Sarajevo, reported by the Ministry of the Army and Navy;[165]
- July 19, 1929, Courts Section of the central command of the first army district in Novi Sad;[166]
- July 24, 1929, Courts Section of the central command of the second army district in Sarajevo;[167]
- August 10, 1929, Sixth Gendarmerie Regiment from Niš;[168]
- On August 12, 1929 the Chief of the Courts Section ordered the commander of the Gendarmerie to submit a full report on "whether the adherents of the pure Adventist sect swear the oath and accept arms, that is, whether there are any cases of refusal to answer the call to military service on their part on the grounds of their religious teaching, paying regard in this to the true Nazarenes, adherents of the Nazarene sect, who are fundamentally opposed to swearing the oath when entering the forces, and to the bearing of arms…" [169]
- On August 13, 1929, the Gendarmerie Regiment in Ljubljana reported that "there are no *Nazarenci* [sic] on the territory of this regiment."[170]
- On August 15, 1929, the acting commander of the Gendarmerie reported on the situation in the Fourth Regiment (Split), the Fifth Regiment (Cetinje) and the Eighth Regiment (Ljubljana), as well as on the situation in the territory of the Belgrade Gendarmerie Battalion…[171], while the Skoplje Regiment sent a telegram;
- September 10, 1929, Prefect of Travnik District.[172]

---

[165] S. Br. 504 of 18 July 1929.
[166] S. Br. 489 of 19 July 1929.
[167] S. Br. 514 of 24 July 1929.
[168] J.B. Br. 1865 of 10 August 1929.
[169] S. Br. 14816 of 12 August 1929.
[170] J.B. Br. 299 of 13 August 1929.
[171] J.B. Br. 5975 of 15 August 1929, and K. Br. 4983 of 6 August 1929.
[172] Broj 920, pov. 24 of 10 September 1929.

Although the persecution on the part of the state authorities lasted several years, some local officials nevertheless recognized that the punishment and persecution of Nazarenes was excessive. The High Captaincy of Novi Sad, as early as 1929, filed its opinion[173] that adherents of the Nazarenes sect were in all respects upstanding and loyal citizens, and that their places of worship ought to be opened, a position it had held to since the beginning.[174] However the centralized state authorities in Belgrade always held up "higher interests" as a shield before it. A police report from Kovin in July 1931 described a now-familiar sequence of events: "Twenty-one persons maintaining the place of worship of the forbidden Nazarene sect...books were not found on their person and they state that these had previously been confiscated by the gendarmes...the suspects were interrogated, and consistently stated...and admitted the crime... [and] were released and charges were filed with the state prosecution service..."[175]

The WRI archive contains a request sent by this organization to members of the British Parliament, from November 1930, in which they state that their attempt to correspond with General Petar Živković, then Prime Minister of Yugoslavia, had been unsuccessful and that the documents (a petition for thirty-one Nazarenes serving repeat sentences to be pardoned) had not even reached him. The WRI was therefore requesting that members of Parliament forward this list for the attention of the Yugoslav government, in the hope that communication between high officials would not be intercepted or hindered.

---

[173] Archive of Serbia and Montenegro, fond 14, fascikla 3, jedinica opisa 10, document 3-1100, 7 November 1929, broj 8081/1929. Copy of document in possession of author.

[174] Relevant to this question is an accompanying document sent by the Ban of the Danube Banovina to the Bačka District Prefect in which he briefly states that a report has been sent regarding the opening of Nazarene places of worship. Archive of Serbia and Montenegro, collection 14, binder 3, description item 10, document 15407/II dated 24 January 1930. Copy of document in possession of author.

[175] Vojvodina Archive F-126.II-65529/1931. Copy of document in possession of author.

КОМАНДА ЖАНДАРМЕРИЈЕ
Ј.Б.Бр. 597
15. августа 19__ год.
БЕОГРАД

ГОСПОДИНУ МИНИСТРУ ВОЈСКЕ И МОРНАРИЦЕ (СУДСКО ОДЕЉЕЊЕ).-

26. јула текуће године, одмах по пријему наређења С.Бр. 14816 од 25. јула 1929. године, најхитније сам - шифром - наредио свима жандармеријским пуковима и батаљонима (сем 2. пука, који је поднео извештај), да најхитније доставе извештај: колико на њиховим територијама има адвентиста (суботара). Да ли је било случајева да се не одазивају војној дужности; да не полажу заклетву и не примају оружје, као и да приликом подношења ових извештаја разликују адвентисте од назарена.

Ови су извештаји до данас стигли од 4.пука (Сплит)5.пука (Цетиње) и 8. пука (Љубљана) и Београдског жанд.батаљона. Извештаји 4. и 5. пука и Београдског жанд.батаљона негативни су, а извештај 8. пука гласи:

»Извештавам, да има гласком добивених извештаја од подређених ми чета на територији овог пука укупно 9 адвентиста (суботара) и то 3 мушких и 6 женских лица.

Сви мушки адвентисти (суботари) одазивали су се војним дужностима, положили су заклетву и примили оружје. Исти су врло лојални и добри држављани.

Назаренаца на територији овога пука нема.«

14. овога месеца под ЈБр. 5934 - поново сам наредио депешом и осталим пуковима, да се ови извештаји најхитније пошаљу и чим се буду добили, доставиће се Министарству.

Напомињем, да за прикупљање ових извештаја треба више времена, јер пукови ове морају прикупљати од чета, а чете од станица.

С молбом на увиђај и надлежност.

Заступа Команданта
Бригадни Ђенерал,

171

Translation:

Gendarmerie Central Command
15 August 1929
Belgrade

TO THE MINISTER OF THE ARMY AND NAVY (COURT DIVISION)

On 26 July this year, immediately upon receipt of order S. Br. 14816 dated 25 July 1929, I most urgently sent a ciphered order to all regiments and battalions of the gendarmerie (except the Second Regiment, which had filed a report), to most urgently report on how many Adventists (Sabbatarians) there were in their territory, whether there had been any cases of them failing to respond to the call of military duty, swear the oath or take up arms, and also, when filing these reports, to distinguish Adventists from Nazarenes.

So far, reports have come in from the Fourth Regiment (Split), the Fifth Regiment (Cetinje) and the Eighth Regiment (Ljubljana), as well as the Belgrade Gendarmerie Battalion. The reports of the Fourth and Fifth Regiment and the Belgrade Gendarmerie Battalion were negative. The report of the Eighth Regiment states:

"I can report from verbally received reports from companies subordinate to me in the territory of this regiment that there are a total of nine Adventists (Sabbatarians), three of them male and six female.

All of the male Adventists (Sabbatarians) have answered the call of duty, sworn the oath and taken up arms. They are very loyal and good citizens.

There are no Nazareans in the territory of this regiment."

On the 14th of this month, under reference number JBBr. 5934, I again sent a dispatch ordering the remaining regiments to send these reports most urgently, and as soon as they are received they will be forwarded to the Ministry.

I would like to note that collecting these reports will take a little more time, since regiments need to collect them from companies, and companies from posts.

I hereby request your understanding and further action in accordance with your authorization.

For the Commander
Brigadier General

**Report from the central command of the
Gendarmerie to the Army Minister in response
to the question of Adventists refusing arms**

The New 1931 Constitution

Despite all the efforts by the Nazarenes at home, friends from abroad and delegates to the League of Nations, no concessions were made to the Nazarenes in Yugoslavia. The new constitution of the kingdom of Yugoslavia in September 1931 continued with this practice, and Article Eleven expressly states the following: "The enjoyment of civil and political rights is independent of the exercise of religion. No one may claim exemption from civil and military obligations and duties by reason of the prescriptions of his religion."[176]

Although the War Resisters International (WRI) archive gives no indication that their petition was acted on at the state level, the complaint of the Nazarenes to the League of Nations did have occasional local effects. During 1930, The Danube Banovina revised three rulings by county prefects, as well as shorter prison sentences, monetary fines and forced labor that had been handed down by the lower courts, ruling them to be unfounded and seeking their revision – these were sentences against sixty-two Nazarenes in Ilok, forty Nazarenes in Kula, and thirty-one Nazarenes in Novi Bečej.[177]

The state evidently found it easy to admit to technical and administrative errors on the part of the lower courts and to revoke shorter prison and misdemeanor sentences. However, the appeals of Nazarenes sentenced to long-term prison sentences had no effect and the sentences were not altered. Another point of interest is that county prefects responded to these decisions by the higher authorities by enquiring whether this meant they could now allow the Nazarenes to meet together, and if not, what could they do to prevent them in this, if they could not punish them in this way? Many local government agents found it difficult to arrest and punish their

---

[176] Constitution of the Kingdom of Yugoslavia, 1931:5.

[177] Vojvodina Archive F-126.II-6145/1931. Pov. K. Broj. 278/30 dated 13 January 1931, Royal Administration of the Danube Banovina in Novi Sad. Copy of document in possession of author. For the report of the Danube Ban, see Appendix 3 to this chapter. Further documents show that the administration sought hard for a definite answer to these issues, right up until May 1931, but with no response that can be found in the archives.

neighbors—farmers and craftsmen—who were Nazarenes and who everyone knew as diligent and upright folk.

In the 1931 census, 7,000 people publicly and fearlessly, declared themselves as belonging to the Nazarenes, which can be seen from the attached document.

ПРИЗНАТИХ ВЕРОИСПОВЕСТИ И СЕКТА

ПО ПОСЛЕДЊЕМ ЗВАНИЧНОМ ПОПИСУ ИЗ
1931 ГОДИНЕ У ЈУГОСЛАВИЈИ ИМА И ТО:

1 *Православних* 6,785.501 душа (сада има преко 7 милијона)

2 *Римокатолика* 5,217.847

3 *Гркокатолика* 44.608

4 *Старокатолика* 7.273

5 *Јерменокатолика* 63

6 *Протестаната*, и то:

а) Евангелика аугсбуршког исповедања (лутерани немачке народности) 113.218

б) Евангелика аугсбуршког исповедања (лутерани словачке народности) 62.061

в) Реформати хелветског исповедања (калвини) 55.890

7 *Протестанаских секата*, и то:

а) Назарена 6.990

б) Адвентиста (суботара) 983

в) Баптиста 1.231

г) Методиста 993

8 *Других хришћанских вероисповести* 6.011

9 *Мојсијеваца* (Јевреја), и то:

а) Мојсијеваца сефардског обреда 26.168

б) Мојсијеваца ешкеназког обреда 39.010

в) Мојсијеваца ортодоксних 3.227

10 *Муслимана* (исламска вероисповест) 1,561.116

11 *Других вероисповести* (будиста и др.) 264

12 *Без вероисповести* (конфесије) 1.107

13 *Неозначатих* 427

Свега 13,934.038 душа. Ове су се цифре у току прошлих 7 година знатно увећале и измениле. — Податци су добивени у Државној статистици при Министарству Унутрашњих Дела.

107

Translation:

RECOGNIZED CONFESSIONS AND SECTS ACCORDING TO THE LAST OFFICIAL CENSUS FROM 1931 IN JUGOSLAVIA, THERE ARE:

1. *Orthodox* 6,785,501 souls (now there are more than 7 million)
2. *Roman Catholics* 5,217,847
3. *Greek Catholics* 44,608
4. *Old Catholics* 7,273
5. *Armenian Catholics* 63
6. *Protestants*, as follows:
   a) Evangelicals of the Augsburg Confession (Lutherans of German ethnicity) 113,218
   b) Evangelicals of the Augsburg Confession (Lutherans of Slovak ethnicity) 62,061
   c) Reformed Christians of the Helvetic Confession (Calvinists) 55,890
7. *Protestant sects*, as follows:
   a) Nazarenes 6,990
   b) Adventists (Sabbatarians) 983
   c) Baptists 1,231
   d) Methodists 993
8. *Other Christian confessions* 6,011

176

> 9. *Members of the Mosaic faith* (Jews), as follows:
>   a) Jews of the Sephardic rite 26,168
>   b) Jews of the Ashkenazic rite 39,010
>   c) Orthodox Jews 3,227
> 10. *Muslims* (the Islamic faith) 1,561,116
> 11. *Other faiths* (Buddhists and others) 264
> 12. *No faith* (confession) 1,107
> 13. *Unknown* 427

The source of this information was state statistics, the publication *Crkva – Kalendar Srpske pravoslavne crkve za 1939. godinu* [*Calendar of the Serbian Orthodox Church for 1939*]. This number may not reflect the real numbers of Nazarenes, and there may have been more.

За сада се код поменутих није могло ништа сумњиво приметити. Над именованим води се такође стална дискретна контрола. На подручју среске испоставе у Бос Броду постоји Назаретска секта са члановима Ивановић С.Симеуном и Ивановић С.Власо оба из села Полоја те Пејичић J.Бранком из Колиба доњих.
Именовани не шире никакву пропаганду нити одржавају какве састанке. Њихов вођа је Селтер Јаков из Слав.Брода гдје се и одржавају предавања. "
Предње је част доставити Министарству у вези Пов. Бр.1696/34 тога Министарства с молбом на надлежност.

По наредби
Министра унутрашњих послова
Пол.Инспектор,

ДБ.

177

Translation:

For the time being, nothing suspicious has been observed concerning the aforementioned. Ongoing, discreet monitoring of them is being maintained.

The Nazarene sect is present on the terrority of the county office in Bos[anski] Brod, with members Simeun Ivanović and Vlaso Ivanović, both from the village of Poloj, as well as Branko Pejičić from Donje Kolibe.

The above-named do not disseminate any propaganda, nor do they hold any meetings. Their leader is Jakov Selter from Slavonski Brod, where lessons are held.

It is my pleasure to report the foregoing to the Ministry in connection with Pov. Br. 1696/34 of this Ministry and to request further action in accordance with your authorization.

On the order of
Minister of the Interior
Pol[ice] Inspector
[signature]

Ongoing, discreet monitoring
– memorandum from the State Protection
Department, August 2, 1934.

The WRI archive currently also contains three lists of Nazarene prisoners in Yugoslavia, one from 1934 with the names of thirty-one people who were in prison in Požarevac, the second with twenty-eight names from Sremska Mitrovica. The third list is from 1936 and lists the names of 251 people, the length of the sentence, the number of children they have and the prison where they are serving their sentence. The shortest sentences were seven years, while the large majority were ten years imprisonment[178], served in the following prisons:

---

[178] In an article published in 1990, one of the old Nazarenes, born in 1907, wrote of the prison time he served in pre-war Yugoslavia. For his refusal to serve in the

Sremska Mitrovica, Požarevac, Zenica, Petrovgrad (Zrenjanin), Sombor, Zagreb, Vinkovci, Lepoglava, Pančevo, Beograd, Zemun, Šabac, Valjevo, Niš and Skoplje.[179]

Sentences continued to be handed down up until the eve of the Second World War. One witness from the book of testimonies collected by Kathleen Nenadov tells of how he was sentenced to eight years of solitary confinement, and how this was later increased to eleven years. He served his sentence in prison in Niš with around twenty-five other Nazarenes. Soon after being imprisoned, he became a prison trusty and worked in the book-bindery. According to his account, when the German occupying forces took control the commander released them all saying that they were a threat to no one.

Tomislav Branković talks about an interesting partnership between the Nazarenes in the Sremska Mitrovica prison and communist prisoners, with whom they usually shared accommodation in the cell-blocks.

> According to an account by Dušan Tubić, who was leader of the Nazarene community in the 1970s, the Nazarenes were allowed leave to go into town and often served as postmen or couriers for prominent party workers. Thus, for example, the Nazarenes and their relatives took parts of Marx's voluminous *Das Kapital*, which was being translated by Moša Pijade and Rodoljub Čolaković[180], prisoners in Sremska Mitrovica. *Das Kapital* was most often conveyed out by the Nazarenes when their relatives would visit them

---

army, Ranko Nedeljkov had spent nine years in prison (Jeftić, 1990:83).

[179] "Verzeichnis," "Nazarenes imprisoned in Jugo-slavia," "Letter to General Pera Zhivkovitch from 29 November 1930," "Letter from H. Ruhnam Brown to a 'Dear Friend' from 19 November 1930." Copies of documents in possession of author. International Institute of Social History, War Resisters' International Archive, binder 420. For the lists of prisoners, see Appendix 4 to this chapter.

[180] Both later to become household names in post-war Communist Yugoslavia (t/n).

at the weekends from the villages of Srem bringing them bags and baskets of food. The empty
baskets, after the visit was over, were a convenient
way to hide materials to be taken out (Branković,
2006:48).

The *Novonazareni*

Soon after the Nazarenes (and Adventists) were formally prohibited in 1924, some individuals began to waver, and some took
individual decisions to serve in the military after all and thus avoid
jail. In 1927, the authorities notified all the district prefects that a
splinter movement among the Nazarenes was gathering momentum
and that it had resulted in internal strife concerning control over
places of worship and over members, and that the state could and
should help these so-called *Novonazareni* [New Nazarenes] by tolerating them and reopening their buildings for worship services. The
first divisions arose, which were later to deepen.

The first Nazarenes to acquiesce in regard to taking the oath
and accepting arms were young men from Beška, Nova Pazova, and
Stara Pazova.[181] Having seen the efforts of the elders to have the oath
replaced with a ceremonial pledge, they realized that this matter of
principle could be changed by way of decisions at the local level,
and so they took the decision not to languish in jail but to accept
their civil, military duty in accordance with law. And although the
authorities accepted this decision, some remained suspicious towards
the Nazarenes, such as priest Jovan Buta from Beška (Buta, 1928:8).

This topic is addressed in particular detail and strong emotion
in a book from 1936 published in Belgrade under the pseudonym
"Hadžija." Feelings were running so high among the Nazarenes on

---

[181] Supposedly at that time there were 383 Nazarene congregations in the kingdom of SCS, but it is quite possible that this number included very small and
dying fellowships, and so the number itself still tells us little of the numbers of
Nazarenes, other than that there were still 380 fellowships that had yet to accept
this new understanding of the oath and the bearing of arms.

this matter that the author (probably a New Nazarene) felt compelled to publish a text pseudonymously on numerous moral issues and dubious decisions on the part of some elders. Hadžija laid out a range of examples of inappropriate behavior on the part of individuals, from financial abuses to sexual sins to lies and concealment of the truth. Several of his examples shed light on the power struggle amongst elders. Hadžija also devoted some of his writing to the changes to the Nazarene way of life and the pursuit of comfort that arose after the Great War among the Nazarenes.

This was probably prompted by the expulsion of young Nazarene men from membership for swearing the oath in the military, as well as "several hundred imprisoned men and thousands of members of their families left without anyone to provide for them." The author did not focus just on this, however, but meted out criticism left, right, and center. The main thrust of Hadžija's argument was that the elders of the "old" Nazarenes had allowed young men to receive long prison terms for refusing the oath and arms, that they encouraged them in this, and indeed ordered them, while they themselves found excuses and continued with their lives undisturbed by the authorities. At a meeting with the military authorities, held in 1924, even the representatives of the army inquired as to why the Nazarenes punished those who took the oath and accepted arms.

> As long as the Nazarenes held to the maxim, "gather together the weak, help those in need," they grew, as long as the congregations of the believers took care of spiritual matters but also economic matters. The chaos of war, and post-war circumstances led the Nazarenes into crisis (Hadžija, 1936:3).

According to this author, on receiving his call-up papers, an elder from Kisač sent his "unbelieving" son to the authorities, knowing that he would swear the oath. Because they had the same name and surname, he knew the authorities would leave him in peace after that. An elder from Mramorak was tricked by others into signing a statement which was later held against him and used to remove him, since he was very popular with all nationalities. There are also stories of financial irregularities, and so on. The author was evidently very well-informed regarding goings-on in Nazarene circles, particularly those less savory.

Inspector Hranisavljević, on the order of the Ministry of Justice, informed the Ministry of the Army and Navy in 1929 that the Adventists too had to be equated with the "Old Nazarenes" since they were not included in pov. No. 167/27 – which made public the division amongst the Nazarenes.[182]

The county prefect in Kula reported to Novi Sad in February 1930 that all Nazarenes under his jurisdiction belonged to the "Old Nazarenes" and that their places of worship should not be opened "until such time as they show the inclination to take up arms in the army as the New Nazarenes do."[183] Old Nazarenes were arrested and penalized for holding funeral services at the gravesides of their deceased,[184] for the sale of Scriptures, for holding night-time meetings,[185] for conducting baptisms by immersion in the canal,[186] their believers were not allowed to perform burials without all the religious trappings,[187] and so on. During 1930, these pressures let up and the arrests became less frequent.

After the Death of the King

After the assassination of King Alexander in Marseilles in 1934, the Yugoslav government demanded that its subjects swear allegiance

---

[182] Archive of Serbia and Montenegro, collection 63, binder 144, v. br. 16106/29 – XV Ministry of Justice. Copy of document in possession of author.

[183] The following four footnotes are from the Archive of the Danube Banovina, F 126. This document II 23430/930. Also attached is the negative report of the county prefect. Copies of documents in possession of author.

[184] II 44078/930.

[185] II 18374/930.

[186] II 18881/930.

[187] II 38026/930.

to the new boy-king Peter II, which posed a new yet familiar problem for the Nazarenes. New imprisonments began. However the New Nazarenes (as the authorities had earlier dubbed them) decided to go along with this and agreed to the new oath, and so there was once again division among the Nazarenes, and this only a few years after things had calmed down following the events in 1924. A new group detached itself, one that was prepared to go along with the authorities in this matter. This group contacted the Army Minister in October the following year promising that their young people would take the oath:[188]

> We have come from far-off places to request that the authorities take action regarding the petition submitted to the Army Ministry on 24 June 1935. In our homes and among our relatives and friends there is great concern for our people since in just one day, on the 19th of this month, the Military Court in Belgrade handed down 42 sentences totalling more than 400 years' jail. We request that the authorities summon our elders and order them to sign the proposed statement, which we will later show to our members in the jails, and we believe that the majority will then agree to take the oath.

The New Nazarenes agreed to military service and for this reason were expelled from their congregations. However if they were to repent they would, after a certain number of years, be rebaptized and received back into fellowship. This practice provoked indignation on the part of "those Nazarenes who had languished in prison for years, refusing to submit to the authorities." While they were still in jail, these penitent New Nazarenes had the freedom of their old congregations, having avoided state imprisonment and yet still being considered believers.

---

[188] You can see the text of the oath in Appendix 2 at the end of this chapter.

Because of this division the Nazarene movement decided that those people who had initially been baptized as Nazarenes and subsequently gone over to the New Nazarenes and were now asking to be readmitted, having repented, could be received back into fellowship, but no longer as a "free and full member." If someone had been first baptized as a New Nazarene and wanted to become a Nazarene, they first had to give their testimony before the fellowship and be rebaptized into the Nazarene faith.

Господину

Б А Н У Д У Н А В С К Е Б А Н О В И Н Е

Краљевине Југославије   Нови Сад

Доле подписани припадници Назаренске Секте, слободни смо
најпонизније умолити Господина Бана, да би нама наше Богомоље отво-
рио, да би и ми могли уживати слободу вере и савести, које припада
сваком човеку у задужење да се моли Богу за Његово Величанство Краља
и за све који су у власти а и за себе самог.

Са обзиром да је затварање Назаренских Богомоља насту-
пило из недовољног тумачења закона од јануара 1929. год. о распу-
штању свих политичких и политичко-верских удружења,то Назаренска
Секта не припада никаквом политичком удружењу но једна високо ло-
јална (Етичка) установа која се придржава чврсто Светога Писма.

Пошто је и делегација Државе Југославије при јесењем са-
станку у Цириху 1929.год. при Савезу Друштва Народа исто изјавила
да су Назаренске Богомоље чисто из недовољног тумачења горе споме-
нутог закона уследиле. те наводно и изјавили да се надају исправци
горње погрешке.

У нади да ће Господин Бан схватити колико је нама непра-
вде учињено досадашњом забраном, те да ће Господин Бан наредити да се
Назаренске Богомоље што пре отворе.

У напред Благодаримо на овом племенитом делу остајемо са нај-
дубљим понижењем у име свих Назарена.

Ст. Врбас 2.фебруара 1930

поданички одани

Мика Иванчевић
стг Пазуба
Милан Добросовац
Бдадра
Јанко Јабо
кивас
Лазар Накшијан

КРАЉЕВСКА
БАНСКА УПРАВА
ДУ...
НОВИ САД
II № 18360   9.II 1930
1-Зел.

КРАЉЕВСКА
БАНСКА УПРАВА
ДУНАВСКЕ БАНОВИНЕ
НОВИ САД

Translation:

[5-dinar stamps]

To the Esteemed
BAN OF THE DANUBE BANOVINA
of the Kingdom of Yugoslavia
Novi Sad

We the undersigned members of the Nazarene Sect have found fit, with all humility, to entreat the Esteemed Ban to open our Houses of Prayer, that we too might enjoy the freedom of faith and conscience that is the right of every man, including the duty to pray to God for His Highness the King and for all those who are in government, and for himself too.

In view of the fact that the closure of Nazarene Houses of Prayer came about as a result of flawed interpretation of the January 1929 law regarding the dissolution of all political and politico-religious associations, since the Nazarene Sect is not part of any political association, but rather is a highly loyal (Ethical) institution which adheres firmly to Holy Scripture.

Since also the delegation of the State of Yugoslavia at the fall 1929 meeting in Zurich of the League of Nations stated that [the closure of] Nazarene Houses of Prayer had happened purely because of flawed interpretation of the above-mentioned law, and had supposedly also stated that they hoped for the above error to be remedied.

In the hope that the Esteemed Ban will appreciate the injustice that has been done to us by this prohibition thus far and that the Esteemed Ban will order Nazarene Houses of Prayer to be opened at the earliest opportunity.

We thank you in advance for this noble deed, and remain, with the deepest humility, on behalf of all Nazarenes,

Your loyal subjects
St. Vrbas, 2 February 1930

[signatures]
Mika Ivančević
Stara Pazuva
Milan Doroslovac
Beodra
Janko Sabo
Kisač
Lazar [illegible]

[official Banovina stamp of receipt]

**A letter from a group of Nazarenes to the Ban
of the Danube Banovina, in which they request
the opening of their place of worship**

СРЕСКО НАЧЕЛСТВО У КУЛИ.

Број 1501/1930.

Предмет: Иванчевић и друг.молба за отварање назаренске богомоље.

На број:18360/II-1930.

КР.БАНСКОЈ УПРАВИ

Управно оделење

НОВИ-САД.

У поврат молбе част ми је следећи извештај поднети:

У подручном ми срезу сви назарени припадају секти старо назарена,код којих по њиховом верском тумачењу постоји најстрожија забрана одузимања туђег живота ма у којим приликама.Из тих разлога припадници те верске секте непримају оружје и због тога од стране војних судова су и кажњавани.

Из горњих разлога мишљења сам,да неби требало дозволити отварање њихових богомоља све дотле док неби били склони да приме оружје у војски као што то раде нови назарени.

Част ми је позвати се на моје већ раније поднешене извештаје у том предмету под бројевима 1363/1930.на тамошње наређење II.Бр.13151/1930.

К у л а,14.фебруара 1930.

срески начелник.

COUNTY PREFECTURE IN KULA
No. 1501/1930
Re: Mika Ivančević and others – request for opening of Nazarene place of worship.
Ref: 18360/II-1930

TO THE ROYAL ADMINISTRATION OF THE BAN
Administrative Department
NOVI SAD

In response to your request it is my honor to submit the following report:

In my local district these Nazarenes belong to the sect of the old Nazarenes, in whose religious interpretation the taking of another's life under any circumstances is most strictly forbidden. For this reason the members of this religious sect do not accept arms and have indeed been punished by the military courts for this.

For the above reasons, I am of the opinion that opening their places of worship should not be permitted until they show an inclination to bear arms in the army as the new Nazarenes do.

I have the honor of referring to my earlier reports in regard to this case, filed under numbers 1363/1930 in response to local order II.Br. 13151/1930.

Kula, 14 February 1930
County Prefect

Opinion of the county prefect, refusing permission for the opening of a place of worship since the worshippers belong to the so-called Old Nazarenes

For their part, many New Nazarenes coming home to their fellowships from having served in the military and learning that they were no longer "free and full members" petitioned the authorities to forcibly secure this right for them. The state made the most of this, closing many Nazarene churches (Nenadov, 2006:8-9). For example, on January 3, 1936, D. Tadić, police inspector of the State Protection

Department of the Ministry of the Interior informed the Danube Ban that one Danilo Velker, a New Nazarene elder, had petitioned the Ministry for the "old" Nazarenes to have their places of worship closed and "sealed" because they were meeting together freely, while "us New [Nazarenes], who have submitted to the authorities and allowed our young men to take up arms, they even mock…and inflict great harm and grief on us. And we who have submitted to the military and civil law, we are obliged to register every meeting with the police and pay a tax of 5 dinars for this, and 5 dinars to the city, while no-one touches the old [Nazarenes], they meet openly both in houses and in those places in which their places of worship are open to them." The letter further mentions Old Nazarenes in Stari Sivac, Kać, Temerin, Novi Sad, Zemun, Stapar, Buđanovci, Ruma, Kovilj, and Silbaš.[189]

Many of the churches closed at that time did not reopen right up until 1945, even though the state had softened its stance on the Nazarenes because of the New Nazarenes. A letter from early 1938 talks about how these events from the late 1920s transpired.

> Circular no. 167/1927 made null and void the order of the Ministry of Religions of 5 May 1924 no. 8765 forbidding the activities of the Christian sect of Nazarenes and Adventists and decreeing that their places of worship be closed. One of the primary reasons for the prohibition on the activities of the Nazarenes was their stubborn refusal to bear arms and take the military oath… The prohibition of the Nazarene sect, and the especially harsh punishments on the part of the military authorities, resulted in a number of Nazarene conscripts accepting arms and swearing the oath, for which reason such Nazarenes, on their return from military service, were expelled

---

[189] Vojvodina Archive, F-126.II-6145/931, dopis 39292, dated 31 December 1935. Copy of document in possession of author.

by their community from the Nazarene faith and
were thus compelled to establish a new community under the name of New Nazarenes.

Noting this favorable state of affairs and correctly anticipating
its consequences, the Ministry of the Interior decided, as they put it,
in accordance with their obligations under law and in the interests
of the state, to assist in this matter by allowing places of worship
to be reopened and New Nazarenes to meet in them, thus bringing
back into force those legal regulations that until order 8765/1924
had applied to the Nazarenes, on condition that access to places
of worship and participation in New Nazarene fellowships could
only be extended to those Nazarenes who had met their military
obligations.[190]

In this extensive letter, there is also mention of the fact that in
the enactments and decisions issued by the Ministry of Justice there
is no recognition of the organized religious communities either of
the Nazarenes or the Adventists. As tolerated religious sects, they had
neither the status of legal entities (public corporations), as recognized religious communities did, nor any rights in that respect. The
same letter forbade the preaching of the faith and the acceptance of
new members, the dissemination of religious literature for the purposes of proselytism, collecting tithes and other practices. There was
also provision for persecution to be employed against members of
these religious communities from a particular area if they were to
be caught disobeying any of these prohibitions. The New Nazarenes
and Adventists were permitted to meet in private homes, but only
members, and only if they had registered the meeting with the local
police authorities the day before. Although very restrictive this decision was a step forward in allowing the Nazarenes some freedom,
even if only within their congregations and circles of believers.

---

[190] SCG Archive, fond br. 63, fascikla 144. State Protection Department, Ministry
of the Interior, Pov. I broj 1647, 24 January 1938. Copy of document in possession of author.

There is no doubt that the many pressures brought to bear by the state, and probably the extended family too, as well as by the public, in addition to mistakes made by the Nazarene leadership and the application of double standards, all resulted in some Nazarenes turning to other religious communities, and others returning to the traditional churches. During the 1920s and 1930s many of them became Adventists and Pentecostals, as was the case with one new fellowship established by two brothers from a Nazarene family.[191]

> While conflict raged amongst the Nazarenes over obedience to the decisions of elders and the motives behind them, serving or not serving jail time, subsequent repentance etc., the state for its part worked actively to stifle the Old Nazarenes and their stance on refusing to take oaths and bear arms. The authorities used illegal and ethically dubious methods to do so.
>
> In 1953, the state security service gave this assessment of the Nazarenes in the period between 1932 and the beginning of the Second World War (Verske zajednice..., 1953:658):
>
>> Thus from 1932 until the surrender of the former Yugoslavia, most members of the sect voted for the incumbent regime of the time. Besides other factors, this stance on the part of the sect leadership in relation to these matters, whereby they proved themselves inconsistent in their beliefs, contributed greatly to the numerical decline of the sect. This also led to the division into "old" and "new" Nazarenes. The "old" held fast to dogma while the "new" favored abandoning certain prohibitions such as the prohibition on voting, oath-taking and bearing arms, and leaving these to the conscience of believers. However this schism did not last long but was smoothed over, in a way that favored the views of the "new."

---

[191] Aleksandar Birviš, interview, Steele, 1995:24-40.

Masthead of a Nazarene journal published in Beška in German
up until the Second World War

Der Kleine Nazarener-Bote, Marz 1940, Nr. 3.

WHY DID A GREAT EVIL BEFALL THE NAZARENES IN YUGOSLAVIA IN 1924?

In 1924, a great evil befell the Nazarene community in Yugoslavia. We all know what that evil brought with it. The entire community suddenly fell silent. The spiritual life, previously so beautifully cultivated, was suddenly extinguished, love grew cold and the old leaven once again took its place in the hearts of members. Many fellowships were deceived, the youth no longer attended and so some once again came to love the world.

The reason for all this can be found in insincerity alone. When in 1924, the order was issued regarding swearing the oath to the King, it was clear to all Nazarenes what this meant for them. The law envisaged ten-year jail sentences for refusal to take the oath. Several thousand Nazarenes were jailed.

The Nazarenes did everything they could at the time to free their imprisoned brothers. After long negotiations at various levels, an agreement was finally reached that the brothers could make a pledge instead of taking the oath. This pledge consisted of speaking the entire text of the required oath, word for word, except instead of the words "I swear" [zaklinjem se] they were allowed to say "I pledge" [zavetujem se (could also be translated "vow") – t/n]. It took several months before they were allowed to make this pledge. During that period, quite a number of brothers agreed to take the oath and were afterwards released.

Before making the pledge, the brothers had this act explained to them in detail. The general would stand before the brothers and explain to them that making the pledge was equivalent in meaning to taking the oath. He would liken it to the comparison between a cap and a hat [kapa and šubara – t/n]. Nobody was in any doubt as to the act he was to perform and each was conscious of his intent in doing so. All were happy that such a solution had been arrived at and all gladly accepted it. After making the pledge, each received a release document from the military authorities saying that such-and-such had taken the oath.

This solution would have remained in place and the Nazarenes, instead of taking the oath, would have been able to make the pledge. But then a major, grave mistake was made. All those brothers who had taken the oath before the pledge and were released were simply excommunicated. That these brothers erred in taking the oath there is no doubt.

But did they deserve excommunication for that? Could those brothers not simply have been disciplined and then later reinstated? This would have been far more reasonable. For how are you, dear brother, so much better for having made the pledge and yet having a paper in your pocket that says you took the oath? All those who stood with their brothers against excommunication were themselves condemned and excommunicated. This was the cause of the division.

After this division, and after many brothers had been expelled, it became apparent that among these deeply embittered brothers there were even those who fell so low as to seek revenge upon those who had judged them by accusing them before the military authorities.

Another mistake made at the time was the failure to adhere to the pledge. And now we arrive at the answer to our question: The reason for the great evil that befell the Nazarenes was firstly the expulsion of fallen brothers and secondly the failure to adhere to the pledge.

Those were the first two mistakes that were made. Everything that happened later was more a consequence of the first two errors. It is the same as when a believing soul sins. If it did not expose the sin but sought to conceal and cover it up, then this first, usually minor error would become the cause of new, much worse errors, which could then lead to apostasy. It was the same here, too. Instead of the pledge being accepted at face value the exact opposite was done. Sincerity was lacking, and in its place were constant attempts to present the pledge as being something other than it was… What was the consequence? The [option of the] pledge was immediately withdrawn and every Nazarene was compelled, when called to do so, to first take the oath – and then he would be offered arms. Of course many again found themselves in jail at that time.

From the article above we can clearly see how there was a constant effort to deceive the authorities. Do you believe, dear brother, that if you fool the authorities you are clean before God? So we ask all Nazarenes to abandon this way of insincerity and to rid themselves of such ideas, so that the same fate would not befall us as those teachers of the law. Our dear Savior rebuked them, telling them that because of their schemes they did not respect the commands of God. Let us abandon this and all unite under one motto: The matter of arms and oath should be left to each brother individually and he should do as his conscience allows him…

This commentary was published in March 1940 in the magazine *Der Kleine Nazarener-Bote* in the German language. No author was credited. We can assume it was written by Filip Knizl from Beška, publisher of the magazine. There was a note accompanying the text saying it would "be sent solely to believers as we do not want anyone else reading it."

Nazarenes Among the German Ethnic Minority

Rüegger's short report on Yugoslavia (Rüegger, 1962:185-188) gives us several pieces of information about the Nazarenes among the German minority in Vojvodina. From the foreign visits to Nazarene congregations during 1939[192] we learn that the larger churches were in Kraljićevo, today Kačarevo (Franzefeld), Nova Pazova and Crvenka, and that they had several hundred members each. There were smaller congregations in Mramorak, Pančevo, Novi Sad and Vrbas. New believers mostly came from the Protestant churches – according to

---

[192] The Nazarene delegation in 1939 was comprised of: Robert Leimgruber, Edwin Baer, Andreas Schenk and Paul Kambly.

the 1931 census, in Yugoslavia the Germans were seventeen percent Lutheran and three percent Reformed.

In other towns, smaller groups met mostly in each other's houses. There was one such group in Beška.[193] In early October 1944, when the German army began evacuating the German-speaking population, around a hundred Nazarenes, including small children and grandchildren, left the war zone and moved to Austria and Germany.[194] Their accommodation was directly taken care of by the humanitarian organization HILFE from Zurich, and by Paul Kambly, who had visited the German Nazarenes in Bačka and Banat districts two years before the war.

Rüegger reported that in 1962, in the congregations mentioned in Kraljićevo, Nova Pazova and Crvenka, there were just a few dozen Nazarenes of German origin.

---

[193] Their meeting was described as follows: "For a long time after the First World War, believers were dubbed *štundisti* [from German *stunde* – hour/class, referring to Bible studies – t/n]. Perhaps because that is how they referred to their meetings. But even before the First World War a schism emerged when some prominent families broke away… These families then joined the Nazarene community and that is how a Nazarene congregation was formed in our town," – from an interview with Nikolaus Betschel conducted by Tihomir Vekić in 1996 and published in his master's thesis (Vekić, 2003:59).

[194] According to data cited in Maričić, 1995:14, p. 64 and 73, there were around half a million citizens of German origin in the kingdom of Yugoslavia, many of them in Vojvodina. The withdrawal of the German army in autumn 1944 also saw the beginning of an exodus of Germans. The first to leave Vojvodina were the families of people who had served in the German army – 35,000 from Banat and around 40,000 from Bačka. Later there were more. It is estimated that around 200,000 *Volksdeutsche* fled to Austria and Germany. While new rule was being consolidated in the liberated territories, court proceedings were brought resulting in sentences of anything from six months' jail with forced labor to ten years…members of military groups were sentenced to death…it is thought that through 1948 some 300,000 people – German prisoners-of-war and *Volksdeutsche* – passed through various camps in Yugoslavia. At the same time, just in Vojvodina, 68,035 estates were confiscated, comprising 389,256 hectares of arable land.

Nazarenes Among the Romanian Ethnic Minority

Romanians in Vojvodina are still today concentrated primarily around Vršac, as well as Pančevo, Kovin and the area around Zrenjanin. With the break-up of the Austro-Hungarian monarchy, around forty settlements remained in the new state in which there were Romanians living. A state census in 1921 tells of 69,000 ethnic Romanians in the kingdom.

The Romanian Orthodox Church, too, worked hard on supressing the Nazarenes among the Romanian population in Vojvodina. The Nazarene movement reached the Romanians living in the Banat district in the last decades of the nineteenth century. In the village of Lokve (Sveti Mihailo) the Nazarenes amassed a considerable number of believers. Regarding the spread of the Nazarenes, the Romanian Orthodox Church indignantly observed that "sectarianism of the most dangerous kind possible has been insinuated into the Romanian masses: Nazareanism, a blight on the Church and the nation" (Đurić-Milovanović, 2011:26).

Between the two World Wars, the Nazarene movement gained new impetus among the Romanian population in Banat, although the anti-Nazarene backlash was fierce, too. In Vladimirovac in 1934, for example, the Romanian Orthodox priest Valeriu Filaret Perin succeeded in returning some twenty Nazarene children to the Orthodox faith, and baptizing them, which was even reported on in the interwar press.[195]

Towards the end of this period, on the eve of the Second World War, we find more data on the number of Nazarenes in the villages, also from Romanian Orthodox Church sources. The largest number of Nazarenes was recorded in Lokve—518, as compared with 3,950 Orthodox Romanians; in Banatsko Novo Selo there were eighty-five *sektaši* (Nazarenes and Adventists), as compared with 4,718 Orthodox Romanians; in Kuštilj there were fifty Nazarenes as compared with 1,753 Orthodox Romanians; in Dolovo there were seventy-seven Romanian and 211 Serb Nazarenes, as compared with

---

[195] *Nădejdea*, Vršac, issue 25 of 24 June 1934, page 7.

1,664 Orthodox Romanians and 2,788 Orthodox Serbs; in Nikolinci there were thirty-one Nazarenes as compared with 3,443 Orthodox Romanians; in Vojvodinci there were six Nazarenes as compared with 1,329 Orthodox Romanians, to cite just some of the data (Đurić-Milovanović, 2011:27).

Conclusion

With the consolidation of power, and with the inevitable division of the royal government on national and religious grounds, at a time when the Ministry of Religions was occupied by prominent Orthodox politicians, the decision was taken to finally put a stop to the Nazarenes (and Adventists), particularly because both religious communities had gained significant ground in Vojvodina. Decisions made at the highest level led to prohibitions on meeting for worship, the closure of houses of prayer and the confiscation of property. Around the same time, the army began to issue call-ups for military exercises, at which reservists were required to retake an oath of allegiance to the new state, and to accept arms and other military gear. Nazarenes were immediately singled out and first tried for misdemeanor and then by the criminal courts. The Nazarene movement itself remained an enigma to the authorities, who did not even try to understand what was happening with regard to this section of its citizenry. Repressive measures were employed across the board, through the police, the education system, the army, and the courts.

The Nazarene movement—which instead of being national in character spread primarily within social classes rather than according to mother tongue and ethnicity—was never perceived as something positive and diverse, but rather as an attack on the new regime and a potential source of weakness. The public were regularly served scare-stories, with unrealistic figures speaking of hundreds of thousands of *sektaši*, of their immoral gatherings, their foreign connections and their secretive nature.[196] For this reason, the persecution of the Nazarenes in peacetime was even harsher than the sanctions they endured in wartime, a contradiction in itself.

Another unique aspect of the situation the Nazarenes found themselves in under the new regime is described by Aleksov in his 2010 work (p. 294). In the kingdom of SCS, the majority of Nazarenes were of Serb ethnicity, and they were no longer an ethnic minority in the new state as they had been in Austro-Hungary. The state expected the Nazarenes to change their stance toward the bearing of arms and swearing the oath to the state. Their reservations towards the Hungarians were one thing, but now this was their state and their ruler. The authorities did not understand the Nazarene movement.

In order to put a stop to the Nazarene movement and to destroy it, the state formed an alliance at highest level. The Ministry of Religions issued orders—albeit of dubious legality and legislative backing—and then sought the cooperation of the local state authorities in putting them into practice. These local authorities—county prefects, mayors etc.—had to make use of the police and gendarmerie, and frequently the army got involved too, especially in trying and punishing the Nazarenes.

The division amongst the Nazarenes left its mark, not only in terms of their internal relations but also on their growth and progression. In some cases, they became scattered and disenchanted, and so the state got the results it wanted after all. However, the feeling remains that the persecution of the Nazarenes in the period under consideration (1918-1941) could have been averted had a different

---

[196] It is interesting to note that this author has noticed very similar patterns of behavior on the part of the authorities, and media outlets close to them, towards minority religious communities in the early 1990s and beginning of the twenty-first century in Serbia. Minority religious communities were accused of collusion with foreign powers, of having hundreds of thousands of converts and of acting systematically to compromise state security. As it transpired, no prosecutions were ever brought for such activities. The media hue and cry was primarily a calculated distraction from the real problems of the day – war, refugees, etc.

approach been taken towards the authorities, and had dialog been initiated. In the new state, in which separatist tendencies were a real threat, the executive powers were not able to respond adequately to the sociological challenge, and the challenge to the state itself, presented by the Nazarene movement.

Appendix 1 – Order of the Royal Provincial Government of Croatia, Slavonia and Dalmatia

Order of the Royal Provincial Government of Croatia, Slavonia and Dalmatia, Department for Religion and Education and Department for Internal Affairs, dated 12 November 1895 no 12.200, amending and supplementing some provisions of the order of 15 December 1893 no. 8940 on uniform procedures to be adopted in regard to the sect of the Nazarenes and Baptists in the Kingdoms of Croatia and Slavonia.

Since experience hitherto has shown that some enactments of the Royal Provincial Government's Department for Religion and Education and Department for Internal Affairs, dated 15 November 1893, no. 8940, ordering a uniform procedure to be adopted in regard to the sect of the Nazarenes and Baptists in the Kingdoms of Croatia and Slavonia, have given cause for wrong interpretation both on the part of the adherents of these sects and on the part of spiritual and subordinated secular authorities, the Royal Provincial Government has found it necessary to decide as follows:

I. § 3 of the above-named order shall be revoked and replaced by the following provision:

Assemblies of the adherents of the sect of the Nazarenes and the sect of the Baptists, regarding the law of 14 January 1875 concerning the right to meet, shall not be permitted; however they shall be free to congregate for the purposes of joint prayer on the following conditions:

1. that the meeting shall be held in the house of one of their fellow adherents;

2. that the meeting shall be limited only to persons known to the house owner and whom he has particularly invited and
3. that the house owner register the day and hour of the meeting, at least one day prior to the meeting, with the Royal County or town authorities. No decision is to be issued in regard to such application.

II. § 4 shall be supplemented with the addition of the following three new paragraphs:

Children born either before or after the apostasy of their parents to the Nazarenes or Baptists shall until their eighteenth year be considered adherents of the legally recognized confession to which their parents officially belong.

Accordingly, such children shall be brought up in the confession to which their parents officially belong, as per the existing regulations on religious upbringing. Such children must thus also be christened, attend catechism in school, attend church and be buried according to the rite of the confession in question.

Where parents refuse to abide by these regulations and duties, the local authority, upon learning of this, shall report this to the competent local court, which shall initiate proceedings against such parents pursuant to civil code regulations §§. 140 and 178, and take appropriate action to compel them to carry out their duties, or order the loss of parental rights.

Appendix 2 – Letter to all Nazarene congregations

To all Nazarene congregations in the Kingdom of Yugoslavia.

[For] those called upon in these days by the military authorities in Belgrade who are imprisoned having refused to take the military oath, we have taken a decision as spiritual leaders and elders, without whom no member or house of prayer may take a decision amongst themselves until we as elders have given our consent to the matter, which can best be seen in the book published by the elders in 1919 in Stara Pazova.

From this day each member of ours who is a military conscript may freely take the oath and take up arms in the army, and will not be punished for this with exclusion from our midst as previously, neither by us as elders, nor by those of our congregations in which we have the final say.

No longer will anyone be prevented from coming to our meetings who has taken the oath, as was previously the case, fearing that we will publicly exclude him, for which reason someone might report us to the authorities as happened last year in Belgrade.

We take upon ourselves the obligation to send this statement to our members in various jails so that they would know how to conduct themselves, and whoever should not submit to this order of ours and to the military authorities shall be excluded, for we shall no longer walk the wrong path in regard to our government. We will immediately set to work on reconciling our people who are in turmoil and have become divided over the military issue.

(Submitted along with a letter to the Ministry of the Army and Navy in Belgrade of 26 October 1935)

Appendix 3 – Order of the Danube Ban

Order of the Danube Ban to the Administrative Department for Nazarene sentences to be reduced

КР.БАНСКА УПРАВА ДУНАВСКЕ БАНОВИНЕ

Пов.К.Број: 278/30.

13.јануара 1931 год.

НОВИ САД.

ПРЕДМЕТ: Жалба Назарена на незаконско поступање наших власти.

УПРАВНОМ ОДЕЉЕЊУ

Кр.Банске Управе

НОВИ САД.

Назаренски кругови у иностранству поднели су жалбу Лиги Народа против наше државе ради незаконитог поступка наших власти према њима.

Министарство унутрашњих послова под Пов.I.Бр.42874. од 13.децембра 1930 наредило је да један бански инспектор утврди,на лицу места све евентуалне неправилности,почињене од месних власти и да према томе сва Управе даље по закону поступи.

Бански инспектор,којему је овај посао поверен,доставио је извештај у којему,између осталог казаћа ово:

I. 62 Назарена кажњено је од стране Среског Начелства у Илоку на 14 дана затвора и то ради преокршаја "по §.7 Наредбе од 20 априла 1854 у вези са чл.67 закона с унутрашњој управи",а казна је одмерена "на основу § 11 цитиране Наредбе и чл.69 З.У.У." 11-орица од осуђених изјавила је да се подвргава казни и одриче жалбе.Остали нису ништа изјавили,а колико сам могао дознати Мачетић Рада жалио се је против те пресуде Кр.Банској Управи.

Цитиране наредбе од 20.априла 1854 (т.з.Бахов патент) у овој пресуди погрешно је,јер та наредба,по домовену З.У.У.није више на снази,исто је тако погрешно примењен и чл.69 З.У.У. јер тај чланак предвиђа кажњене санкције за наредбе које власти опште управе могу да издаду на основу чл.67 З.У.У. а из пресуде се не види да је у конкретном случају издата таква наредба.Сем тога по чл.69 ЗУУ може срески начелник да изрече казну затвора до 10 дана и то субсидијарно док је овом пресудом то законско овлашћење препоручено.

Будући да је проти овој пресуде поднета жалба имаће Кр.Банска Управа пригоде да оцени незаконитост ове пресуде Ср.Начелства у Илоку.

II. Општинско поглаварство у Кули,пријавило је Среском Начелству у Кули,40 Назарена што се без дозволе сакупљају у кући Ненада Вукмића да врше назаренске обреде.

По преслушању,Среско Начелство је ове окривљене осудило на 200 Дин.глобе,и то пресудом Бр.396 од 1 октобра 1930 ради преступа по чланку 9 закона о заштити јавне безбедности и поретка у држави.

Ниједан од кажњених Назарена није се жалио против те пресуде те је иста постала правоснажном и сви су осуђени већ платили глобу од 200 Динара.

Мишљења сам да је Среско Начелство у Кули у конкретном случају неисправно поступило, јер пошто је сакупљање Назарена квалификовало као деликат по закону о заштити јавне безбедности и поретка у држави,имало је да ствар уступи надлежном суду,јер су по пропису предспоменутог закона,надлежни да суде по свим кривичним делима по том закону,државни судови.

Сем тога у мотивацији пресуде Среског Начелства у Кули, наведен је међу осталим као разлог казни и тај,што су се Назарени сакупљали да се "моле Богу по назаренском обреду,што им је забрањено", а таковва је мотивација,по мојем мишљењу,не само неумесна него,нема ни законског ослона.

Мислим да би ослоном на пропис чл.76 З У У,требало да Кр. Банска Управа,по праву надзора затражи тај акт од Среског Начелства у Кули и да га подвргне мериторној ревизији.

III. Истина је да је 31 Назарен кажњен од стране Среског Начелства у Новом Бечеју на глобу од 100 Дин. 20 Динара таксе за пресуду и 21 Динар на име трошкова поступка јер је поступак проведен - у корист самих окривљеника,на лицу места у Беодри.

Казнену пријаву доставила је општина у Беодри под Бр.134. две 9 фебруара 1930,ради недозвољеног сакупљања.Среско Начелство у Новом Бечеју уступило је пријаву Среском Суду у Новом Бечеју,који је под

Бр.К.П.С.75/30. ради ненадлежности вратио акт Среском Начелству. Услед
тога је Среско Начелство поступило против Назарена и издало пресуду о
казни коју сам горе споменуо под Бр.изгр.333/930. Казна је изречена на
основу чл.74 З.У.У.у вези алинеје 1и2 наредбе бившег угарског Мин.ун.
посл.Бр.1136 од 1898.

Осуђени се Назарени нису жалили и 26 њих од 31 колико
их је кажњено платили су глобу, а петорици који ради сиромаштва нису могли да плате глобе, претворено је у затвор, односно мулук.

Мишљења сам да је у конкретном случају Среско Начелство
у Новом Бечеју погрешно цитирало у својој пресуди чл.74.З.У.У. који се
није могао применити, јер се тај чл.односи на казне изречене у заштити
јавних органа и ради недостојног поступања на јавним местима а то у
конкретном случају није био објекат кажњивог дела.

Непознајем горе споменуту наредбу угарског Мин.унутр.пос-
лова из год.1898, али мислим да се она по доношењу З.У.У.не сме више при-
мењивати (чл.204 З У У).

Част ми је предложити госп.Бану да нареди да и ова пре-
суда буде подвргнута мериторној ревизији од стране Управног одељења Кр.
Банске Управе.

Предње достављам том Одељењу с тиме да од односних срес-
них начелстава затражи горе наведена акта, да подвргне мериторној реви-
ји поступак среског Начелника те да, у дивом случају, даље поступи по сми-
слу чл.75 З.У.У.и да ме о томе извести.

БАН:

Translation:

ROYAL ADMINISTRATION OF THE BAN OF THE DANUBE
BANOVINA
Ref. no. Pov.K.Broj: 278/30
13 January 1931
NOVI SAD

Re: Complaint by the Nazarenes regarding unlawful actions by our authorities.

TO THE ADMINISTRATIVE DEPARTMENT
of the Royal Administration of the Ban

NOVI SAD

Nazarene circles abroad have filed a complaint with the League of Nations against our state for unlawful actions by our state towards them.

The Minister of the Interior, under ref. Pov. I.Br. 42874 dated 13 December 1930 ordered that an inspector of the Ban go and look into any irregularities carried out by local authorities and that this Administration take further action in accordance with law.

The Ban inspector to whom this task was entrusted filed a report in which, *inter alia*, he states the following:

I.   62 Nazarenes were sentenced by the Country Prefecture in Ilok to 14 days' imprisonment for a misdemeanor "pursuant to § 7 of the Order of 20 April 1854, with reference to Art. 67 of the Law on Internal Administration [Z.U.U.]," the sentence being determined "pursuant to § 11 of the above-cited Order and Art. 69 of the Z.U.U." 11 of the convicted stated that they would accept the sentence and waive appeal. The others did not make any statement, and as far as I was able to learn, Rada Ničetić did appeal the ruling before the Royal Administration of the Ban.

Citation of the order of 20 April 1854 (the so-called Beating Patent – *Prügelpatent*) in passing this sentence is wrong, since that order ceased to have force upon the promulgation of the Z.U.U. Also wrongly applied is Art. 69 of the Z.U.U., since this article lays down penalties for orders which the general administrative authorities may issue pursuant to art. 67 of the Z.U.U., whereas from the ruling it cannot be seen that such an order was issued in the case in question. Additionally, pursuant to Art. 69 of the Z.U.U., the County Prefect may hand down a sentence of up to 10 days, and only in a subsidiary sense, whereas this ruling has overstepped this legal authorization.

In view of the fact that an appeal has been lodged against this ruling, the Royal Administration of the Ban has the opportunity to remedy the unlawful nature of this ruling of the Country Prefecture in Ilok.

II. The municipal administration in Kula reported to the County Prefecture in Kula that 40 Nazarenes were meeting without permission in the house of Nenad Bukvić for the purposes of conducting Nazarene rites.

After questioning they were all fined 200 dinars, by ruling no. 396 dated 1 October 1930, for a breach of Article 9 of the Law on the Protection of Public Security and Order in the State. None of the fined Nazarenes appealed the ruling and it was made final and all those fined have already paid the fine of 200 dinars.

It is my opinion that the District Prefecture in Kula acted improperly in this case for summarily deeming the meeting of the Nazarenes a crime pursuant to the Law on the Protection of Public Security and Order in the State. This case should have been referred to the competent court, since according to the above-mentioned law it is the state courts which have jurisdiction to hear all cases relating to crimes pursuant to this law.

Additionally, the motivation for the ruling of the District Prefecture in Kula included the reason that the Nazarenes were gathering to "pray to God according to the Nazarene rite, which is prohibited to them," a motivation which, in my opinion, is not only inappropriate but does not even have legal grounds.

I think that pursuant to the provision of Art. 75 of the Z.U.U. the Royal Administration of the Ban should invoke its supervisory rights and require the District Prefecture to forward this decision to it for qualitative review.

III. It is true that 31 Nazarenes were fined 100 dinars by the District Prefecture in Novi Bečej, plus 20 dinars tax for the verdict and 21 dinars against costs, since the proceedings were conducted locally in Beodra at the request of those charged. The charges were filed by the municipality in Beodra under ref no 134, dated 9 February 1930, claiming unlawful gathering. The County Prefecture in Novi Bečej delegated the charges to the County Court in Novi Bečej, which under ref. no. K.P.C. 75/30 returned them to the County Prefecture citing a lack of jurisdiction. Consequently, the County Prefecture took action against the Nazarenes and issued a ruling handing down the previously mentioned fine, ref. no. 333/930. The fine was issued pursuant to Art. 74 of the Z.U.U. in relation to paragraphs 1 and 2 of the order of the former Austro-Hungarian Minister of the Interior, no. 1136 of 1898.

The convicted Nazarenes did not appeal, and 26 of the 31 that were sentenced paid the fine, while for five who were not able to pay the fine for reasons of poverty the sentence was amended to a term in jail and forced labor.

In my opinion, in this specific case, the County Prefecture in Novi Bečej improperly invoked Art. 74 of the Z.U.U. in its ruling. This article was not applicable since it relates to penalties handed down for the protection of the public authorities and for inappropriate behavior in a public place, which in this specific case was not the subject of the punishable offense.

I am not familiar with the above-mentioned order of the Austro-Hungarian Minister of the Interior from 1898, but I believe that with the passage of the Z.U.U. it may no longer be applied (Art. 204 of the Z.U.U.).

It is my honor to propose to the esteemed Ban that He order this ruling too be subjected to qualitative review by the Administrative Department of the Royal Administration of the Ban.

I am submitting the foregoing to this Department with the request that it seek the above-mentioned rulings from the county prefectures in question, to subject the actions of the County Prefect to qualitative review and, in the specific case, take further action pursuant to Art. 75 of the Z.U.U. and keep me notified in this regard.

Ban:
[signature of the Ban]

Stamp: Ban of the Danube Banovina, Novi Sad

Appendix 4 – List of Nazarene prisoners

List of Nazarene prisoners in the Požarevac penitentiary from 1934 from the WRI archive

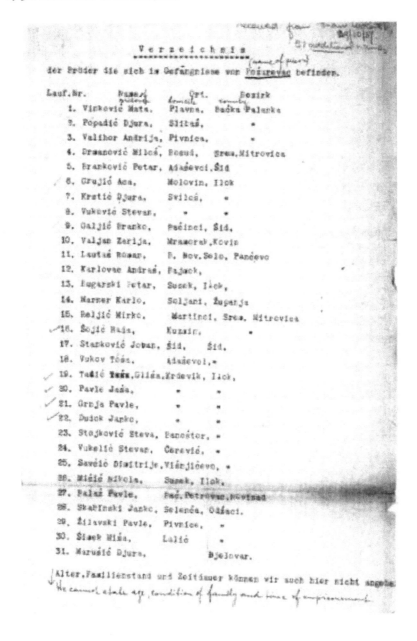

List of 251 Nazarene prisoners from 1936. The list gives each prisoner's age, number of children, length of sentence and the name of the prison. From the list, we can see that some Nazarenes served their sentences in military prisons.

Kenewied Pee 1936.

251 imart
61 s.d.f.
16
373

NAZARENES IMPRISONED IN JUGO-SLAVIA.

Surname & christian name	age	sentence	children	prison.
1. Olympió Milan	28	----	---	Srem.Mitrovica
2. Jovanov Streva	50	10 y.6 m.	8	" "
3. Koler Bara	---	----	---	" "
4. Savin Zivko	24	9 years	---	" "
5. Kovač Ištvan	47	----	2	" "
6. Vinkovic Mate	42	----	---	" "
7. Galik Stevan	44	----	---	" "
8. Ciboš Marije	---	10 years	---	" "
9. Balaš Pavle	43	11 years	5	" "
10. Trovski Joven	---	10 "	---	" "
11. Shrendjer Pavle	36	----	---	" "
12. Hajka Janko	41	----	5	" "
13. Costven Pavle	41	----	6	" "
14. Strepak Jano	41	----	4	" "
15. Sperak Jano	34	----	3	" "
16. Hojka Jano	39	----	3	" "
17. Kahlec Jano	34	----	3	" "
18. Dadva Jano	33	----	4	" "
19. Pacovski Mišo	37	----	1	" "
20. Sinek Mišo	37	----	5	" "
21. Vašara Sara	47	----	5	" "
22. Metalka Jano	46	----	4	" "
23. Slabinski Jano	39	----	4	" "
24. Sinkoski Stefan	50	----	---	" "
25. Srankov Dušan	28	7 y. 7 m.	---	" "
26. Slach Janoš	39	10 years	7	" "
27. Sarga Janoš	42	10 years	7	" "
28. Karlovic Andreš	32	10 years	3	" "
29. Gal Isidor	43	----	12	" "
30. Sandrak Lukaš	47	----	8	" "
31. Sinstvaš Petar	50	----	10	" "
32. Simul Jefta	50	----	10	" "
33. Sratea Mila	43	----	7	" "
34. Bogšan Sava	33	----	4	" "
35. Sarba Joca	40	----	---	" "
36. Sloc Vran	34	----	4	" "
37. Rasalin Joca	34	----	2	" "
38. Sandra Bika	36	----	3	" "
39. Sandra Faja	34	----	3	" "
40. Sandra Gavrila	27	----	4	" "
41. Taljan Sacheja	37	----	5	" "
42. Tfiš Jano	32	----	7	" "
43. Chalok Jano	33	----	4	" "
44. Marko Milo	32	----	2	" "
45. Chuško Mišo	34	----	---	" "
46. Janoš Sara	31	----	4	" "

- 2 -

Surname & christian Name	age	sentence	children	prison.
47. Špefak Paja	80	----	4	Srem.Mitrovica.
48. Lautaš Roman	46	----	5	"
49. Semiš Lazar	50	----	2	"
50. Manošan Velemir	35	----	4	"
51. Suvošar Slavko	27	----	2	"
52. Sodin Alexander	26	----	2	"
53. Miloji Jovan	35	----	4	"
54. Taro Janoš	--	10 years	--	"
55. Kristijan Zlatov	26	10 "	--	"
56. Radovanov Charko	34	----	--	"
57. Nemesohajmar Dušan	35	10 years	--	"
58. Kolariš Obrad	41	11 years	2	"
59. Krstonožiš Branko	27	10 y. 2 m.	--	"
60. Sebuliš Živan	40	10 y. 6 m.	2	"
61. Crajiš Petar	47	10 y. 6 m.	--	"
62. Milovac Obrad	37	10 years	3	"
63. Cekiš Penta	47	9 years	6	"
64. Chereviš Laza	38	9 years	6	"
65. Svilokma Nedžlko	41	9 y. 8 m.	9	"
66. Stapovski Samo	35	10 y. 2 m.	2	"
67. Tardaj andrija	47	10 y. 2 m.	1	"
68. Tordaj Janko	34	10 y. 5 m.	2	"
69. Peleš Miša	31	10 y. 2 m.	1	"
70. Mocho Semo	45	10 y. 8 m.	8	"
71. Bedžla andrija	42	10 y. 8 m.	8	"
72. Martinski Jano	44	10 y. 3 m.	8	"
73. Mišiš Nikola	36	10 years	2	Požarevac
74. Jakiš Simiš Dušan	23	10 years	2	Srem.Mitrovica
75. Sagarski Pera	32	10 years	5	Požarevac
76. Jaremiš Laza	40	9 "	9	Niš
77. Popoviš Lazman	49	10 "	--	Srem.Mitrovica
78. Dragojloviš Miloš	42	10 "	5	Požarevac
79. Pejiš Lazman	42	10 "	6	Niš
80. Vikoviš Steva	37	9 "	6	Požarevac
81. Rankov Nedžlko	29	10 "	inprisoned	second time in Zenici.
82. Maarini š Rada	47	5 years 6 m.	7	"
83. Jefta Rankov	42	----	--	Srem.Mitrovica
84. Mišloviš Milodar	34	9 years	--	"
85. Čiboš andrija	34	9 y. 8 m.	1	Petrovgrad
86. Taro Janoš	32	10 years	3	"
87. Milostrašiš Vila	42	----	--	osodb r
88. Simon Jozef	51	9 y. 9 m.	10	"
89. Liloviš adam	32	----	--	Zagreb
90. Klajiš Ivan	42	----	--	"
91. Mišloviš Ilija	36	10 y. 8 m.	--	Vinkovac
92. Pešanoviš Steven	44	9 y. 8 m.	2	"
93. Lemajiš Dušan	41	9 y. 8 m.	5	"

- 3 -

Surname & christian name	age	sentence	children	prison.
94. Lemajiš Jovan	42	9 y. 8 m.	6	Vinkovce
95. Radosevljeviš Milutin	41	10 y. 6 m.	5	"
96. Kamm Michal	31	5 y.10 m.	1	Lepoglava
97. Aron Falko	26	11 years	---	"
98. Lapiš Stjepan	22	5 y.10 m.	2	"
99. Bocka Sandor	45	5 y.10 m.	1	"
100. Kapetan Milovan	38	----	---	"
101. Stamaniš Sreta	26	----	---	"
102. Falčin Gantner	43	----	---	"
103. Somorja Mira	46	----	---	"
104. Brankoviš Dimitrije	22	----	---	"
105. Jdukoviš Toša	51	----	---	"
106. Posavac Mirko	50	----	---	"
107. Pavloviš Nikola	51	----	---	"
108. Vesely Rudolf	42	----	---	"
109. Bočiš Michajlo	42	----	---	"
110. Markoviš Jovan	32	----	---	"
111. Mirko Iakoš	29	9 y. 8 m.	--	"
112. Gišša Sorše	34	----	---	"
113. Prekin Velko	28	----	1	"
114. Bališa Branden	27	----	1	"
115. Šla Miše	26	----	--	"
116. Toman Janko	27	10 y. 2 m.	---	"
117. Junkoviš Boža	46	10 y. 6 m.	3	"
118. Rajchard Filip	47	----	8	Pančevo
119. Rišman Chrisman	45	----	7	"
120. Rišman Jochan	43	----	7	"
121. Bauman Jochan	43	----	7	"
122. Stanijer Bara	36	----	2	"
123. Tiriš Laza	42	----	1	"
124. Valšev Mateja	48	----	5	"
125. Baracka Jano	49	----	6	"
126. Nemšak Miša	36	----	--	"
127. Grvar Jovan	33	----	2	"
128. Joca Grajiš Molovin	49	10 y. 2 m.	---	Požarevac
129. Caran Joca	50	----	8	"
130. Cheader Jovan	50	10 y. 6 m.	2	"
131. Rešiš Mirko	50	10 y. 6 m.	3	"
132. Šijoš Rade	38	9 years	4	"
133. Grša Falko	48	10 y. 2 m.	1	"
134. Falko Jašo	41	10 y. 2 m.	--	"
135. Tadiš Giga	48	10 y. 2 m.	3	"
136. Budak Janko	33	10 y. 2 m.	4	"
137. Gečiš Branko	28	18 y. 2 m.	--	"
138. Falkenburger Jakob	41	10 y. 3 m.	3	Beograd 2.pešpul
139. Duniš Rima	46	10 years	2	" "
140. Uchrik Jozef	34	16 years	3	" "

214

- 4 -

Surname & christian name	age	sentence	children	prison.
141. Bori** Svetozar	47	10 years	6	Beograd Z.pešpuk.
142. Rabni** Joca	48	10 years	5	" "
143. Blamu** Milovoj	45	10 years	--	" "
144. Grbi** Doka	48	12 years	4	" "
145. Kratin Đura	47	10 years	6	" "
146. Zichlavaki Pavle	46	10 years	4	" "
147. Valichori .Marija	43	10 years	5	" "
148. Zala Nikola	44	14 years	--	" "
149. Petarajac Pavle	49	10 years	2	Beograd18 pešpuk.
150. Jovanovi** Božidar	48	10 years	3	" "
151. Jung Georg	30	10 years	3	" "
152. Jut Petar	49	10 years	1	" "
153. Križan Janko	38	14 years	4	" "
154. Nikoli** Dragutin	41	----	5	" "
155. Crānskij Radivoj	48	----	8	Ljepoglava
156. Rojka Janko	49	----	3	"
157. Droběevi** Luka	50	----	3	"
158. Zala Nikola	45	----	3	"
159. Zaaljac Janko	--	----	6	Beograd .RT. Puk.
160. Sverak Janko	--	----	5	" "
161. Doša Janko	--	----	4	" "
162. Brankovi** Milan	--	----	3	" "
163. Sopalo Pepa	47	9 y. 10 m.	3	Balina
164. Aleksandar Graji**	48	10 years	1	Zemun Z. peš. pluk
165. Rojka Janko	42	10 years	5	" " "
166. Castven Pavle	41	10 years	6	" " "
167. Strepak Jano	42	10 years	4	" " "
168. Stanojevi** Živan	4.	10 years	11	" " "
169. Joki** Milinko	41	10 years	5	" " "
170. Pavi Janko	41	10 years	1	" " "
171. Stojkovi** Jefta	43	10 years	--	" " "
172. Milinči** Milivoj	67	10 years	4	" " "
173. Mormar Karlo	45	10 years	7	" " "
174. Stankovi** Javan	49	10 years	4	" " "
175. Vukovi** Ilija	48	10 years	4	" " "
176. Rinči** Rada	41	10 years	6	" " "
177. Vukov Toša	43	10 years	6	" " "
178. Fučenov Sava	50	10 years	1	" " "
179. Ragojev Dušan	27	----	--	" " "
180. Teodorovi** Nikola	--	----	4	Rapos
181. Patnikov Jovan	--	----	3	"
182. Aladislavljevi** Mitar	--	----	5	"
183. Vitis Đura	--	----	6	"
184. Ruja Nikola	--	----	7	"
185. Jovanovi** Aleksandar	--	----	--	"
186. Feld Jochan	--	----	6	"
187. Negovanovi** Žika	--	----	6	"

- 8 -

Surname & christian name	age	sentence	children	prison
188. Jević Dragomir	36	----	4	Zabela
189. Đurić Čeda	36	----	1	"
190. Mihaljević Mladen	39	----	---	"
191. Mićaljović Milutin	---	----	4	"
192. Petrović Nikola	36	----	5	"
193. Gojić Žoja	47	----	3	"
194. Gretenović Draja	50	----	2	"
195. Grođević Đoka	---	----	2	"
196. Šarp Adam	50	----	6	Valjevo
197. Struher Mišo	48	----	8	"
198. Ranđen Palko	38	----	7	"
199. Sejanković Vaca	48	----	7	"
200. Timić Jovan	31	----	2	"
201. Ignatović Milan	41	----	4	"
202. Martinko Janko	43	----	7	"
203. Milee Palko	50	----	3	"
204. Stojković Steva	42	----	4	"
205. Marić Mile	51	----	8	"
206. Jerisavljević Mile	39	----	6	"
207. Gojić Toša	47	----	4	"
208. Đurđić Slavko	38	----	7	"
209. Pešen Adem	39	----	3	"
210. Jandrić Rajko	31	----	4	"
211. Stugovski Samuel	36	----	3	"
212. Stojković Jovan	38	----	2	"
213. Nešić Miloš	31	----	3	"
214. Vukolić Petyen	39	----	---	"
215. Stojčić Grol	42	xxxxxxxx	xxx	Valjevo
216. Moreo Rajko	--	9 y. 6 m.	---	Niš
217. Matvajn Henrich	--	10 years	---	"
218. Trpić Dušan	--	9 years	---	"
219. Jović Novak	--	9 y. 5 m.	---	"
220. Betejanac Giršde	31	9 y. 8 m.	---	"
221. Jović Đorđa	39	9 years	2	"
222. Ljubo Ilija	--	9 y. 6 m.	---	"
223. Živanović Đoško	--	11 years	---	"
224. Merjanski Milan	--	11 years	---	"
225. Stokin Miloš	--	9 y. 8 m.	---	"
226. Župljev Spasa	23	9 y. 6 m.	---	"
227. Dubrovski Marija	--	11 years	---	"
228. Palko Aron	--	4 years	---	"
229. Despotov Tošor	--	10 years	---	"
230. Serinov Vladimir	--	9 years	---	"
231. Gutvajn Henrich	47	10 years	4	"
232. Milković Čeda	43	1 year	2	"
233. Gojić Đorđe	47	9 y. 8 m.	3	"
234. Vučko Janko	23	10 years	-	"

216

- 8 -

Surname & christian Name	age	sentence	children	prison.
235. Gečiš Milivoj	44	10 years	--	Niš
236. Drakenović Mate	--	8 years	--	"
237. Šal Jano	28	7 years	--	y Šoplju
238. Tasnković Živa	--	7 years	--	" "
239. Bognar Joven	--	7 years	--	" "
240. Jovin Jova	--	9 years	--	" "
241. Krščanov Milan	--	1 years	--	" "
242. Ter Martin	--	9 years	--	" "
243. Miladinov Manojlo	27	10 years	--	" "
244. Galjan Viša	24	1 years	--	" "
245. Periškiš Lazar	23	11 years	--	" "
246. Borta Ilija	--	11 years	--	" "
247. Cigoriš Proša	23	11 years	--	" "
248. Markov Mirko	--	13 years	--	" "
249. Vitomirov Dušan	--	11 years	--	" "
250. Krneljan Vasa	28	11 years	--	" "
251. Šipoš Mišan	29	9 years	--	" "

NAZARENE CONSCIENTIOUS OBJECTORS DURING THE SECOND WORLD WAR IN SOCIALIST YUGOSLAVIA

During the Occupation

The occupation authorities commonly imprisoned Nazarenes and members of other minority religious communities, consigning them to forced labor[197] and forbidding their meetings. The same was done by the collaborationist Nedić government in Serbia.[198] Many Nazarenes spent the war in labor and concentration camps in Serbia, Croatia, and Germany.[199] Some were released by the authorities only to be recalled to the military by other local authorities, ending up in prison again. Some were held in jails by the Soviets until as late as 1947.

On the other hand, some Nazarenes volunteered in partisan units. They served as medics, in the stores, as cooks and as auxiliary

---

[197] One such account can be found in Appendix 1 at the end of this chapter.

[198] On 1 May 1941, all church assemblies, fairs and councils were forbidden, and the order decreeing this was published in *Obnova*, issue 63, 16 September 1941 (Radenić, 1961:352). Religious communities could secure permission to gather together for worship only with great difficulty.

[199] We can see how commonplace forced labor was in the occupied areas of the former Yugoslavia from the fact that in 1943, from Belgrade alone, around 11,000 male persons aged between seventeen and forty-five were consigned to forced labor. Of this number, 3,560 men were sent to forced labor in the Bor mines, 238 to Kostolac and more than 1,500 to the surrounding area of the same town (Glišić, 1969:72).

workers in the NOB[200] on the Partisan side, and some were decorated for their dedication and bravery. Because of them, many Nazarene houses of prayer were reopened in 1945. The Republic's Commission for Religious Matters in the NOB[201] determined that more than 100 young Nazarenes had participated in the war and that ten had died. Another seventy-four Nazarenes had died who had served as couriers and food runners for the Partisans.[202] Another 800 persons whose parents were Nazarenes had taken part in the war, and around 200 of them had died. Many survivors later served as officers in the army, the police, and in other state institutions. Particularly active were Nazarenes from Vojka, Grgurevo, Paćinci and Laćarak. Branković states that Nazarenes from Srem were most common in the Partisan

---

[200] *Narodnooslobodilačka borba* – People's Liberation War, referring to the armed struggle against the Axis occupying forces in Yugoslavia during the Second World War (t/n).

[201] This Commission was established by decision of VASNOS (*Velika antifašis-tička skupština narodnog oslobodenja Srbije* – the Great Antifascist Assembly of People's Liberation) on 26 February 1945, titled *Verska komisija pri pretsed-ništvu ASNOS-a* [Religious Commission of the Presidency of ASNOS], its function being to act as an advisory body and study the relationships between individual religious confessions and churches and questions of the relationship between church and state. Soon after the end of hostilities, on 21 August 1945, the Presidency of the Council of Ministers of the DFJ (*Demokratska Federativna Jugoslavija* – Democratic Federal Yugoslavia) issued a decree establishing a state commission for religious matters. Its task was to investigate all matters relating to the public activities of religious communities, to give opinions and proposals regarding all matters concerning the relationship between religious communi-ties and the state, and to concern itself with the implementation and proper application of all legal regulations.

[202] For more on this subject, see Branković 2006:54-56. In the report on the Nazarenes from Srem, figures are given of sixty Nazarenes who died or were executed, eighty who were sent to camps, 130 Nazarene homes that had been burned down, as well as other data. The report also talks of the children of Nazarene parents who had taken part in the war on the Partisan side and had later become JNA [Yugoslav People's Army] officers and become actively involved in the political and public life of the new state.

units, whilst some Nazarenes from Banat were "loyal to the occupying forces" (Branković, 1986:35).[203]

The Nazarenes also had contact with the communists in the pre-war period when they helped in the Sremska Mitrovica penitentiary with the removal of parts of the translation of Das Kapital from the jail, and in other cases. Communist leaders held in the same prison sent parts of translations of communist literature in empty food baskets brought by Nazarene women to their husbands, brothers or sons. Checks on leaving jail were not as rigorous as when entering it, and this activity went unnoticed. The manuscripts would then be collected by communist party couriers.

During the war, Nazarenes had been permitted to serve without bearing arms, so it was not entirely clear how the new authorities would treat this issue in peacetime.[204] The Nazarenes themselves,

---

[203] When it became clear that the Nazarenes were taking a position of non-cooperation with the new state in regard to voting, cooperatives, common ownership, and the distribution of Volksdeutsche estates etc., by the time of the 1953 police report, somehow the wartime merits of the Nazarenes "evaporated," and the war years were depicted in a very negative light. The phrase used by the State Security service was "*neprijateljski stav prema Narodnoj vlasti*" ["a hostile attitude towards the People's Government"]. Unable to pin wartime misdeeds on the Nazarenes, they accused them of collaboration with the enemy and in their report concluded that many Nazarenes, and especially their elders, who were mostly "wealthy men," had cooperated economically with the occupying forces and used the opportunity for wartime profiteering. Doroslovac (see later) is accused of having frequently had German officers as guests in his home. *Verske zajednice u FNRJ*, book 2, 1953:662.

[204] An account from the testimony of Rada Nikolić is of interest here:

> This was something told to us by our Auntie Rada, and it included this:
> After liberation they called Jaćim, her husband, who was a Nazarene servant, to the SUP [*Sekretarijat unutrašnjih poslova* – local police station]. He was not at home so she went to find out why they were summoning him. The SUP guy asked her: When and how did this faith come here, and where did it come from? She said: from Austro-Hungary. My father used to travel 'over there' [to Vojvodina, author's note] and he was first to believe. The policeman said: You

however, appeared to be happy. The first year after the war, and the following year – 1946 – were "good years" for the Nazarenes. The following anonymous account bears this out:

> When the sergeant came to me I said to him: Sir, I cannot accept arms, I am a Nazarene and that is against my faith. He replied that I had to bring a document from my local town administration certifying that I was a Nazarene. I got in contact with my family and my mother brought the necessary papers. When I had got them I handed them over to the commanding officer. He examined them and then said to his officers: "This man is a Nazarene. Do not give him arms." That was a good time for the Nazarenes (Nenadov, 2006:52).

---

don't allow your children to defend their fatherland, they will not swear the oath and they will not bear arms. Our aunt replied to him: I wish our children were with us, but nobody comes to us by force, only of their own will, if they want to. Then she said to him: My husband was a *solunac* [served on the Salonica Front in WW2 – t/n], he was away from home for five years, he worked in supplies (he carried around food, wounded soldiers and the sick) without swearing the oath or bearing arms when they were retreating before the enemy through Albania, while your people, who swore to king and country, wanted to go no further so they called my husband: Come on Jaćim, let's go back to our homes! But Jaćim replied: I will not – you do as you please but I will go with my brothers, and may whatever befalls them befall me too. Soldiers who had taken the oath threw down their arms and scattered, while my husband, without oath or arms, reached Salonica and was there the whole time. The policeman said to aunt Rada: I have no further questions (Nikolić and Milovančev, n.d.).

The Great Assembly in Vrbas

That same year, 1946, at a gathering in Vrbas (*Velika Vrbaska Skupština* – the Great Vrbas Assembly), which brought together the large majority of Nazarene elders who had previously made peace with one another, three new decisions were taken that led the authorities to quickly change their stance towards the Nazarenes. Nazarenes could not, it was decided, vote in elections, join farming cooperatives, associations or trade unions, nor accept any of the confiscated German property that was being distributed. And in addition to all this, the decision regarding the refusal to bear arms remained in place. All of these decisions brought them in direct conflict with the new authorities who, having learned of these decisions, completely changed their attitude towards the Nazarenes and decided only to support Nazarenes that were in favor of working with the new government, those headed by Živko Vanka[205] and Dušan Tubić. The forced closures began again. Many elders were interrogated and subjected to physical torture. They were pressured to revoke these decisions, while those who happened to be in the army at the time were immediately arrested and sentenced to terms of between six and ten years jailtime for refusing to bear arms. Nazarenes of German origin were already in jails and concentration camps anyway, mostly imprisoned for their nationality, while those who succeeded in getting out would typically leave for the West. In the wake of this change in attitude towards the Nazarenes, during the first two years after the war, the authorities sentenced more than 350 people to jail terms, some of them for repeat offenses. This practically meant that the state was jailing the same people again for the same crime.

In 1949 in Austria, there remained some 400 Nazarene refugees from Yugoslavia who later emigrated to the USA, with a smaller number going to Canada. This was facilitated in large part by the Swiss Nazarenes, who had maintained close ties with the movement in Vojvodina. Nazarenes of German origin were also included in this

---

[205] In the mid-1960s, Vanka was removed from his position as elder for a "doctrinal error."

large group of refugees. Data from this period suggests there were 15,000 Nazarenes in Serbia and another 300 or so in the area around Osijek in Croatia. The Swiss organization HILFE, founded in Zurich in 1921 in the effort to help the Nazarenes after the First World War, was behind this drive to evacuate them. The activities of HILFE continued after the Hungarian political crisis of 1956, too. When the Yugoslav authorities relaxed restrictions on crossing borders and on its citizens traveling to the West in 1957, the opportunity was also taken by Nazarenes who had decided to leave the country and never return. The HILFE organization helped them relocate to Canada, Switzerland, and Australia, as well as Germany. The trend of emigration continued for a number of years, and a significant number of believers left the country. Some estimates put the number of young Nazarenes leaving Yugoslavia, predominantly men, at more than a thousand. One of the primary reasons were the prison terms handed down for failure to answer the call to military service and to the reserves.

Intensive emigration led to a decline in the number of believers in the country, since these were young people just beginning their adult, working, family and church lives. The Nazarene movement lost an entire generation within a period of a few years. With many in jail and many leaving the country, the number of active members of the Nazarenes fell drastically. On the other hand, even though the authorities knew that a section of the population would emigrate, especially its political rivals (in fact they were counting on it), the fact that a large number of young people left the country later negatively impacted the overall attitude of the state towards the Nazarene movement. The consequences were far-reaching.

The Doroslovac Movement

By late 1947, the situation had again become difficult, and many elders sought a new council at which the problems could be discussed. In March 1948 in Stara Pazova, a gathering of forty-two elders was held, and a decision taken to allow Nazarenes to vote and to join collectives, to accept nationalized assets and to cooperate with the People's Front.[206] However a group of elders headed by the lead elder, Milan Doroslovac, who had chaired the previous assembly in Vrbas, decided not to go along with this. The state had harbored suspicions against Doroslovac since the war, because he had run a mill under the German occupation, which was considered collaboration with the enemy.[207] After this, Doroslovac tried to organize another council in Kisač, but the authorities (the State Security Service) prevented this.

The secret police employed a variety of methods to attempt to weaken Doroslovac's influence. There is mention of "our various measures," but also the influence of international organizations that encouraged the Nazarenes to consider cooperating with the authorities. In the book *Verske zajednice* on page 667, it is even claimed that the council held in Kovačica was organized "on our initiative, with the aim of persuading members of the Nazarene sect to take part in the forthcoming elections." In any case, the authorities took a keen interest in the many Nazarenes and their families within Serbia's territory. The state actively interfered in the life of this religious community, punishing and persecuting some of its members and tolerating and assisting others.

This *druga strana* (the "other side," as Nazarenes of both parties call each other), the Doroslovac party, decided to separate from the Nazarene congregations into a new group named *Nazarenski Dom*

---

[206] The Yugoslav Communist Party used the People's Front organization to promote its views to ordinary people. The People's Front consisted of several smaller political parties and movements (when this was still allowed) which were close to the government. The Democratic Party and the People's Radical Party, later both banned, were not members. In 1953, the People's Front was merged from a federation of parties and movements into a single organization called the SSRNJ (*Socijalistički Savez Radnog Naroda Jugoslavije* – Socialist Alliance of Working People of Yugoslavia), popularly known as the *soc-savez*.

[207] In the second tome of *Verske zajednice u FNRJ* [Religious Communities in the FNRJ], page 662, published by the Security Institute in Belgrade, no author or editor named, it is claimed that the Nazarenes under Doroslovac's influence joined the German *Kulturbund* and other *Volksdeutsche* organizations, and took a position of loyalty towards the occupying forces and its "quislings."

Molitve [Nazarene House of Prayer], with some 3,000-4,000 follow-ers. The schism was huge. The state dubbed this group "negative" and the group of Nazarenes willing to partially cooperate with the authorities "positive."

> Over time intolerance arose between the two groups, with fuel added to the fire by the Novi Sad DSUP (State Secretariat of the Interior). The "positive" group ostracized the Nazarenes of M. Doroslovac... Doroslovac then split off and continued alone with a group of followers. The majority group then several times requested official assistance from the Federal Commission for Religious Affairs in the struggle against Doroslovac (Radić, 2002, knjiga 2:631).

Ties between the two Nazarene factions were cut off in 1959 after five elders were elected to the Executive Board in 1958 who were inclined towards cooperation with the authorities. The state looked on this in a positive light since some people from this group had taken part in the NOB. The conflict culminated with Doroslovac's excommunication at a council held February 5, 1961, a development which the Commission for Religious Affairs immediately reported back to the higher powers.[208]

The state had noted back in 1952 that the Nazarenes did not have a unified church structure with a leadership, but that each local congregation seemed somewhat independent, an assessment that applied to central Serbia and Vojvodina. Their total number at the time was estimated at 15,650, with only 650 in Croatia and the remainder in Serbia.[209]

---

[208] Information from the Republic Commission for March 1961. Copy of docu-ment in possession of author.

[209] Arhiv Srbije, Zemaljska komisija za verske poslove NRS, G-21, f-14. Copy of document in possession of author.

One report on a visit to the Nazarenes from Switzerland[210] mentions three hundred believers gathered for worship in Novi Sad with a children's choir, and strong local churches in Belgrade, Pančevo and Vrbas, as well as a still-numerous group of German believers and services in Belgrade and Vojvodina at which songs were sung in both Serbian and German. The Doroslovac group was heavily attacked and pressurized (internally) by the Swiss, Hungarian, and other Nazarenes, and this left a mark on their relationships which persists today. One state report from 1968 tells of the efforts to reconcile the two sides:

> The process of reconciliation between the two groups continues, with the mediation of Nazarene groups from abroad. The positive group proposed that the mediators in this dispute be Nazarenes from Hungary...it was agreed that a meeting of delegates from both groups would be held 23 March 1968 in Hungary, but the negative group refused to attend this meeting, probably because the Nazarenes there were required to join collectives, trade unions and other organizations, while the negative group from our country expressly forbade this.211

A report by the state commission from 1978 on the situation in the municipality of Pančevo says that there were only "Nazarene"

[210] Georg Davatz, *Bericht uber die Reise nach Jugoslawien vom 26. Juli bis 2. August 1952 (Georg Davatz)*, HILFE archive, Zurich, in Bojan Aleksov: *The Dynamics of Extinction*. There are records of visits by Dr. Albert Marquis and Arnet Schepp from Switzerland, and others. Visiting foreigners mostly favored the positive Nazarene movement and encouraged cooperation with the authorities. This later led to the breaking of ties between the "negative" Nazarenes and the Swiss Nazarenes and their organizations.

[211] Arhiv Vojvodine, F 198/I kutija 879. *Informacija o delatnosti verskih zajednica Pokrajinske komisije za verska pitanja* [Information on the activities of religious communities of the Provincial Commission for Religious Affairs], Pov. br. 35 dated 8 April 1968, Novi Sad. Copy of document in possession of author.

or "Nazarene Christian" congregations, but that the congregation in Dolovo still bore the name "old Nazarene fellowship" (*stara nazarenska zajednica*), which was meant to emphasize its separation from the "other party," although legally speaking it did not exist. All the Nazarene congregations were formally registered by the state under a single designation.

"In documents in the Pančevo SUP [local police] archives this division into 'old' and 'new' Nazarenes was sometimes equated with the division into 'negative' and 'positive' Nazarenes – those unyielding in their old, Nazarene orthodox principles and those more flexible, more inclined to cooperate with the authorities and the social and political institutions" (Pavković, Bandić & Rakić, 1978:30).

Persecution, Threats, and Pressure

Reports from the 1940s mostly tell of three-year prison sentences, accompanied by attempts at rapid "re-education," by force, beatings, and death threats. The first registered cases mention two-year sentences, and one four-year sentence, handed down to a military conscript by a court in Skopje. Reports from Kragujevac tell of one Nazarene being threatened with the firing squad if war were to break out, while other reports mention small groups of Nazarenes in prisons in Sisak and Banatski Karlovac. It is interesting to note that in the early 1950s, sentences began to get somewhat more severe. In Foča, one Nazarene was sentenced to four years, while another in Istria got five years of hard labor with two years' loss of civil rights. Another report tells of a five-year sentence handed down to a newlywed young man, while in Idrizovo (Macedonia) a sentence of four years was handed down in a repeat trial—more severe penalties were often given to those appealing to the higher courts.

However the worst treatment was reserved for those who were being convicted for the second time for the same offense. For a repeat offense they would be given at least the same sentence, and often a more severe one, with one Nazarene being tried on three separate occasions and spending a total of ten years in different jails. Often they would serve their jail sentence together with other members of their families who had been convicted of the same crimes.

During the 1950s, some Nazarenes were sent to the Goli Otok[212], where the Communists tried to ideologically reform them, but later resorted to torture and mistreatment. A chance occurrence led to a letter containing a report on the brutal treatment of the Nazarenes being smuggled out of the camp in 1954, and the situation improved a little when the Nazarene elders went to Belgrade to talk to police general Svetislav "Ćeća" Stefanović, who was himself of Nazarene background. Because of this report on the mistreatment of prisoners (the letter smuggled off the island), a delegation from the United Nations[213] visited Goli Otok[214] in 1954.

Reports from the late 1950s once again tell of long prison sentences—one such, a four-year term, was handed down in Sarajevo in 1957, and the prisoner shared a cell with four other Nazarenes. One Nazarene had initially been sentenced to three years and had served his term, was convicted for a repeat offense (the next time he was called up to do military service) to a seven-year sentence; how-

---

[212] A notorious island penal colony, reserved primarily for political prisoners (t/n).

[213] Nazarene elders tried to appeal on a number of occasions to high-up officials and the authorities in general. For example, in November 1953, Cveta Gićanov and Šandor Popov wrote to the president of the FNRJ, Josip Broz Tito, on behalf of the Nazarenes. The Nazarenes asked to be allowed to do military service without bearing arms, giving numerous examples from the Partisan struggle, and making an offer – that the Nazarenes could serve a double term of military service, four years instead of two. *Arhiva Komisije za verska pitanja NR Srbije* [Archive of the Commission for Religious Affairs of the People's Republic of Serbia, broj 1109, dated 11/11/1953. All their efforts were in vain.

[214] The testimony of Venko Markovski, Macedonian and Bulgarian poet and writer, who spent five years on Goli Otok as a political prisoner, makes interesting reading. In his memoirs, Markovski tells of Nazarene brigade leaders, who were badly thought of for their exceptional faith in God and their unrelenting commitment to reporting every lapse on the part of the other prisoners to the administration, sometimes also taking part in administering punishment. Markovski says that they diligently recorded every breach of the prison rules on the spot and reported them, since this was their duty. They would also report in a positive light on prisoners who worked well. They were not well-liked. For more information, see Markovski, 1984:63-65.

ever after serving eighteen months, he was pardoned on Day of the Republic, November 29.

Since Nazarenes were considered incorrigible political prisoners, in some jails they had trusty status, while in Gradiška they were sent to vocational schools.

The Federal Commission for Religious Affairs' archive material[215] speaks in very precise terms – of 339 Nazarenes convicted for conscientious objection between 1946-57. Of this number, 265 were convicted for the first time, sixty-five for a second time and eight people for a third time. Sentences of more than ten years were handed down to fifteen Nazarenes. One believer, Pavle Ožvat, spent a total of twelve years behind bars over three terms, and then was sentenced to four years on a fourth occasion. During this period, forty-five individuals took up arms the second time they were called up to military service, having served a prison term the first time. For them, a repeat sentence and jail time was too high a price to pay. The army also registered forty-one individuals who emigrated. In the following six years, up to 1965, a further ninety-two men were convicted.

> There were cases of some individuals who upon reporting for military service immediately refused arms, citing their religious convictions. In cases like these the men would be given jail sentences, but in line with the National Defense Law (Article 77), military service was suspended and then resumed upon completion of the term or release on parole. Generally, those convicted of this offense, after having served their sentence (1-5 years of strict imprisonment was the stipulated term), would again be called up to military service and then, again refusing to take up arms, convicted again. Since the same course of events

---

[215] Arhiv SCG, fond/faksimil broj: 144-32-324 and 42-389. In 1959, there were thirty-five Nazarene convicts on Goli Otok, nine in Sremska Mitrovica and two in Belgrade. During that year, some twenty young Nazarenes emigrated.

would repeat itself – the refusal to take up arms – there were Nazarenes who were even convicted multiple times in succession for the same offense (Radić, 2002, book 1:429).

Another International Initiative

In October 1958, during a visit to London by the Yugoslav State Secretary for Foreign Affairs, Koča Popović, there was an attempt at personal contact by representatives of pacifist organizations advocating for the plight of the Nazarenes in the FNRJ – but it was unsuccessful. However, dialog was conducted in written form, and later continued via the Yugoslav ambassador to Great Britain, Ivo Vejvoda in 1959. 216 State officials were forced to respond to pressure exerted by some parts of the international community.

In March 1959, the Yugoslav State Secretary for Foreign Affairs of the FNRJ held an advisory meeting in Belgrade, attended by representatives of the army, the police and the Ministry of the Interior, in order to discuss the many objections lodged with the government from abroad in relation to the prison sentences meted out to the Nazarenes and to others who refused to serve in the military, to bear arms and similar cases. At this meeting, the Nazarenes were effectively declared enemies of the state.[217]

---

[216] Koča Popović wrote to Arlo Tatum, General Secretary of WRI, on 31 October 1958 from the Yugoslavia Embassy in London. He said that the Yugoslav government had always taken a keen interest in the advancement of human rights and would continue to do so, but underlined that full respect would be maintained for applicable Yugoslav law. Copy of letter in possession of author. See Appendix 3 at the end of this chapter. International Institute of Social History, War Resisters' International Archive, binder 420.

[217] The authorities tried other ways of getting the Nazarenes to cooperate. For example, some local nationalization committees in Vojvodina would inform local Nazarene congregations that their houses of prayer would be nationalized unless they could present a document confirming their right to conduct religious activities in Serbia. The People's Republic of Serbia Commission for Religious Affairs issued such a document and afforded the Nazarenes protection

> It has been concluded that no changes to regu-
> lations or practice can be considered with regard
> to the persons in question, and that in respond-
> ing to foreign organizations it should be stated
> that these are not people who refuse arms for rea-
> sons of conscience, but rather this is a sect that
> is using the religious convictions of its members
> in a direct attack on the socialist order in the
> FNRJ.218

In the early 1960s, some Nazarenes were sent to serve their prison sentences on chain gangs, including some who worked on the construction of New Belgrade.[219] Two reports from this period men-tion two six-year sentences served in Požarevac, with two believers serving three years each in Sremska Mitrovica and Valjevo and one recent convert, who had already previously completed military ser-vice, being sentenced to just six months imprisonment. A consider-able number of believers were also imprisoned in Idrizovo, in Skopje, where the average sentence was four years, and there was conflict with the prison administration because of their demand to work on Sundays. Some individuals requested transfer to Sremska Mitrovica, especially from prisons in Zenica, Foča, and Sarajevo, since there were more Nazarenes in Mitrovica and so the administration took this into account, and prison life seemed somewhat easier.

In March 1960, the Nazarenes held their Zemaljska Skupština [General Assembly], which was the highest body of this religious community in Yugoslavia, and sent the Federal Executive Council Commission for Religious Affairs proposals for resolution of the sit-uation: that the Nazarenes be allowed to serve in medical or other

---

in respect to the Law on Nationalization. Cases like this contributed to the atmosphere of insecurity and ongoing state repression of the Nazarenes. Other Protestant religious minorities had similar problems with the local authorities. Arhiv Komisije za verska pitanja NR Srbije, broj 369 dated 6 October 1959.

[218] Radić 2002, knjiga 1, page 431, per ASMIP, PA, 67/29, br. 48227.

[219] A major post-war development project to expand Belgrade to the other side of the Sava river (t/n).

units without taking up arms, that after serving their first sentence they be transferred to the reserves and—the most important proposal—that the state pass new legislation that would be favorable towards the Nazarenes. The state responded somewhat positively to these proposals. A contributing factor to this was a letter sent by the President of the FNRJ, Tito, in October 1960, to the federal authorities, asking for a solution to be found for the Nazarenes, in view of their contribution to the National Liberation War (see footnote 219). The army immediately responded by deciding to no longer prosecute those who had already been convicted of the same offense[220], but to immediately transfer them to the reserves. However there were problems here, too, especially when they were called up for exercises and had to collect their equipment. However, during 1961, some young Nazarene men were indeed released.

In the late 1950s and throughout the 1960s, numerous international organizations petitioned the Yugoslav government, its embassies abroad, and the United Nations on behalf of the Nazarenes. When President Tito visited Norway in 1965, a human rights organization took the opportunity to approach him. These efforts seem to have paid off as that same year, on the Day of the Republic, the Nazarenes serving nine and ten-year sentences on Goli Otok were reprieved. They were allowed to go home after their sentences were commuted to four years of imprisonment – these they had already served, and so there was no further basis for them to be held.

The organization WRI exerted constant pressure on the Embassy of the SFRJ in London, and its newspaper Peace News published several articles on the treatment of the Nazarenes by the SFRJ. In mid-1964, some British Members of Parliament

---

[220] A meeting at the SIV (*Savezno Izvršno Veće* – Federal Executive Council) in December 1960 was attended by top state officials: Edvard Kardelj, Aleksandar Ranković, Vladimir Bakarić, Svetislav Stefanović, Boris Krajger, Otmar Kreačić, General Ivan Gošnjak, and others. A decision was taken to adopt a more lenient attitude towards Nazarenes refusing to bear arms. Arhiv Komisije za verska pitanja NR Srbije, br 11/1-61.

got involved, Laborites Lord Russell and Frank Allaun, who approached the Yugoslav Embassy in London regarding the same issue. The efforts continued in the years that followed.221

Influential in securing the release of these Nazarnes was also a meeting between "positive" (as the authorities referred to them) Nazarene elder Dušan Tubić with General Gošnjak at the celebration of the Day of the Republic in 1964.222 The Federal administration was then given the go-ahead to try to find a new solution to the Nazarene question, and during a visit to the Commission for Religious Affairs in March the following year, Tubić was told that the opinion of the army and police had been sought.223 Consequently in 1965, the Federal Commission for Religious Affairs recommended more lenient sentencing of Nazarenes, to a maximum of four years, to which the army agreed. It seems that this was immediately put into practice by the courts, as testified in a letter written by Delbert Gratz in September 1965 in which he confirms that prison sentences are now shorter, three to four years on average.224

However, that very same year, this practice of more lenient sentencing changed again. Around the middle of the year persecution reintensified and sentences became longer once more.225 During 1965, nine young Nazarenes were sentenced by military courts to between six and nine years. Sources abroad, especially Pacifists International, were unable to arrive at accurate information such as names and locations of prisoners. The Nazarenes were not open to

---

221 Radić, 2002, book 1:432. See also the text of a confidential report from Yugoslavia kept in the WRI archive – see Appendix 2 to this chapter.

222 Army General Ivan Gošnjak was Federal National Defense Secretary of the FNRJ and then of the SFRJ from 1953-1967.

223 Vojvodina Archive, F 198/I – 879. Bilten Savezne komisije za verska pitanja [Federal Commission for Religious Affairs bulletin], 29 March 1965. Tubić requested that the Nazarene petition and their proposal for more lenient sentencing of Nazarenes be addressed.

224 Letter dated 31 May 1965 to Devi Prasad, see Appendix 2.

225 "Pacifists Imprisoned in Yugoslavia and other Communist Countries" – statement 65:289 of 15 October 1965. European Baptist Press Service.

communication as they felt at the time that the pressure from abroad was doing more harm than good to their cause at home.

After the authorities took the general decision in 1966 to sentence Nazarenes, and any others refusing to bear arms, to a maximum of four years' imprisonment, five Nazarenes who had been sentenced to between eight and ten years were immediately released. However, three believers, Tomaš Đemrovski, Milivoj Popović,[226] and Janoš Ipač, who had only been convicted in 1964-5, were kept imprisoned until 1967, when it was hinted to their families that they should apply for a reprieve.[227] On one visit to the Provincial Commission for Religious Affairs in 1968, Dušan Tubić told them that there were around 8,000 "positive" members and around 4,000 "negative."

Amnesty International also got involved in attempting to secure the release of religious conscientious objectors from Yugoslav jails, having begun monitoring the situation in 1960. In the 1980s, military service for recruits was still compulsory. According to Article 214 of the federal criminal code, concealment or any other attempt to avoid military service carried a five-year sentence, while those who went abroad to avoid conscription could expect harsher sentencing of up to ten years. Amnesty published a book in London in 1985 titled: *Yugoslavia, Prisoners of Conscience*, in which they could not give firm information on any Nazarene prisoners but it was stressed that there probably were some (Yugoslavia: Prisoners..., 1985:57).

Nevertheless, the authorities did take steps towards alleviating the situation, not just for Nazarenes but for other conscientious objectors (be they political or religious.) As of 1985, permission was given for individuals to opt for auxiliary military duties, but it still had to be in uniform and in a military institution. On December 24, 1986, the state news agency Tanjug announced that since 1970, only 152 citizens had been convicted for refusing military service, and that the majority of them had been Jehovah's Witnesses.

---

[226] It is interesting to note that Tubić petitioned in writing only on behalf of Đemrovski and Ipač, and not for Popović, from which we might conclude that he belonged to the "other side."

[227] Vojvodina Archive F198/I-877. Savezna komisija za verska pitanja, broj 100/1

The Last Conscientious Objectors

In the period which followed, the mid-1980s to the late 1990s, there were individual cases of Nazarenes being imprisoned, but as the state weakened, so did the persecution and punishment. During that period, a great many young Nazarenes left the country for the West and so sidestepped the issue of military service and, therefore, the oath and arms-bearing. During the 1980s, a number of cases were recorded of repeat prison sentences, and in 1986, one believer was sentenced to five years of imprisonment for a third time, which did provoke public debate, and several articles were published abroad.[228] In 1987, another young believer was sentenced to two-and-a-half years of imprisonment.[229]

In 1985, the Nazarenes again requested a meeting with the state leadership, petitioning the President of the Federal Conference of the Socialist Alliance of Working People of Yugoslavia, the President of the SFRJ National Assembly and the Federal Secretariat for National Defense. The Nazarenes complained:

> ...although we cannot understand how during the NOB [People's Liberation War] the Nazarenes were able to serve with the Partisans without bearing arms, to receive medals for bravery and awards for service to their people, and yet today,

---

[228] The Nazarenes issued a statement on this occasion, publishing the content of a letter they had sent to the Yugoslav leadership stating that they were not protesting in principle against the prison sentences for the refusal to bear arms but were rather protesting the fact that the decision of the President of Yugoslavia, Tito, was not being adhered to. The decision referred to was Tito's order to the Chief of Staff of the third administrative district, no. 265, dated 28 October 1960. In this order, Tito requested an end to the practice of repeat convictions for the same crime, see Newsdesk, Keston News Service, 19 March 1987; also AKSA of 7 November 1986.

[229] According to the news report the believer in question was Milorad Doroslovac from Baranda. He served his sentence in the prison in Slavonska Požega. News Roundup. Keston News Service. 1 December 1988.

in a time of peace, they are not able to usefully
serve their country without bearing arms...

Despite pressure from the public and a number of smaller organizations that advocated for the rights of conscientious objectors,
the authorities were unyielding.[230] Thus on January 15, 1987, the
Presidency of the Socialist Alliance announced that it had decided
to refuse all initiatives regarding alternative military service and said
that there would be no further debate on the matter.

In 1990, *Vojno-politički Informator*, the journal of the Yugoslav
People's Army, published an article in which they concluded that the
number of young men refusing military service on religious grounds
was very small, and that it ought to be kept in mind that they did
so out of deep-seated religious convictions and not out of a desire to
avoid military service using their faith as an excuse (Jevtić, 1990:79).
The climate was changing in the country as a whole.

The 1994 FRY Army Law brought about reform in the attitude of the army towards conscientious objection.[231] Some articles
of the law were amended in 1996 and then in 1999 and in 2002.
Conscientious objection was finally also enshrined in the Serbian
Constitution. Article 45 states: "No person shall be obliged to perform military or any other service involving the use of weapons if this

---

[230] *Novosti* of 30 October 1986 reported that the Federal leadership had supposedly
agreed to allow such conscientious objectors to be sent to serve in quartermaster
and medical units; later events proved this optimism unfounded, however. One
of the reasons for this optimism lay in the fact that a relatively small number of
people were punished for these offenses during the 1980s, mostly in violation
of Articles 201 (refusing orders), 202 (refusing to accept and bear arms) and
214 (refusing the draft) of the federal criminal code. For more information, see
Conscientious Objection... 1987:332

[231] The first attempt was in 1989 when the Yugoslav government proposed changes
to the regulations on recruitment. One of these changes concerned people who
refused to bear arms for personal religious reasons. It was proposed that they
serve a double term in the army – two years instead of one. See News Roundup,
Keston News Service, 13 April 1989. The next Keston report talks about the
law being voted through but seemingly not satisfying conscientious objectors,
who did not want to do military service in the army but in a civilian institution
instead. See News Roundup, Keston News Service. 11 May 1989.

opposes his religion or beliefs. Any person pleading conscientious objection may be called upon to fulfil military duty without the obligation to carry weapons, in accordance with the law." (Constitution, 2006).

It was only a large-scale general amnesty in 1995 that finally reprieved the great number of young Nazarenes who had avoided the draft during the "non-war" early 1990s in Serbia.[232]

The last two Nazarene conscientious objectors in Serbia were Pavle Božić from Stari Banovci and Goran Žižić from Leskovac. In 1993, Pavle Božić had served six months of a nine-month prison sentence for his religious convictions and his refusal to bear arms, to wear a uniform or to take the oath of loyalty, and then in 1997 he was again called up to military service at the Karađorđevo military facility. Having refused, he was again sentenced to a year's imprisonment in 1998, which he served and was thus twice jailed for the same thing—conscientious objection and military service.

> "I was sentenced to nine months' in jail in Niš when I was 23. This happened in 1993. I knew from an early age that I would end up in jail because my father and my grandfather and who knows how many more of my relatives went through the same. This state couldn't deal with us and found the most unpleasant ways they could to punish us," says Božić.
>
> When he was called up for military service a second time, which he also refused, the court sentenced him—in 1997—to a year's imprisonment, and in one of the strictest penitentiaries at that: Zabela in Požarevac, on the rationale that he was a "repeat offender."

---

[232] For more about this period, see Aleksov, 1999.

"In prison they treat you like the worst kind of criminal, regardless of your story. They are trying to kill you psychologically... I felt like they had convicted me for driving 60 [kilometers per hour] through a residential area," says Pavle Božić. (Leđenac, 2011).

In 1996 and 1997, state policy towards conscientious objectors was once again relaxed and a pardons commission commuted long prison sentences handed down to eight Nazarenes.[233]

Goran Žižić was sentenced to two years' imprisonment in Niš in 1999 for failing to answer a call-up to the reserves (he had completed his military service in 1982/3 when, as he puts it, he was "not fully formed as a person"), and had also served a forty-day jail sentence in Leskovac in 1992 for refusing to collect a uniform (Lilić, 2001:96).

In a report dated April 3, 2003, by Forum 18, an organisation based in Oslo, Norway, an anonymous Nazarene elder from Belgrade is cited as saying that more than twenty young Nazarene men were serving in the military in noncombatant units at that time.

---

[233] Arhiv Vojvodine, fascikla 198, kutija 877. See document on following page, filed under no. 100/1, dated 3 April 1967. The document is a reaction to the memorandum sent by the Council of Elders of the Christian Nazarene Community in the SFRJ, with headquarters in Novi Sad, signed by Dušan Tubić, to the Autonomous Province of Vojvodina Commission for Religious Affairs in March 1967. Copy of document in possession of author.

SAVEZNA KOMISIJA
ZA VERSKA PITANJA
Broj:100/1

3.IV.1967.

BEOGRAD
Zgrada Saveznog izvršnog veća
Tel. 22-461

POKRAJINSKOM IZVRŠNOM VEĆU APV
Komisiji za verska pitanja

NOVI SAD

Veza Vaš pov.br.20/67 od 20.III.o.g.

Od strane ove Komisije nikome iz Starešinstva Nazarenske verske zajednice nije saopšteno da se, prilikom odlaska pripadnika Nazarenske verske zajednice u JNA, obraćaju komisijama za uputstvo i sl.

U pitanju kažnjavanja lica koja odbiju da prime oružje u JNA, bez obzira da li pripadaju Nazarenskoj verskoj zajednici ili ne, postupiće se po Zakonu.

U vezi sa zauzetim stavovima, koji su poznati samo našim organima /komisijama za verska pitanja, unutrašnjim poslovima i vojnim organima/, kazne za ovo krivično delo izriču se, kao što je poznato, do 4 godine zatvora. To je već u praksi počelo da se i primenjuje.

Isto tako, u skladu sa ovim stavom prošle godine sniženjem su - na predlog ove Komisije - pomilovana 5-orica Nazarena koji su bili osuđeni na visoke kazne zatvora, od 8-10 godina. Medjutim, predlogom tada nisu bila obuhvaćena sledeća lica, a koja su takodje osuđena na visoke kazne: DEMROVSKI TOMAŠ, rodjen 1944. godine osuđen na 10 godina strogog zatvora, FILIPOVIĆ MILIVOJ, rodjen 1945. godine osuđen na 10 godina zatvora i IPAČ JANOŠ, rodjen 1946. godine osuđen na 9 godina zatvora. Njih nismo uzeli u obzir za pomilovanje zbog toga što su im kazne bile izrečene tokom 1964. odnosno 1965. godine.

Pošto je od tada proteklo relativno duži period, to je ova Komisija 30.III.o.g. predložila da se i ovoj trojici kazne pomilovanjem snize do 4 godine zatvora.

Mišljenja smo da bi, u vezi s tim, trebalo da i porodice napred spomenutih, takodje, podnesu molbe za pomilovanje /Komisiji za pomilovanje putem Saveznog sekretarijata za pravosudje/, neovisno od našeg predloga. Na taj način, verovatno bi se slučaj Džemrovskog mogao izdvojeno razmatrati obzirom na zadobijena teška telesna oštećenja za vreme izdržavanja kazne.

Ovo bi, na određen način, trebalo sugerisati Starešinstvu Nazarenske verske zajednice, nespominjući da je Savezna komisija uputila predlog za pomilovanje.

POMOĆNIK PREDSEDNIKA,
Petar Šegvić

P. Šegvić

FEDERAL   3 April 1967
COMMISSION FOR   BELGRADE
RELIGIOUS AFFAIRS   Headquarters of the
No: 100/1   Federal Executive Council

TO THE PROVINCIAL EXECUTIVE COUNCIL OF THE
AUTONOMOUS PROVINCE OF VOJVODINA
Committee for Religious Affairs

NOVI SAD

Re: your ref no. 20/67 of 20 March this year.

Nobody from the Eldership of the Nazarene religious community
has been informed by this Commission that they should approach
the commissions for instructions or similar in the event that members of the Nazarene religious community are called up to the JNA
[Yugoslav People's Army].

In regard to the question of the sanction of those persons refusing to accept arms in the JNA, regardless of whether they belong to
the Nazarene religious community or not, the Law will be acted on.

In regard to the stance that has been taken, known only to these
authorities (commissions for religious affairs, interior ministry and
military authorities), penalties handed down for this crime are up to
4 years' jail. Application of this has in fact already begun.

Accordingly, last year, at the proposal of this Commission,
five Nazarenes were pardoned (their sentences commuted), who
had been sentenced to long jail terms of 8-10 years. However, the
proposal at the time did not encompass the following persons, who
had also been sentenced to long jail terms: TOMAŠ ĐEMROVSKI
(born 1944), sentenced to 10 years' strict imprisonment, MILIVOJ
FILIPOVIĆ (born 1945), sentenced to 10 years' imprisonment and
JANOŠ IPAČ, (born 1946), sentenced to 9 years' imprisonment.
We did not take them into account for pardoning only because their
sentences had been handed down during 1964 and 1965.

Since a relatively long period has now passed, on 30 March this year this Commission proposed that these three too have their sentences commuted to 4 years by way of pardon.

In our opinion, in this connection, the families of the aforementioned should also file petitions for pardon (to the Pardons Commission, via the Federal Secretariat for Justice), regardless of our proposal. In this way separate consideration might be given for the case of Džemrovski [sic] in view of the serious bodily injuries he has sustained whilst serving his sentence.

This should be hinted at in some way to the Eldership of the Nazarene religious community, without mention of the fact that the Federal Commission has filed a proposal for pardon.

DEPUTY CHAIR
Petar Šegvić

**Proposal of the Commission for Religious Affairs
to the Provincial Executive Council in Vojvodina in
1967 for a number of Nazarenes to be pardoned**

Organizational Structure

It is important to note that Nazarene congregations function independently at the local level and that there is no hierarchy or central administration. The Elders' Assembly (*starešinski zbor*) deals with spiritual matters while the Council of Elders (*starešinski savet*) deals with all other issues and with the organization internally. The local church is called *skupština* (congregation or assembly) and the building in which they meet *dom molitve* (house of prayer). They are usually led by an elder, with several deputy elders, while preachers are called *sluga* (servant). Non-members attending or visiting services are referred to as *prijatelji* (friends). Local congregations do not keep registries of baptisms, deaths or ex-members.

The division of Nazarene congregations along the old lines (the Doroslovac party and "the other side") is still an issue, albeit in somewhat reduced form, especially after the introduction of alternative military service. The Provincial Commission for Religious Affairs divided the Nazarenes into "positive" and "negative," in line with their attitude towards the authorities. The report from 1968 mentioned in the section on the Doroslovac movement (p. 146) says that the "positives" claimed to have 8,000 members and that the "negatives" had 4,000.[234] This report tells of an attempt at reconciliation between the two groups, when the "positives" proposed a meeting with the others in Hungary. However the "negatives" rejected this initiative on the grounds that Hungarian Nazarenes were mostly members of trade unions, collectives etc., which was forbidden to them.[235]

It is hard to determine the membership figures for this religious community, both historically and today. One undergraduate dissertation from 1975 (Makaji, 1975) talks of a division into a Petrovaradin and a Novi Sad congregation, and says that the largest Nazarene congregation is in the Romanian village of Lokve, with some 600 members, followed by the Novi Sad congregation with around 200 members, and then the Petrovaradin group with somewhat fewer. It was estimated then that there were four to five thousand Nazarene congregation members.

In Switzerland and other European countries, there is a union of Nazarene churches (who in translation from the German are called

---

[234] A report by the Commission for Religious Affairs of the Alibunar municipal assembly, which in early 1967 reported to the Autonomous Province of Vojvodina on the existence of twenty "other" religious communities ("sects," as they put it), of which the following were Nazarene:
- *Nazarenska hrišćanska verska zajednica* [Nazarene Christian religious community] – old, Lokve;
- *Nazarenska hrišćanska verska zajednica* – new, Lokve;
- *Nazarenska pravoslavna skupština* [Nazarene orthodox community], Janošik
- *Nazarenska verska zajednica* [Nazarene religious community], Vladimirovac;
- *Nazarenska verska zajednica*, Nikolinci;
- *Nazarenska verska zajednica*, Seleuš;
- *Nazarenska verska zajednica*, Alibunar;

[235] Vojvodina Archive F198/I-879. Informator o delatnosti verskih zajednica. Copy of document in possession of author.

the Evangelical Baptists). In 1983 an initiative was launched to found a union of the congregations of Evangelical Baptists, which was done on June 1, 1985. This union comprises:

Twenty-two local congregations from Switzerland;
Twenty-one local congregations from Germany;
Six local congregations from France;
Four local congregations from Austria and
Two local congregations from Sweden.

Commenting on their ties, Professor Ott believes that thirty-six congregations are actively involved in this union, working together in the areas of missions, mutual assistance and identity-building (Ott, 1996:260-268). In Switzerland, there is also a group of Nazarenes who do not cooperate with any other faith community, including the Evangelical Baptists.

Today the Christian Nazarene religious community is recognized by the state, and although only one side is registered—the "Novi Sad" party—this official registration applies to all Nazarenes in Serbia.

Conclusion

The Nazarene movement suffered greatly in the Second World War and in the period immediately afterwards. In addition to the fact that some Nazarenes died in the war, there was a wave of persecution of all those of German nationality after the war, as well as interference by the communist authorities in the organization and leadership of the movement itself, which led to further divisions. The model for work and life in traditional village environments in Vojvodina, where the Nazarenes were strongest, was significantly affected by the efforts of the new regime to get the Nazarenes to accept the *kolkhozian* model of collectives, to become part of the "organized people" through the trade unions and People's Front, to agree to vote, to distribute the property of *Volksdeutsche* who had been exiled, had fled, or been killed.

After the Second World War, it is evident that the Nazarenes were persecuted by the state. This time, however, matters of the state church, registry books and oath-swearing to the ruler were not the issue, rather it was the Nazarene refusal to submit to the Communist regime and their concept of rule. The Nazarenes not only rejected arms, they also rejected the collectivization of land, the distribution of *Volksdeutsche* property, voting in elections, (state) trade unions and cooperatives and more besides.

From the available sources, it can be seen that the Socialist/Communist regime did not understand the Nazarene movement, its motives and its principles of faith and living, and failed to take into account historic facts regarding this movement. The need and intent to secure complete control over public life, seen from outside as strength and unity at work in the new socialist state of "peoples and ethnicities," resulted in the secret services operating within religious communities and attempting to rig internal elections and get "loyal" or "positive" people into the leadership of these organizations. This external influence only contributed to further division within the movement and to its decline.

Some relief came with changes in the social and state system and the introduction of alternative military service. In 2010, the Republic of Serbia abolished compulsory military service and thus the question of conscience objection became a matter solely for states of emergency or war. It is still not clear today what the attitude of the state of Serbia would be towards the Nazarenes if the country were put on a war footing. In the opinion of this author, democratic processes and Serbia's efforts to align its legislation with that of the European Union with a view to future membership, have sufficiently progressed that in the future Nazarene conscientious objectors would not be jailed.

From a major movement—with probably more than 20,000 members immediately before and during the Second World War—with the departure of the German minority, the emigration of young men and the natural mortality rate, the number of Nazarenes declined fourfold over a period of sixty years. In 1968, the authorities estimated that there were no more than 12,000 of them. An optimistic estimate today would be that there are no more than 4,000 on "both sides," although it is likely that there are in fact 1,500 members at most.

Appendix 1 – An account from captivity

Excerpt from Nenadov, 2006:27

In 1943, the Germans took control of our prison unit (from the Hungarians) and put us together with a group of Jewish believers. After a while, the Germans loaded us onto a boat and sent us down the Danube to Bor in Yugoslavia. There was a huge group of people there, including 70,000 prisoners from Serbia, France and Italy, as well as Jews. There were also Christians: eighty Jehovah's Witnesses, eighteen Adventists and seven Nazarenes. They kept us seven Nazarene brothers together in a hut and we did not have to work on Sundays, so one of the brothers would preach, another would pray and another would lead singing. It was our little church. When the Belgrade church found out about us, one brother came to visit us. He brought each of us a Bible with our names engraved on the title page. Four days later, he came again with other brothers and they brought us a big package full of warm clothing, and 10,000 dinars at the bottom of the package. They said that everyone in the church had given what they could.

All of us Nazarenes were assigned to blasting duties. Two of us had the job of setting off the explosives. In this way we cut down a mountain and moved it. The Germans had plans to remove some mountains because of the copper found underneath. In September 1944, the Germans fled and left us there. We heard that the Russians were coming to help Tito and the Partisans get free of the German occupation...

Appendix 2

Excerpt from a letter from Delbert Gratz[236], librarian of the Mennonite Historical Library at Bluffton College in Bluffton Ohio in the US, to Devi Prasad, Secretary of War Resisters' International in Enfield, Great Britain, dated May 31, 1965 and filed on September 10 the same year.[237]

> I recently returned home, where your letter of 27 April awaited me, which concerned the Nazarenes in Yugoslavia. One thing is clear to me, regarding all my contacts with Nazarenes in Easter Europe, is that there is nobody who can provide answers to all the questions we have. They have no centralized organization at all. What I did manage to learn came from many sources, and even now I cannot be sure that all my information is accurate. The Serbian mind is an interesting one and does not think or speak as precisely or in as much detail as we might like.
>
> I had the opportunity to get very close to them, being as I am a Mennonite and our beliefs are very similar. I was invited to and participated in worship services, and spoke before their groups in Yugoslavia and Hungary. Thus I had the opportunity to gather information. All I wish is to return there in order to continue developing the contacts made, and now I have first-hand information, I can collect this wealth of information and testimony and at the same time establish its veracity. Since the information I received was confidential I am not willing to forward it, even though I would

---

[236] Dr. Gratz was a historian of the Anabaptist and Mennonite movements in Switzerland and of their migration to the US.

[237] Document found in WRI archive. Copy of document in possession of author. Note for this English edition: the original English letter was unavailable at the time of publication and the text has been translated back from the Serbian translation.

like to do so. I think you will understand my situation. However I would be happy to answer any questions you may have as long as I am sure that I would not be breaking the word I gave.

To answer your questions, I can only say that I have heard that sentences are now shorter, from three to four years on average. Of course they have been re-imprisoned, two or even three times, adding up to 6-10 years, and even more in some cases. Several people told me that the situation in this regard was better under Tito's communism – oh the irony – than it was under the "Christian Habsburgs." They are all together in one jail and have some opportunity, albeit very limited, to meet together.

Their numbers are declining for various reasons. Some of these are as follows: many young men are waiting to finish military service before joining congregations, thus avoiding church discipline. Many skilled young people are finding employment abroad and thus leaving the scene. A small colony has even been established in Israel.

I have always wished to contact leading figures in the United Nations or in Yugoslavia in connection with their suffering. I have constantly asked Nazarene elders what I can do to help. All of the ones I talked to discouraged me from my efforts to establish those kinds of contact abroad, explaining that they were convinced that this would only make the situation worse – they assured me that things would then be even worse than they are now. They gave me some examples from the past in order to clarify this...

Actually, the situation is much worse in Romania, where they are forbidden from meeting...

Appendix 3 – Letter from the Yugoslav Embassy

Two letters written in response to Arlo Tatum from the Yugoslav Embassy in London, on the subject of the Nazarenes in Yugoslavia. The 1958 letter was sent by Koča Popović, then-Minister of Foreign Affairs of the FNRJ, the January 1959 letter was sent by Yugoslavia ambassador to the UK, Ivo Vejvoda.

YUGOSLAV EMBASSY

25, KENSINGTON GORE,
LONDON, S.W.7.

31st October, 1958.

Dear Sir,

Thank you for your letter of the 29th October. I am very sorry indeed that I am unable to see you, but my many engagements and the shortness of my visit here prevent me from doing so.

I would like to say that I am familiar with the subject which you have raised in your letter. The Yugoslav Government, which has always paid special attention to the furtherance of human rights, is constantly endeavouring to find solutions having regard for personal convictions and similar considerations and at the same time ensuring respect for the existing Yugoslav laws.

I may assure you that I shall continue to take an interest in this matter.

Yours faithfully,

Koca Popovic

Mr. Arlo Tatum,
General Secretary,
War Resisters' International,
Lansbury House,
88, Park Avenue,
Enfield,
Middlesex.

YUGOSLAV AMBASSADOR

London, 14th November, 1958.

7 - JAN 1959

Dear Sir,

Thank you for your letter of the
11th November.

I shall of course be glad to see you
at any mutually agreeable time and be a ready
listener to whatever you might wish to explain,
but should like to say that I am not in a
position to tell you more on the subject than
what my Foreign Secretary said in his letter to
you.

Yours sincerely,

Ivo Vejvoda

Mr. Arlo Tatum,
General Secretary,
War Resisters' International,
Lansbury House,
88, Park Avenue,
Enfield,
Middx.

END MATTER – NAZARENE FAITH AND PRACTICE

Rules from 1919

In 1919, the Nazarene movement passed a number of decisions and rules regarding their internal structure, in accordance with "the Gospel,"[238] as they put it in the document. Eight elders from the districts of Bačka and Srem held a series of meetings during November 1919 in Stara Pazova and came to an agreement over eighteen points. However, since this document was published together with the Nazarene articles of faith which are dated 1920, this author believes that both documents were approved at the same time: the articles of faith in order to explain the Biblical basis for the Nazarene faith and practice, and the rules of the organization which were meant to clarify how decisions were to be taken and life was to be lived among the Nazarenes at the local level.[239]

---

[238] One of the earliest documents – probably the first – on the Nazarene faith, was put together by Lajos Hencej in 1841 in Budapest. This document was never translated into Serbian, although it was commented on in 1870 by Paja Dimić in the magazine *Pastir* in the 1869 edition (Szeged). The title loosely translates as *A Short Outline of the Nazarene Articles of Faith*. Both in 1870 and in 1880 in the expanded edition, Dimić criticizes Nazarene beliefs which, since they have not changed significantly since then, are analyzed separately in this chapter based on published editions of the articles of faith, beginning in 1919.

[239] The anonymous author "Hadžija," probably a member of the Nazarene eldership, in his book published in 1936, talks about this document as something of a secret, which many Nazarene fellowships were not even familiar with, as well as that it was partially incorrect. We can only guess at what aspects are being referred to here since no other details are given.

In several of the points of the document on decisions and rules from 1919, there is discussion of the responsibility of the local congregation as the highest body in terms of decision-making, as well as of the responsibility of the eldership and of usual practice in everyday life and ministry.

The elders are required to respect the decisions of local congregations and may not take decisions independently except regarding minor and unimportant issues. The elders are the ones who determine what issues the congregation will take decisions on, and must be in agreement with this. In the event that meetings have been held and an agreement reached without the presence of the elders, the elders need to give their consent for the decision to be implemented, otherwise the agreement will not be considered valid.

There are three types of elder or minister in the Nazarene congregation. Anyone who is a member of the congregation can be elected to this position by a simple majority. If it is determined that a minister or elder has not been faithful and has acted contrary to decisions taken by the congregation, he withdraws from the ministry and another person is appointed to the position. Ministers and elders serve the entire congregation on a voluntary basis (with no recompense), except when they are in need. Then they are helped, just as any other member would be. The Nazarenes have the following types of elder and minister:

- Those who preach from the Bible: known as servants [*sluga*], and
- those who conduct ceremonies (acceptance into the congregation, the Lord's Supper, organization and decision-making): elders [*starešina*].
- Those who are concerned with the material assets of the fellowship, and with communal life and providing assistance (diaconal ministry) to members who are in financial hardship, to the helpless and to the sick too; they are normally called: stewards [*staratelji*]. The person tasked with taking care of the money, who has two or three assistants, must record all income and expenditures in written form

"in the books"; he is usually referred to as the *rukovatelj sa novcem* [manager of money].

It is interesting to note here that according to the 1919 rules, the congregation does not hold meetings to discuss the financial situation since "we trust one another." Nevertheless, the congregation can call upon the treasurer at any time to give a financial report. The most senior elder in terms of years of service in the ministry is usually asked first for his opinion and advice.[240]

A collection is taken up every Sunday after the service is over; there are no compulsory taxes, nor is personal wealth taken into account. The elders only act if someone is observed to be "stingy." Such people are generally given a warning. The money collected is used by the treasurer and his assistants to buy food and heating fuel for those under the care of the fellowship. It is important to note that the Nazarenes take an attitude of solidarity not just towards members of the congregation but to non-members too. The stewards are expected to be sensitive and able to assess the needs of those in hardship and then to take a decision regarding assistance to be provided.

Solidarity is also expected on the part of larger Nazarene congregations towards smaller ones. Since smaller congregations only have one elder and one minister, the nearest large Nazarene congregation has a duty of care over them. Where there are few Nazarenes they usually meet in private houses (they call them *mirne kuće* [peaceful houses], which probably refers to the fact that meetings are held in homes in which the entire family is part of the Nazarene movement), while larger congregations collect money for a church building, or house of prayer. It is also mentioned that some congregations have their own small graveyards, while in other cases local churches have been given plots of land for burials by the local authorities.

---

[240] Kraljik notes that when a "brother" is called to the ministry as a "servant," the calling is initially for a trial period which ends with his "confirmation" by the elders. From among the "servants" of a congregation, the council of elders chooses an elder. The usual phrase used here is "to raise (someone) up as an elder" [*podići za starešinu*] (Kraljik, 1995:28).

Every year, or as required, there is a meeting or convention (referred to as a *dogovor*) of all elders (and lower-ranked servants) in one of the larger churches. This convention can choose elders and ministers for smaller congregations, and guests from abroad are frequently invited who are "likeminded in faith." Guests are listed from a variety of countries: Switzerland, Germany, America, Hungary, and Austria. The purpose behind these meetings is stated as being to motivate the believers to faithfulness, love for God, and love for one another. This *dogovor* is also the highest decision-making body for issues that cannot be resolved at the local level, and it is emphasized that the decisions and conclusions of this convention are binding for local congregations.[241]

The State and Its Attitude Toward Nazarene Beliefs

In the early years after the First World War, it was common for the Nazarenes and the Adventists to be confused with one another. Not only did the authorities in the kingdom of SCS, and later in the kingdom of Yugoslavia, initially think that the Adventists and the Nazarenes were a single sect with the same beliefs and act accordingly, certain misunderstandings about Nazarene faith and practice have remained to this day. For example, as recently as early 2000s, historian and expert on religious life in Serbia, Dr. Radić, expressed her belief that the Nazarenes "celebrated the Sabbath, adhered literally to the teachings of the Gospels and did not recognize the sacraments of baptism or communion. They evaded and condemned the swearing of oaths, court disputes, warfare and academic research..." (Radić, 2002:631). This author knows of no case in which the Nazarenes celebrated Saturday as the "Sabbath" in the sense in which the Adventists do (as the seventh day and the day of rest and the peace of God). It is more likely that the Nazarenes met on Saturdays

---

[241] Kraljik says that these conventions are called *starešinska skupština* [assembly of elders]. *Op cit.*

in isolated cases, which had nothing to do with the practice of the Sabbath.

And although we can say that the **Nazarenes did not recognize infant baptism**, but required adults to decide of their own free will to be followers of Christ and to clearly express this conviction through water baptism, this had not always been the Nazarene practice. Reports from the nineteenth century talk of (sporadic) Nazarene recognition of infant baptism. There were a number of reasons for this, some of them being the lack of a published articles of faith until 1920, the pietistic nature of the movement which in its early days attracted adherents from the Lutheran and Reformed churches in which infant baptism was normal practice, and the fact that children were automatically entered, on birth, into the births registry of one of the existing faiths, which all, without exception, baptized infants.[242]

There is some additional confusion relating to the act of baptism itself. Dimitrijević first suggests, in his 1894 study, that during

---

[242] Froehlich himself was of course against the practice of infant baptism, this being one of the reasons for his leaving the state (Calvinist) church in Switzerland. In his commentary on Hebrews 6 – collected from various sermons and compiled into a single work after his death – Froehlich gives theological arguments for the baptism of adults. He believed that so-called Confirmation, claimed by the state church to be a renewal of the covenant of baptism, never actually happened. Froehlich was of the opinion that this covenant was frequently violated and therefore renewal was effectively impossible. In this sense, infant baptism was nothing more than "deception," from which the believer could be set free through repentance, faith and baptism, creating a new foundation in Christ, where the believer is in a relationship with the risen Christ. Froehlich also says that the laying on of hands was related to baptism, like the dedication of a temple, where the laying on of hands symbolized God entering the new temple and taking residence there, having driven out the devil. From Fröhlich, 1978:201-212.

In one of the earliest commentaries on Nazarene beliefs from 1899, Jug Stanikić talks about how the Nazarenes "disagree with our…church on the teaching on infant baptism." Stanikić says that the Nazarenes do not believe small children should be baptized, while older children are not allowed to be baptized for just one reason – because children are not mature enough to understand Christ's teaching on repentance and faith, without which there can be no baptism. Stanikić says that the Nazarenes believe that even if a child is baptized this has no value, since the act of baptism does not save (Stanikić, 1899:121).

baptism the Trinitarian formula is used: "in the name of the Father, the Son and the Holy Spirit." Just a few years later, Dimitrijević amends his claim and now says that the Nazarenes are baptized using the following formula: "I baptize you with water for the forgiveness of sins," according to the Gospel of Matthew 3:11 (Dimitrijević, 1894/2:755). After baptism with water somewhere outside, everybody returns to the house of prayer, where the elder calls on the Holy Spirit to baptize the newly-baptized believer. Then they partake of the Lord's Supper.

However, in the early days of the movement, Baptist leader Oncken took issue with Froehlich's followers for baptizing adults by sprinkling or pouring water on them, instead of by full immersion underwater (Bächtold, 1970:55). Oncken also objected to the Nazarenes' regenerative understanding of baptism, in which baptism was integral to salvation and renewal in regard to prior sins. Froehlich's followers at the time believed that the person was not saved if they were not baptized in this way. However, since Stanikić does not back up this claim in his report, it remains unclear for now what the early practice was amongst the Nazarenes with regard to baptism. It may be that initial uncertainty crystallized over the years into the beliefs that are held today.

Even though at first glance the attitude of the Nazarenes towards others, and even towards their own children, may resemble a theology of predestination, it is more likely that this is a theology of free will, whereby the Nazarenes are concerned not to impose their beliefs on anyone and thereby interfere in the lives of others. The Nazarenes witness to their faith through their lives, through their dedication to reading the Scriptures. and through the witness of the Holy Spirit to those around them. The moment of conversion is of exceptional importance, as is the preparatory period prior to baptism, in which the candidate appears to go through a period of depression and liberation.

Since Froehlich's time, the Nazarenes have believed that regenerative baptism is effective only when conversion as an event is experienced before baptism, and when the conversion can be shown to be "solid." For this reason the conversion experience is very carefully considered. The pre-baptism interview was earlier even referred to as the baptismal "examination" [*ispitivanje*]. The usual way this functioned was that there was a period of repentance, dedicated to public confession of every sin the candidate could possibly think of. After that, every member of the church had the right to publicly question the candidate on every aspect of his or her life, and all the time the degree of public repentance in the examinee was subject to scrutiny. After all this, the entire local congregation would consider whether the candidate's conversion experience was to be accepted, and it would then take a decision regarding candidate's baptism and their church membership.

The older congregations even had a custom whereby, after the elder had announced that there was a candidate for baptism, and after the candidate had given a testimony of their conversion and repentance, each member of the local congregation would stand and give a statement on their acceptance of the candidate as a member. If even one member of the congregation had something against the candidate, baptism and acceptance into membership would not proceed. It is not hard to imagine that local custom among some Nazarene groups was even more stringent.

This practice came about from the teaching on a **church of the true believers, the church of the "remnant,"** that is, a holy and indeed perfect church, in which there are no longer any sinners. This is a theological distinctive of the Mennonite churches, and Froehlich probably took this on board whilst working with Mennonite, Anabaptist congregations in Switzerland later on in his ministry. This is also the origin of the Nazarene refusal to swear oaths and take up arms. When we read Froehlich's letters to congregations we can see that one of the topics that constantly comes up is the discussion of how to raise standards for membership in the local church so that the church would truly only be comprised of holy people. This is the reason for the drawn-out process of repentance, the importance of the conversion experience and the pre-baptismal examination period – and all this is required of people who have already proven themselves worthy of being members of the Nazarene church.

In the event of continued sin in the congregation, and in view of the fact that the Nazarene church is supposed to be a community of holy and sinless people, harsh church disciplinary measures are employed. Just by observing the customs of Nazarene congregations, we can see the significance of these two moments in the life of the church – entry into membership and departure from membership. All these decisions are taken out of the desire to keep the church holy and secure. In this process, Nazarene elders—and the congregation itself—take on the responsibility of addressing the deepest and most private secrets in the life of a person, such as that of their repentance. Because of this theological standpoint, the questions that have come to the fore in the Nazarene church are how to ensure "entrance" is only allowed to the holy, how to keep the holy holy and how remove those who are not—and these are indeed the issues the eldership is most concerned with.

When minister Janjić issued the decision in 1924 to forbid the activities of the Adventists and the Nazarenes, he did so in the belief that they were one and the same religious group. Police and later military reports gave the opposite picture. Yet it took the state authorities a full decade to understand the basic differences in the beliefs and practices of these two religious communities. Of course, the chief concern of the state was to ensure that its subjects swore allegiance to king and fatherland, that they were prepared to take up arms and go to war if needed, and that they would swear the oath in court that would compel them to speak the truth under penalty of perjury. The state could not seem to grasp that the Nazarenes, following biblical principles, did not wish to swear loyalty to anyone, even though they have been loyal citizens under every government because they believe that authority is conferred by God. Likewise the Nazarenes, although opposed to bearing arms, were not against military service in unarmed and noncombatant units. There is also no indication that the Nazarenes were opposed to academic study – it was simply an area that did not interest them.

Radić's claim regarding their literal adherence to the teachings of the Gospels is also odd, since this is nowhere stated. However this impression might be gotten in conversation with Nazarenes, who often cite Bible verses in support of their beliefs and practices.

Nevertheless, this author cannot help but observe that certain state bodies deliberately perpetuated the confusion between these two religious communities, even after all had become clear with regard to the differences in beliefs and practices between them, especially in terms of their attitudes towards the state. If we read certain official documents over an extended period, it seems clear that the police and military authorities realized fairly early on that the *subotari* (Sabbatarians—Adventists) were willing to swear oaths and accept the uniform and arms, but that they would not accept duties on Saturdays, they did not eat pork, etc. The Ministry of Religions continued to insist that the Adventists were a threat to the state as they were not willing to defend the country. Doubtless the Ministry of Religions wanted to confuse the issue and try to leverage the repressive measures employed by the state authorities—the police and army—by way of a response to demands for action on the part of the Serbian Orthodox Church leadership against the Adventists who, like the Nazarenes, were experiencing rapid growth. It is also possible that those in charge of religious matters lacked the information and theological knowledge to appreciate the distinctions between the Nazarenes and the Adventists.

Sociologists of religion have the following to say on the Nazarenes in Serbia—that they are the **oldest and most enduring** of the sects in existence today, with strong roots in Vojvodina; that **women predominate** among its membership, as do the middle-aged, with a low percentage of young people. The most common occupations among them are craftsman, housewife, pensioner, and farmer.

The regulation specially emphasized in Section 18 of the 1919 Articles of Faith (see later in this chapter) is not a purely Nazarene distinctive: "We believe that sisters in the Lord wear a shawl or head covering during prayer or worship as a symbol of their submission to God's command at the time of Creation—1 Cor. 10:16; 11:17, 32." This practice has also been noted in the *Hristova Crkva Braće* [Church of Christ Brethren] who are small in number in Serbia, in some Pentecostal groups and in a few other dwindling smaller churches.[243]

Observers have also noted their pronounced rejection of society at large, and their refusal to do their civic duty and take part in the electoral process. Strict personal morals are also preached with regard to sexuality and money matters (Flere, 1986:28).

In 1981 Dušan Lončar published a paper in which he described the Nazarene attitude towards society as follows:

> One of the more significant traits in the behavior of members of these religious communities is an elitism which not infrequently gives rise to intolerance among believers of differing confessions... Their teachings to a significant degree reject the social (and political) involvement of their members, and some even forbid participation in social and political life... For example, members of the more radical factions within the Christian Nazarene Community in Vojvodina even to this

---

[243] In her graduation paper, Sanja Đorđević describes a local congregation (in the Belgrade suburb of Zemun) as follows:

> The Zemun Nazarene congregation numbers 70 members, predominantly female. The average age of members is more than 40. The youngest members are older than 20, while the eldest are more than 80 years old. The majority of believers have only primary or secondary-level education. Members of working age (they are in the minority) are employed in positions requiring only primary or secondary education, while the majority of members are pensioners and housewives. Long-term members of this congregation joined back in their youth and are typically housewives. All believers consider membership of the congregation their primary task in life, since they thereby satisfy their basic spiritual need of belonging to Christ and achieving personal salvation (Đorđević, 1996:62).

day refuse to take part in elections, swear oaths or
bear arms... (Lončar, 1981:163).244

Their attitude towards society at large can be described as **iso-
lationist**, favoring closed doors against the society around them.
Attendance of and participation in the religious ceremonies of the
Orthodox and Catholic churches are strictly forbidden—even visiting their buildings is not allowed. Friendships are confined to imme-
diate neighbors, to whom believers witness regarding their faith.[245]

Attitudes of the SOC and Others
Toward Nazarene Beliefs

Lazar Milin, a Serbian Orthodox theologian, prominent in the
media as an opponent of Serbs of "foreign faith," described the beliefs
of the Nazarenes in four points, as follows. Of the first belief—concerning Scripture and tradition—Milin says that the Nazarenes, as
Protestants, reject Holy Tradition[246], and favor reading the Sermon on
the Mount, Matthew 23, the Psalms, and the books of the prophets
Isaiah and Jeremiah.[247] Regarding the church, the Nazarenes believe
that only a righteous man can be a member of the church – one who
has been justified through repentance and conversion through faith

---

[244] Lončar elsewhere touches on the publishing activities of the Nazarenes and says:
"It should be noted that there are 'small' religious communities who use no
other printed materials in their religious and propaganda activities than the
Bible and hymnbooks (e.g. the Nazarenes)" (Lončar, 1981:170).

[245] Sanja Đorđević has published a brief sociological study on the Nazarenes in
Serbia (Đorđević, 2003).

[246] The accumulated teaching and customs of the Orthodox Church, passed down
from the first church, considered equivalent in importance to Scripture (t/n).

[247] Dimić comments, interestingly, in 1870, that the Nazarenes do not value the
Old Testament, but this is probably to do with the Nazarene belief that the
teaching on the salvation of man is found in the New Testament, in the message
of salvation through Jesus Christ. It was in this sense that the message of the
Old Testament was not of fundamental importance for the salvation of the soul
(Dimić, 1870).

in Jesus Christ as savior.[248] Concerning the Holy Sacraments, Milin says that the Nazarenes recognize only baptism and communion, and only baptize adults, following a period of testing. Of communion, he says that believers take the bread and wine themselves in remembrance of the Lord's Supper. Regarding prayer, the Nazarenes reject the invocation of the saints and the Mother of God and the veneration of icons and relics, and do not pray for the dead. They also reject the sign of the cross (crossing oneself), and fasting. The Nazarenes reject all oath-taking, the marking of holidays, games and entertainment, and will not bear arms (Milin, 1982:62-3).[249]

From several different sources, we can gain a good overall picture of the Orthodox perception of Nazarene faith and practice. One of the earliest commentators was Orthodox parish priest Jug Stanikić. In the journal *Srpski Sion*, over the course of three years (1897-9), he published no less than sixty-two articles outlining his theological and practical musings on the Nazarenes and "their relatives the Protestants." Stanikić goes into detailed discussion of the Scriptures and Holy Tradition, the church as an organization, the cross, holy days and saints, the baptism of children and the Holy Sacraments, and especially the Sacrament of Priesthood: on binding and loosing, on priestly garments, on the laying on of hands, on the transfer of the priestly ministry to another etc.[250]

---

[248] This may have something to do with the influence of the Holiness movement, which held that the convert/believer was sanctified for a life without sin on earth. The Nazarenes, mindful of the fact that people sin daily, were uncomprising in regard to any sin that was uncovered in their congregations. Nevertheless, one can also point to individual occasions when the Nazarene elders made concessions. For more information see Dimić, 1880 and Hadžija, 1936.

[249] Ivan Cvitković repeats Milin's opinions almost verbatim in his paper *Savez komunista i religija* [*The League of Communists and Religion*] published in 1989 (Cvitković, 1989:223).

[250] Although Stanikić expends a great many words in laying out his arguments, it is the impression of this author that he does not accurately convey even Serbian Orthodox Church theology in certain aspects. Particularly interesting is Stanikić's discussion of baptism as a condition for salvation, and Orthodox chrism as opposed to the Nazarene belief regarding the need for faith and repentance for salvation, where the act of baptism itself plays no role in salvation.

Dušan Petrović talks about how the Nazarenes respect only the Scriptures and not church tradition (Petrović, 1906:17); they observe Sunday and reject infant baptism, baptizing only adults, they do not venerate icons, they do not submit to government, they refuse to bear arms,[251] the Nazarenes have no priests, icons or symbols of the cross on their churches and they do not pay the *parohijal* [church tax] (Milivojević, 1925:39); they do not read books nor the daily newspapers, they do not fast, they do not have catechists etc. Njistor further states that the Nazarenes meet in the evenings, in private homes, that they sing psalms, that their prayers are "as their soul desires" and that of the holy sacraments they have only baptism and communion; also the Nazarenes do not get involved in politics (Njistor, 1940).

After a visit to a congregation, Dimitrijević describes how this looked: the building typically has two rooms, a main one where services are held and a smaller one in which interviews are held with baptismal candidates, in which kerosene and food are kept and so on. Females sit at the right-hand side and are divided into "sisters," members of the Nazarene community, and "friends," female baptismal candidates. On the left are the men, "brothers," and male "friends." The room is very modest, there are no candles or vigil lamps, there is just a desk in the middle where the book is kept containing the list of believers (sometimes with notes on their past sins) (Dimitrijević, 1903/2:5).[252] Zorica Kuburić, sociologist of religion and founder of

---

[251] In his article in which he describes the basic distinctives of the Nazarenes and Adventists, Milivojević also says that the Nazarenes refuse to eat pork, but this is probably a confusion with Adventist beliefs and practices. Another possibility is that the Nazarenes in question had come from Adventism originally and had retained certain customs and beliefs, and Milivojević had wrongly portrayed this as a general characteristic of the Nazarenes. Milivojević incidentally talks about the Nazarenes and Adventists as offshoots of the Baptist movement.

[252] One of the major problems Orthodox authors had, especially those writing in the early days of the Nazarene movement, was the negative attitude taken by the Nazarenes towards the traditional churches, not only the Orthodox and the Catholic, but also the Lutheran and the Reformed churches. Almost all authors wrote about the movement in very heated terms, all the while comparing it with the Orthodox Church and being unable to take a more objective view of the phenomenon. The Nazarenes, for their part, whenever discussing th

the Serbian CEIR (Center for Empirical Research of Religion) also visited a Nazarene congregation:

> While visiting Padina I saw, I think, the loveliest Nazarene congregation in Serbia. These were Slovaks who belonged to the Nazarene community and had a long tradition in this village. The locals told me that in their village the Nazarenes were the biggest religious community and that apart from Nazarenes there were Adventists, Baptists, Pentecostals and Lutherans. It was my first time in Padina. I stood before the beautiful Slovak Evangelical Church, with its built-in organ, and listened to the bell ringing long in the bell-tower. I watched the people passing by, most of them returning from Sunday service in their own churches. I stopped one gentleman and asked him where I could find the other religious communities in Padina. He politely told me that

---

traditional churches, used pejorative terms that were helpful to neither side [approximately translated from Serbian – t/n]:

Church, religious community – Babylon, Tower of Babylon;
Church building, place of worship – mound of bricks, stone grave, synagog of the antichrist, home of Baal etc.
Priest – witch doctor of Baal, servant of the devil, hired hand of sin, scribe and Pharisee
Christians (non-Nazarenes) – unbelievers, the godless
Cross – gallows
Sign of the cross – hand-flapping, swatting flies
Chalice – the devil's goblet
Bell-ringer – bull of Bashan
Bell-ringing – "Hark, the devil is calling"
Observation of Sunday – man's contrivance
State church – state harlot
and so on.
Cited by Stanikić, 1902:46-47.

they were almost all there, close to one another, and pointed the way to me.

I commented to him that there were lots of different religious communities in Padina and asked him which he was returning from. He told me he was a Nazarene and added: "There are many of us, but we all ought to be one" (Kuburić, 2011:197).

As part of his research for his graduation paper in the mid-1970s, Jakov Makaji visited a worship service in Novi Sad and recorded the key details. In the room itself, there were no pictures or inscriptions, the large room was well lit, with pews divided into two sections. The men sat to the left, females to the right. The aisle was empty, leading up to the pulpit, which faced the doors. The believer entered the room in silence, took his place, bowed his head and prayed in silence, waiting for the worship service to begin. On the hour, one of the brothers stood, announced a song from the *Zion's Harp*, and read a few verses from it. After singing several songs, everybody went down on their knees for prayer, while one of the brothers prayed. When prayer was over, one of the elders stood and came out to the pulpit, placed his hand on the Scriptures and prayed silently. He then opened the Scriptures, read some verses and then explained them verse by verse. When the sermon was over, four or five songs were sung, led by one of the brothers. After the songs, one of the elders stood before the pulpit to pray out loud; the other members knelt and followed this public prayer. After this, all stood and gradually left the meeting-place. The Nazarenes in Novi Sad meet three times a week: Thursdays at seven in the evening, Sunday mornings at nine and Sunday afternoons at three. (Makaji, 1975:26).

Important to note is that fact that the Nazarenes consider the use of music and musical instruments in worship services an unnecessary innovation. In this they have theological common ground with some other Evangelical groups who refuse to use musical instruments on the grounds that they are not mentioned in the New Testament (with the exception of one reference in the book of Revelation, which occurs in heaven). Songs are thus sung *a capella*, with someone humming the pitch at the beginning.

With regard to discipline, there are two levels. When a "friend" sins, the matter is discussed before the whole Nazarene congregation. Repentance is public, too, and a verdict is given by the whole fellowship. However when a "brother" or "sister" sins, then discussion is limited to believers, members of the congregation. In the event that guilt is established and admitted, there are three levels of sanction:

- a rebuke, delivered privately
- excommunication from the congregation (for a time)
- withdrawal of blessing[253]

The person being disciplined sits in the last row and walks with head bowed and in doing so publicly expresses their repentance.

Funeral customs are very simple. When a believer dies, the body is prepared by the believers, and before departing for the grave songs are sung in the house. Then the casket is carried in silence to the graveside, and then songs are sung again over the open grave. When this is over the casket is lowered into the grave, covered over, and the funeral is over.[254]

---

[253] The Nazarenes greet each other with the words "*Gospod da te blagoslovi*" [the Lord bless you] – the sinner/penitent in this case is not greeted by members of the congregation.

[254] There is a very interesting written testimony by two Nazarene women, Rada Nikolić and Zora Milovančev, concerning a congregation in Aranđelovac, probably from the period prior to the First World War:

> Just as graveyard funerals were not permitted to those who had not been baptized in [a recognized] church, so marriages were not recognized if the marriage had not been in church, and were considered unlawful. The old regime separated our Rada from her husband, and she had to go to her parents while he was left alone. Sometimes she would go home to her husband. Once, the county clerk saw them together and said, "Are you here again?" She replied, "If we hadn't wanted to be together we wouldn't have got married."

The Basic Articles of Faith of the Christian Nazarene Community in the SFRJ, approved in 1991, state: "The members of the Christian Nazarene Community do not accept arms but are prepared to serve in the Army even in the most difficult and dangerous posts. Loyalty, honesty and integrity are the holy duty of every member of the church. They do not use the word 'oath,' based on the explicit commands of Christ: 'But let your communication be, Yea, yea; Nay, nay: for whatsoever is more than these cometh of evil.'" (Mat. 5:37).

There is another source that talks about Nazarene practice. Maksa Šipoš spent nine years and ten months in jail in the kingdom of Yugoslavia for his Nazarene beliefs. He gave an interview to the Novi Pančevac in 1994, as the assistant elder of the Pančevo Nazarene congregation. Šipoš explains that **the Nazarenes do not accept invitations to social events and parties**. A minority have televisions at home and they only watch educational and factual programs. The Nazarenes do not go to watch movies, theater performances, concerts, or other public events.

When the daughter of Sava Lomić died – she was a grown girl – and when the funeral was to be held and our people set out from the house, they offered all of our believers a cross to carry – first the father and then the rest. All of them got a thrashing, our father the most. He was clubbed all the way to the graveyard. Then they sent them to jail where they were held for a month, one of them a sister. In the early years we would meet in our house, and later sometimes at old Luka Preković's place. The village clerk comes along and says: "I arrest you in the name of the Law!" And my brother Radojica stands up and says, "The law permits prayer to God behind closed doors." The clerk asks him if he is sure about that, and then he gives up and leaves.

Many times the authorities interrupted services and communion and forbade us from meeting. We would meet at dawn, at 4 in the morning, and by the time these esteemed gentlemen woke up our service would already be over.

Šipoš further explains that the individual is saved through faith in God and by His grace: "We believe that we have achieved much through a pure way of life. In this respect we have the most regard for the messages of the New Testament, for the Old Testament is merely a shade and a shadow…"

The local congregation in Pančevo organizes a meeting of the brothers every other year in which all male members of the local congregation, servants and elders participate. Every year a meeting of the elders is held, usually in Novi Sad (Miloradović, 1994).

Nazarene rules issued at a meeting in Stara Pazova in November 1919[255]

1. Internal matters in the Christ-believing congregations (churches), all matters of faith and all related matters are addressed by the whole congregation, of its own accord. Since there are very few of us, in some places we do not have a president etc., our parishes (congregations) have leaders [elders], who may only take decisions and conduct all ongoing affairs by the will of the entire congregation. Without the approval of the congregation they do not have the right to take any decision, other than in minor and less significant cases. Rom. 12:4-5

2. Congregation heads (elders) have the right, under their administration (presidency), to hold advisory meetings, and with the consent of the elders the congregation may conduct any business it wishes.

3. Any [decisions from] such special advisory meetings, when held without the elders, may only be enacted if the elders give their agreement—thus all valid decisions are to be taken by the congregation in agreement with the elders. 2 Tim. 2:1, 3, 15, 16.

---

[255] Photocopy of document in possession of author.

4. These are the kinds of elder and minister we have in our congregation:

    a. Those who preach the Word of God to the congregation and its audience, and conduct necessary ceremonies, related to faith, as in point G) of the Articles of Faith.

    b. Those who manage the material possessions of the community and concern themselves with setting in order those things that are necessary for our corporate body, as in point F).

    c. We have one who has stewardship over money, and two or three helpers in this – they regularly record income and expenditure in the books and are responsible for keeping this faithfully and for care over the property of the congregation.

5. The congregation and its elders have the right and the duty to call to account the money steward and his two or three helpers on request by any member.

6. There is no regular, annual inspection of the accounts since we trust one another.

7. There are helpers of the poor, who take note of whether any of our believers are in want and whether they have sufficient strength to support their families. If he is not able to do so, his way of life is investigated in order to find the reasons for his lack. If he is found to be pure, he is helped from the common goods according to his need. If however it is found that he is careless and wanton he is disciplined. Gal. 2:10 2 Thess. 3:10-12.

8. The greatest duty placed on these stewards is to care for the helpless and the sick.

9. The stewards may perform acts of charity according to their own insight and the need. We also wish to help others in need who are not members of our fellowship.

10. The money required to procure essential items for congregations or parishes are collected from the whole congregation by way of voluntary contributions, and never by personal taxes or according to means. All members of the congregation of believers give of their own good and free will in the amount they wish, each Sunday after the worship service; for they know and believe that God loveth a cheerful giver. 1 Cor. 16:1-2. If, however, it is noted that any one of us is stingy, we warn him of his duty according to Scripture. 2 Cor. 9:5-10.

11. These contributions are taken care of by those who handle the money (4); the money is used to buy various food items, wheat, barley, etc., with which the needs are met.

12. Any member of the congregation can be chosen for these ministries that exist in our fellowship. However, these ministers must be of honest character and be worthy of the trust of the congregation. And only members of the congregation enjoy both active and passive rights. In elections a majority decides. Acts 6:3-6

13. If ministers in the ministry are not faithful, and act contrary to that for which they were called and invested, they are removed from the ministry and others take their place according to the same procedure. Luke 19:24.

14. Our ministers are not so occupied with the ministries that they cannot perform their domestic duties and affairs. These ministries in the congregation are entirely honorary and there is no recompense for them save in exceptional circumstances, when they are in need; in such cases the congregation considers it its duty to help them. 2 Thess 3:7-19; 1 Tim 5:17

15. These ministries do not exist in places where members are very few in number. In those there is one elder and one steward, and small congregations are cared for by larger ones, those which are closest. Acts 20:26-28; 1 Pet 5:2-3. Weekly offerings are used in small congregations to meet needs.

16. Every year, as needed, a convention is held in one of the larger congregations, at which lesser ministers may also be chosen and commissioned. This convention is also attended by those likeminded in faith to us from other countries and states, such as from Switzerland, Germany, America, Hungary and from Vienna. The true purpose of this convention and consultation is that love and faithfulness would be awakened for God and for one another; that we would live a faithful and righteous life towards all men; that we would not lose sight of proper adherence to and preservation of the Gospel; that all those in fellowship with us would be able to grow in equal step.

17. If such events may occur in an individual congregation which this congregation cannot itself discuss or resolve (as per item 16), the whole fellowship takes these matters under consideration and comes to a decision about them. And all such decisions are accepted by smaller fellowships (congregations) with all readiness, and respected. Acts 15:22-26. The attached statement and articles of faith were settled on through just such a common agreement. And we will do so in the future.

18. The larger and more numerous congregations have their own buildings used as houses of prayer, which the parish has raised at its own expense. Where, however, there are few believers, they hold their services in peaceful private houses. Here and there it may be that our parishes have bought burial grounds from their own means, and there are also places where our parish has been given a place to bury our dead by the political municipality or the state authorities.

From the convention of delegates of all Christ-believing congregations in the kingdom of the Serbs, Croats and Slovenes, concluded and confirmed. In Stara Pazova (Srem), November 23, 1919.

Articles of faith

The confessional and Christ-believing fellowships of the so-called "Nazarenes" in the kingdom of the Serbs, Croats and Slovenes, in Ruma, printing press of the Đorđe Petrović company, 1920.[256]

A) Old and New Testament

The main foundation of our faith is the Bible, that is the Holy Scripture of the Old and New Testament.

The Old Testament teaches us that there is One Eternal and Omnipotent God, All-Sustaining, Sabaoth, who created this whole universe with all things on it and in it, both seen and unseen.

The Old Testament further teaches us what the holy Fathers and prophets lived, believed and taught, who prophesized of Christ the Lord and announced His coming, and prepared the world for His teaching. That is why the Old Testament serves as a witness to us. The New Testament of our Lord Jesus Christ serves as a rule and as a guide to eternal blessing for every believer.

B) On God the Father

Regarding God the Father, we believe that He is the Only God, in three persons God the Father, God the Son and God the Holy Spirit, who is worshipped by all the heavenly host, and who has created the race of man and appointed him to worship and exalt Him (God) and obey His Holy Commands according to the teaching of Christ the Savior.

C) On God the Son, that is, Jesus Christ

Regarding God the Son, we believe that He was conceived of the Holy Spirit and born of the Virgin Mary in the flesh, as is written in Matt 1:20, 21. "And she shall

---

[256] Photocopy of document in possession of author.

bring forth a son, and thou shalt call his name Jesus: for he shall save his people from their sins." John chapter 1 speaks in more detail of how by the will of God He was crucified on the cross for those who will turn to Him, through His suffering and blood sacrifice to obtain eternal blessing for every man who truly turns to Him; that happy future beyond the grave that delights the converted soul. What we lost (blessing) through the sin of Adam, our first father, we will be given by Jesus Christ, for by His sacrifice He conquered death.

D) On God the Holy Spirit

Regarding God the Holy Spirit, we believe that Jesus Christ, according to His promise, sends Him to the believers, just as He sent Him to the first Christians in the first times, the fiftieth day after His resurrection, as the promise of God the Father; and later he gave Him through the apostles, when they laid their hands on the heads of the believers, through prayer and faith. Acts 8:17: "Then laid they their hands on them, and they received the Holy Ghost." We believe that the Holy Spirit teaches and preserves those to whom He is given, and remains with them until the end of the age.

E) Worship services

.Worship begins in our churches with singing from the *New Zion's Harp* [*Nova Harfa Siona*], followed by reading from a chapter from *Holy Scripture* and then prayer and thanks to God. One of the fellowship, who is called to do so and who enjoys the complete trust of the members of the fellowship, explains what has been read from Scripture, or teaches by watering in the faith. These duties are performed in the fellowship by members chosen for this, as seen below.

F) Choosing church (congregation) ministers

In our church, as ministers, we first have elders (bishops [*vladike*]) and secondly we have lesser ministers. The Apostle Paul writes to Titus, in 1:5-10: "[O]rdain elders [*priests/servants*] in every city. If any be blameless, the husband of one wife, having faithful children..." and so on – those who are unblemished, of good heart, are not intemperate, are not puffed up, but who spread abroad the glory of God with a pure conscience. Such may be a part of our fellowships, whom the congregation finds sufficiently worthy of trust. 1 Tim. 3: "A bishop then must be blameless, the husband of one wife, vigilant, sober, of good behavior, given to hospitality, apt to teach; not given to wine, no striker; patient, not a brawler, not greedy of filthy lucre... that ruleth well his own house, having his children in subjection with all gravity. (For if a man know not how to rule his own house, how shall he take care of the church of God?)." Such men we unanimously call into the holy ministry – to help the poor, care for the sick, lead the congregation; those who seek to carry out their holy ministry faithfully; for if anyone conducts it unfaithfully his ministry is taken from him.

G) Ceremony of acceptance into fellowship

When one who has believed (in his heart) announces with repentance that he is following the leading of his heart and his firm conviction in faith, with no compulsion, and wishes to become a member of Christ's holy church, and when the believers have fully examined him in regard to his life and works thus far: whether he has shown himself sufficiently unwavering in faith—for we place the greatest importance on constancy of faith—and when we find that he has left sinning behind, and has sufficiently repented and corrected himself—then the congregation agrees in the matter, and he confesses all his prior sins before the congregation elder. The convert is then baptized with water in the name of the Father, the Son and the Holy Spirit for the forgiveness of sins, according to the example of Christ which he left to us. After this, blessing is sought from God through pious prayer and the congregation elder places his hands on his head and he receives the Holy Spirit, as is written in Acts 8:14-17 and again in 2:38, as Peter said: "Then Peter said unto them, Repent, and be baptized every one of you in the name of Jesus Christ for the remission of sins, and ye shall receive the gift of the Holy Ghost." Then the baptized partakes of the Lord's holy supper with the other, previously accepted, members of the congregation. It may happen that believers will partake of the Lord's supper on occasions other than acceptance, where the inner need of the soul requires it. This supper is enjoyed as a mark of the crucifixion of the holy body of Christ and the shedding of his blood, and this reminds us of his death, as is written in Luke 22:14-20: "And he took bread, and gave thanks, and brake it, and gave unto them, saying: This is my body which is given for you: this do in remembrance of me. Likewise also the cup after supper…" As we can see from the above, this cannot easily be attained by anyone, on the contrary, many must wait long before they achieve such worthiness or attain to this act[257].

H)   On the non-baptism of small children

Concerning the above-mentioned rule under G) we cannot practice the baptism of small children since such children cannot yet believe anything, nor know much of themselves, nor can we know in advance whether our children will believe what we believe with the same heart. But we hold that children are, as children, holy, since they do not know sin; additionally, the Lord said: "[O]f such is the kingdom of God." Matt 18:1-6. Here though it should be noted that we properly record the newborn with the authorities for entry into the births register. Therefore,

---

[257] Referring to Holy Communion (t/n).

we only baptize adults and the converted, as it is written in Matt. 28:19-20. Mark 16:15-16: "Go ye into all the world, and preach the gospel to [all nations]. He that believeth and is baptized shall be saved; but he that believeth not shall be damned."

I)   On moral upbringing

Since we do not have our own confessional schools, we send our children to the schools of other confessions, of the state and of the community, since we hold that the schooling of children is entirely necessary and we gladly pay school fees. As far as it concerns us and we are able, we make efforts to supplement the teaching of our children and to bring them up in moral teaching: to be upright, worthy, honest and loyal citizens and people. Our parental duty before God and man requires this. The education of children within the home does not include the requirement that they confess our faith (that of the believers in Christ). Because that is dependent on their conviction and self-determination. We compel no one to believe as we do. Many of the children of our people have gone over to another confession, or to the one to which their parents previously belonged, or to which their inner conviction drew them. Thus not all our children confess our faith.

J)   Marriage ceremony

The young man wishing to marry states this desire to one of the congregation's ministers, and asks him if he would inquire of the girl whom he means to take as his wife whether she might be favorably inclined towards him. If both are so inclined, and if their parents agree to this, the matter is referred to the congregation. The congregation looks into whether these two are able to maintain marital life and to live it in peace and love, as is befitting of reasonable people; and if there is no obstacle, they must go to the appropriate authority and register the marriage.

Then, after 21 days of the marriage, according to civil law, it is confirmed before the appropriate authority by civil law;258 then [they are married] in the congregation, before the whole fellowship, as follows: Having been examined by one of the congregation's ministers, they formally promise themselves to one another, and without swearing any oath they commit to one another and to faithful love, that they will share together all joy and sadness in troubles, and that they will faithfully cherish one another all their lives. Then the whole congregation, along with one member who speaks the prayer out loud, prays to God for those being married, that God would bless their marriage and the promises they have given one another; with this, the act of marriage is completed.

Our acceptance is affirmed with a "yes," and refusal with a "no." Because the only proof of commitment is faithfulness, and faithlessness will trample even on an oath, we hold that true faithfulness is sufficient for promise and obligation, without the need for any oath. Matt. 5:33-39. Also James 5:12: "But above all things, swear not, neither by heaven, neither by the earth: but let your yea be yea; and your nay, nay..." In the courts and on official occasions, when the state authorities require it of us, in confirmation of the honor of our word, we give our hand as confirmation, or place our hand on our heart.

K) On military duty

Since we have already talked about oaths, we would add that our people and young men refrain from taking the oath both before the courts and when entering military service, maintaining the practice explained under J). However, it seems appropriate to mention and recognize that we submit to His Majesty the King and to the state authorities, with the greatest readiness and respect, fulfill-

---

258 Meaning that the act of marriage is complete.

ing the laws laid down, paying taxes, carrying out our military and civil duty and so on – excepting only the killing of people, which we must not do. For in the New Testament it is written: "Love your enemies…do good to them that hate you." Matt 5:43-44, and in the Gospel of Matthew 26:52 it says: "Then said Jesus unto him, put up again thy sword into his place: for all they that take the sword shall perish with the sword." That is why we will take up a gun to clean it, but we can never practice with it, to learn to kill people, for that we can never do.

And to pretend to practice with the gun and then, in the moment of war and battle refuse to shoot, would be to deceive our ruler and the state authority, which we are not willing to do. For this reason the believers in Christ decline to take up the gun or to practice with it. And after all, there are other opportunities and duties in the army where the believers in Christ might serve, such as in caring for the sick, and similar. In such cases we accept weapons (the knife and bayonet), but only as a symbol of military service; this we believe that the military and civil authorities will have the wisdom and understanding to recognize. At all times we are prepared to identify our conscripts so that when these special conditions are applied to them the military authorities may not be deceived by others. And the number of our people in the army is in any case very small, and such cases rare.

L)   Church (congregational) discipline

If any member of the believers in Christ, who has made a covenant and committed himself to do what God requires of us in the Holy Scripture, later goes back on his promise or allows evil intentions to take hold of his heart, and sins, he is rebuked – Matt. 18:15:17: "[I]f thy brother shall trespass against thee, go and tell him his fault between thee and him alone: if he shall hear thee, thou hast gained thy brother. But if he will not hear thee, then take with thee one or two more, that in the mouth of two or three witnesses every word may be established. And if he shall neglect to hear them, tell it unto the church (congregation): but if he neglect to hear the church, let him be unto thee as an heathen man and a publican." Such are excluded from the fellowship, with no regard for person. If through rebuke he corrects himself he may once again be a member, of course if he has not committed some mortal sin, such as in 1 Cor. 5:9-11 and 6:10-11: "[I]f any man that is called a brother be a fornicator, or covetous, or an idolator, or a railer, or a drunkard, or an extortioner; with such an one no not to mix or eat." Therefore our discipline is not fleshly.

M) On burial

When the human body ceases to be the dwelling-place of the soul, we treat it in the simplest way: we place it in a simple coffin, and when the legally prescribed time has passed, we sing a few spiritual songs, read something from the Scriptures, share some teaching with those present, take [the body] to the graveyard and finish with singing and reading form the Scriptures; then we place it in the grave in which it is buried.

N) On the resurrection from the dead

We believe in the words of Christ, our Lord, as is written: John 5:28-29. "Marvel not at this: for the hour is coming, in the which all that are in the graves shall hear the voice of the Son of God. And shall come forth; they that have done good, unto the resurrection [to judgment]." The Apostle Paul says the same in 1 Cor. 15:51-54. The Revelation of John 20:13-15 testifies to this: "And the sea *will* give up the dead which are in it *at the first word of the Almighty God before whom heaven and earth tremble and all will gather before His throne of judgment, each to receive his reward according to God's righteous verdict;* every man

according to his works, *while he was alive, good or evil.*"
[italics indicate their additions]

Note
The paragraphs above give a picture of the simplicity and direction of our beliefs, and in this conviction we will be strongly supported by our firm adherence to that which is written in the New Testament.

The elders of our community:
Milan Dunđerov from Stari Futog (Bačka); Jan Sabo from Kisač (Bačka); Palo Miluh from Petrovac (Bačka); Pavle Milovanović from Jarak (Srem); Steva Nićiforović from Bačinci (Srem); Steva Sisojević from Mitrovica (Srem); Mišo Šarkiz from Stara Pazova (Srem); Milutin Ivančević from Stara Pazova (Srem) and many others of various tongues.

The 1966 Basic Articles

On April 9, 1966, an elders' convention of the "positive group" was held in Zemun, at which new basic articles were laid down, and those from March 30, 1958, annulled. The Executive Board of the Nazarene religious community was disbanded and it was decided that the community would be led by a Board of Elders. The movement also changed its name to Christian Nazarene Community in the SFRJ – Novi Sad [*Hrišćanska nazarenska zajednica u SFRJ* – Novi Sad]. The elders chosen to the Board of Elders were Lajoš Paći, Živko Vanga and Stevan Nenadović.[259] However, for the purposes of contact with the authorities, the number of elders needed to be expanded and so Živko Nenadović joined the board in 1968.[260]

---

[259] Bilten Savezne Komisije za verska pitanja, god 5., br. 3, date 12 October 1966.
[260] Vojvodina Archive, F 198/I 879, Pov. br. 35 dated 4/8/1968. See appendix 1 to this chapter for the text of the Basic Articles.

When the Nazarene delegation visited the Federal Commission for Religious Affairs and presented their new documents and members of the Board of Elders, the state's objection was that item 10 (which mentions the refusal to bear arms) was at odds with the Constitution of the SFRJ and that before approving it at their convention they should have agree things with the Federal Ministry of the Interior – sought approval, essentially. The state still wanted to influence the internal organization and beliefs of this religious community.

The representatives of this group, being of the so-called "positive" Nazarenes, also expressed satisfaction at the improved conditions enjoyed by their members during military service, and special mention was made of this in the Federal Commission's report.

Basic Articles of Faith of the Christian Nazarene Community in the SFRJ (1966)

Article 1

The foundation of the Christian Nazarene Community is the teaching of Christ as expressed in the Holy Scriptures.

Article 2

The Christian Nazarene Community believes that its spiritual leader and High Priest is Jesus Christ himself (1 Pet. 5:4 and Heb. 6:2), while the fellowship consists of all members of both sexes, represented on earth by its highest body, the Elder's Convention [Starešinski sabor] (or Elder's Assembly [Starešinska skupština]).

Article 3

The Elder's Assembly is comprised of all elders, chosen by the members of the Christian Nazarene congregations in the country, whose duty it is to exercise care over all aspects of spiritual life.

Article 4

Christian Nazarene congregations in some places are represented by servants (preachers) who besides preaching Christ's teaching have a duty of care over the members of the local congregation.

Article 5
The Christian Nazarene congregation is completely autonomous in all respects and is independent of all other congregations within the country and abroad, although it has fraternal links in the faith to Nazarene brothers in all nations.

Article 6
Religious gatherings are held publicly, open to all, in premises set aside for the purpose, used exclusively for the study of religious, moral and spiritual matters relating to the religious life of the members of the church.

Meetings are held Sunday mornings and afternoons and one workday evening during the week.

Worship services consist of singing spiritual songs ([unaccompanied] hymns), reading and preaching from the Scriptures, prayers and thanks to God.

Worship is led by elders or servants (preachers).

Preaching is delivered in the languages of the Yugoslav peoples and minorities. All believers are equal regardless of their ethnic background.

Article 7
Acceptance into membership is conducted in the languages of the Yugoslav peoples and minorities, according to the will of the individual, completely freely expressed, along with his testimony that he has fully believed and conducts his life according to God's word.

Article 8
Religious rites are as follows: preaching the Word of God, prayer, [unaccompanied] singing of spiritual songs, sharing the holy supper, baptism of adults, marriage and burial of the dead.

The fellowship recognizes civil marriage before the authorities; after that it calls the couple before the congregation to pledge their faithfulness to one another.

Article 9

The stance of the Christian Nazarene community towards the state authorities, in accordance with Scripture (Rom. 13:1-3) is that government is ordained of God, and our fellowship considers it a duty to respect and submit to the powers in authority and to pray to God for them (1 Tim. 2:1-4), and to do so in all matters which are not in opposition to the teaching of Christ.

Article 10

The members of the Christian Nazarene Community do not accept arms but are prepared to serve in the Army even in the most difficult and dangerous posts. Loyalty, honesty and integrity are the holy duty of every member of the church. They do not use the word 'oath', based on the explicit commands of Christ: "'Thou shalt not kill...' and 'Thou shalt not forswear thyself... But let your communication be, Yea, yea; Nay, nay'" (Matt. 5:21,33,37).

Article 11

Members of the Christian Nazarene Community are not compelled to any material giving, nor to contribute to the congregation, but may do so of their own free will as a gift from the heart (Col. 3:23), which is used for poorer members.

Elders and preachers receive no wage nor recompense; they serve in the ministry from the heart, voluntarily and without pay.

Article 12

The Christian Nazarene Community is a purely religious institution, tasked with preaching and interpreting the Gospel, and in so doing to turn people from sin and towards God through Jesus Christ. It has no ambition to accumulate earthly goods, but seeks to lay up spiritual treasures in heaven (Mat. 6:19-21).

Article 13

Members of the Christian Nazarene Community have a duty to attend all worship meetings and to apply the teaching of Holy Scripture in their own lives (Heb. 10:25).

Article 14

All members of the fellowship have equal rights.

Acceptance and discipline of members is conducted by the congregation in the presence of the elder/s. Members under discipline have no right to participate in decision-making in the fellowship.

Article 15

Revocation of membership [is by]: voluntary withdrawal, exclusion for reasons of a disorderly and incorrigible life and for violation of Christ's teaching.

Article 16

The Elders' Convention (Elder's Assembly) elects a Council of Elders, which represents it in all administrative affairs, while spiritual authority over all churches is concentrated in the Lord Jesus Christ himself, who is the Head of the Church (Eph. 5:23).

Article 17

The Christian Nazarene Community is convinced that its activity and teaching contributes to the nurture of good and upright people who will be of service to those close to them, and to the state.

Article 18

All movable and immovable property belongs to the Christian Nazarene fellowship in the town in question, while the sale and purchase of property is done by the leadership of the local congregation, with the agreement of the Council of Elders.

Article 19

Amendments and supplements to these basic articles of the Christian Nazarene Community in the SFRJ may only be made by the Elders' Convention (Assembly).

Article 20

The official stamp of the Christian Nazarene Community bears the title: "Hrišćanska nazarenska zajednica u SFRJ – Novi Sad."

Article 21

As these basic articles of the Christian Nazarene Community in the SFRJ enter into force, so the prior administrative title of "Glavni izvršni odbor Hrišćanske nazarenske zajednice u SFRJ" [Chief Executive Board of the Christian Nazarene Community in the SFRJ], which was founded on 30 March 1958 with a one-year mandate, is no longer applicable.

Article 22

The Basic Articles of the Christian Nazarene Community in the SFRJ were discussed and unanimously approved by the Elders' Convention of the Christian Nazarene Community in the SFRJ, held 9 April 1966 in Zemun, on which date it enters into force.

Zemun, 9 April 1966
Elders' Convention:

Paći Lajoš, Mućan Đorđe, Kapetan Milovan, Vanka Živko, Tunić Simo, Košut Janko, Babin Sima, Molnar Jožef, Molnar Ištvan, Miklea Đorđe, Jorga Mita, Daku Balint, Turu Janoš, Šandorka Ištvan, Šulja Miša, Nenadović Stevan

Council of Elders of the Christian Nazarene Community:
Paći Lajoš, Vanka Živko, Stevan Nenadović

The 1991 Basic Articles

The last major meeting was held in 1991 in Novi Sad, titled the *Velika Bratska Skupština* [Great Convention of Brothers], at which representatives of both groups/parties gathered. At this meeting, new Basic Articles of the fellowship were adopted, and leadership was entrusted to a three-member Council of Elders, who were selected from among the members of the Elders' Convention, who numbered eighteen. These decisions made null and void the previous enactments and decisions from 1958 and from 1966. The name was also changed to *Hrišćanska nazarenska verska zajednica* [Christian Nazarene Faith Community]. The introduction of alternative military service helped overcome the old schism in the movement, though divisions and occasional suspicion are still present, especially among older members.

HRIŠĆANSKA NAZARENSKA ZAJEDNICA
u SFRJ
N O V I S A D
ul.Valentina Vodnika 12

O S N O V N A   N A Č E L A
HRIŠĆANSKE NAZARENSKE ZAJEDNICE U SFRJ

Član 1.

Temelj Hrišćanske Nazarenske zajednice je Hristova Nauka, koja je izražena u Svetom Pismu.

Član 2.

Hrišćanska nazarenska zajednica veruje da je njen duhovni Poglavar i Prvosveštenik sam Isus Hristos (I.Petr.5,4 i Jevr. 6,20) a zajednicu sačinjavaju svi članovi oba pola, a na zemlji je kao najviše telo zastupa Starešinski sabor (Starešinska Skupština).

Član 3.

Starešinski sabor sačinjavaju sve starešine izabrane od članova Hrišćanskih Nazarenskih zajednica u zemlji, a čija je dužnost da se brinu o celokupnom verskom životu.

Član 4.

Hrišćanske Nazarenske zajednice u pojedinim mestima zastupaju, od članova izabrane sluge (propovednici), koji pored propovedanja Hristove nauke imaju i brigu o članovima dotične zajednice u mestu.

Član 5.

Hrišćanska Nazarenska zajednica je potpuno samostalna u svakom pogledu, i nezavisna od svih ostalih zajednica u zemlji i inostranstvu, iako je u bratskim verskim odnosima sa braćom nazarenima svih zemalja.

Član 6.

Verski skupovi drže se javno, svakom pristupačno, u za to određenim prostorijama, gde se proučavaju samo verska, moralna i duhovna pitanja koja se odnose na verski život članova crkve.

Skupovi se održavaju nedeljom pre i posle podne, i jednim radnim danom uveče u toku nedelje.

Bogosluženja se obavljaju pevanjem duhovnih pesama (pojanja), čitanjem i propovedanjem sv. Pisma, molitvom i zahvalom Bogu.

Bogosluženje obavljaju starešine ili sluge (propovednici).

Propovedanje se vrši na jezicima jugoslovenskih naroda i narodnosti. Svi vernici su ravnopravni bez obzira na nacionalnu pripadnost.

Svaka zajednica u mestu po potrebi može organizovati versku pouku za decu svojih članova.

Član 6/a.

Prema svojim hrišćanskim dužnostima, verska zajednica vodi brigu o svim članovima zajednice:

a) Organizovanjem prikupljanja pomoći u novu, namirnicama,

-2-

odeći i obući, i deljenjem ista potrebnima.

b)Izgradnjom namenskih stambenih zgrada sa više stanova i prostorijom za bogosluženja, i prodajom prava doživotnog korišćenja ovih stanova isključivo starijim vernicima, članovima zajednice po nižim cenama od tržišnih.

c)Izgradnjom staračkih domova za stare, bolesne i iznemogle.

Član 7.

Primanje u članstvo se vrši na jezicima jugoslovenskih naroda i narodnosti, na osnovu potpuno slobodno izražene volje pojedinca uz posvedočenje da se je potpuno obratio, te da svoj život upravlja po Božjoj Reči.

Član 8.

Verski obredi su: propovedanje Reči Božije, molitve, pojanje duhovnih pesama, deljenje svete večere, krštavanje odraslih, venčavanje i sahranjivanje umrlih.

Zajednica priznaje gradjansko sklapanje braka pred vlastima, i na kom toga supružnike poziva pred zajednicu na zavet vernosti jedno prema drugom.

Član 9.

Odnos Hrišćanske Nazarenske zajednice prema državnim vlastima, u saglasnosti sa sv. Pismom (Rimlj. 13,1 - 3) je takav, da su vlasti od Boga postavljena i zato naša zajednica smatra za svoju dužnost poštovati i pokoravati se vlastima koje vladaju, te se i moliti za njih (I.Tim. 2,1 - 4), i to u svemu što nije u suprotnosti sa Hristovom naukom.

Član 10.

Članovi Hrišćanske Nazarenske zajednice ne primaju oružje, ali su spremni služiti u Armiji i na po život najtežim i najopasnijim mestima. Vernost, iskrenost i poštenje jeste sveta dužnost svakog člana zajednice. Neupotrebljavaju reč zakletve na osnovu izričitih zapovesti Hristovih; "Ne ubij i ne kuni se ničim, nego neka Vaša reč bude što jeste "da", a što nije "ne" (Matej 5 Gl. 21,33 - 37).

Član 11.

Članovi Hrišćanske Nazarenske zajednice nisu obavezni ni na kakva materijalna davanja, ni na doprinos skupštini, već to mogu činiti po svojoj slobodnoj volji kao dar od srca (Kološ. 3,23),koji je namenjen za siromašnije članove.

Starešine i propovednici nemaju platu niti nagradu, već se službe vrši od srca, dobrovoljno i besplatno.

Član 12.

Hrišćanska Nazarenska zajednica je čisto verska ustanova za zadatkom da propovedanjem i tumačenjem Evandjelja odvrati ljude od greha i obreda ih Bogu kroz Isusa Hrista. Nema za cilj nagomilavanje zemaljskog imanja, već sabiranje duhovnog blaga na nebu (Mat. 6, 19 - 21).

Član 13.

Članovi Hrišćanske Nazarenske zajednice dužni su pohedjati sve Bogoslužbene sastanke, te nauku sv. Pisma sprovesti u svoj vlastiti život. (Jov. 1o,25)

Član 14.

Svi članovi zajednice imaju jednaka prava.

Primanje i kažnjavanje članova vrši skupština uz prisustvo starešina. Članovi pod kaznom nemaju prave udela u odlučivanjima zajednice.

Član 15.

Prestanak članstva: samovoljnim napuštanjem, isključenjem zbog neurednog i nepopravljivog života, i prekoračenjem Hristove nauke.

-3-

Član 16.

Starešinski sabor (Starešinska skupština) bira Starešinski Savet, koji ga predstavlja i zastupa u svim administrativnim
poslovima, dok je duhovna vlast nad svim crkvama skoncentrisana u
samom Gospodu Isusu Hristu, koji je glava crkve (Efesc. 5,23).

Član 17.

Hrišćanska Nazarenska zajednica je uverena da svojim ra-
dom i učenjem doprinosi da se odgoje dobri i čestiti ljudi, koji će
biti na korist bližnjima i državi.

Član 18.

Sva nepokretna i pokretna imovina pripada Hrišćanskoj Nazarenskoj zajednici u odnosnom mestu, a otuđivanje ili kupovinu imo-
vine vrši rukovodstvo zajednice u mestu preko ovlašćenog predstavni-
ka za imovinsko-pravne odnose na celoj teritoriji SFRJ, a uz saglas-
nost Starešinskog Saveta.

Član 19.

Izmene i dopune ovih osnovnih načela Hrišćanske Nazarenske zajednice u SFRJ može vršiti jedino starešinski sabor (skupština).

Član 2o.

Službeni pečat Hrišćanske Nazarenske zajednice imaće naziv:
" Hrišćanska Nazarenska Zajednica u SFRJ - Novi Sad ".

Član 21.

Stupanjem na snagu Osnovnih načela Hrišćanske Nazarenske
zajednice u SFRJ, prestaje važnost ranijeg administrativnog naziva
"Glavni izvršni odbor Hrišćanske Nazarenske zajednice u SFRJ" koji
je bio osnovan 3o.marta 1958.godine sa mandatnim rokom od godinu
dana.

Član 22.

Osnovna načela Hrišćanske Nazarenske Zajednice u SFRJ su
pretrešena i jednoglasno odobrena od starešinskog sabora (Starešin-
ske Skupštine) Hrišća nske Nazarenske zajednice u SFRJ, koji je odr-
žan 9.aprila 1966.g. u Zemunu od kada i stupa na snagu,a prve izmene
i dopune ovih osnovnih načela su usvojene na velikoj bratinskoj skupštini u Novom Sadu dana 18.maja 1991.godine.

U Novom Sadu, 18.maja 1991.god.

Starešinski sabor:
1. Pači Lajoš, s.r.
2. Nikolić Bogdan, s.r.
3. Gršić Steva, s.r.
4. Čikić Petar, s.r.
5. Murić Veljko, s.r.
6. Dudaš Janko, s.r.
7. Supek Miša, s.r.
8. Murtin Miša, s.r.
9. Varga Geza, s.r.
1o.Golubov Miloš, s.r.
11.Valjan Jon, s.r.
12.Petraš Peter, s.r.
13.Bilek Miša, s.r.
14.Getejanec Pavel, s.r.
15.Keresteš Janoš, s.r.
16.Molnar Ferenc, s.r.
17.Keresteš Laslo, s.r.
18.Hrubik Karlo, s.r.

Starešinski savet:
1. Pači Lajoš, s.r.
2. Nikolić Bogdan, s.r.
3. Gršić Steva, s.r.

M.P.

Za vernost obravka:

TRANSLATION:

CHRISTIAN NAZARENE COMMUNITY
IN THE SFRJ [SOCIALIST FEDERAL REPUBLIC OF
YUGOSLAVIA]
NOVI SAD
Valentina Vodnika street no. 12

BASIC ARTICLES
OF THE CHRISTIAN NAZARENE
COMMUNITY IN THE SFRJ

Article 1

The foundation of the Christian Nazarene Community is the Teaching of Christ, as expressed in Holy Scripture.

Article 2

The Christian Nazarene Community believes that its spiritual Head and High Priest is Jesus Christ Himself (1 Pet 5:4 and Heb 6:20), the fellowship consists of all members of both sexes, and on earth it is represented by its highest body, the Elders' Convention (Elders' Assembly).

Article 3

The Elders' Convention is comprised of all elders chosen by the members of Christian Nazarene congregations in the country, whose duty it is to concern themselves with religious life as a whole.

Article 4

Christian Nazarene congregations in some places are represented by servants (preachers) chosen by their members, who in addition to preaching the teaching of Christ also have a duty of care for the members of the local congregation.

Article 5

A Christian Nazarene congregation is completely autonomous in every respect, and independent of all other congregations in the country and abroad, although it enjoys fraternal bonds of faith with Nazarene brothers of all nations.

Article 6

Faith meetings are held publicly, open to all, in premises set aside for the purpose, where only those religious, moral and spiritual matters are studied which relate to the spiritual life of church members.

Meetings are held on Sundays in the morning and afternoon, and on one workday evening during the week.

Worship services consist of the [unaccompanied] singing of spiritual songs, reading and preaching of Holy Scripture, prayer and thanks to God.

Services are conducted by elders or servants (preachers).

Preaching is conducted in the languages of the Yugoslav peoples and minorities. All believers are equal in rights, regardless of their ethnic background.

Local congregations may organize religious instruction for the children of their members if needed.

Article 6a

The fellowship must show care to all members of the fellowship, in accordance with its Christian duties:

a) By organizing the collection of aid in the form of money, food items, clothes and footwear, and distributing these to the needy.

b) By constructing special residential buildings with multiple apartments and rooms for worship services, and selling lifetime usage rights of these exclusively to older believers who are members of the fellowship, at below market prices.

c) By constructing nursing homes for the elderly, sick and disabled.

Article 7

Acceptance into membership is conducted in the languages of the Yugoslav peoples and minorities, on the basis of the will of the individual, completely freely expressed, along with his testimony that he has undergone full repentance and conducts his life according to God's word.

Article 8

Religious rites are as follows: preaching the Word of God, prayer, singing spiritual songs, sharing the holy supper, baptism of adults, marriage and burial of the dead.

The fellowship recognizes civil marriage before the authorities; after that it calls the couple before the congregation to pledge their faithfulness to one another.

Article 9

The position of the Christian Nazarene community in regard to the state authorities, in accordance with Scripture (Rom. 13:1-3), is that government is ordained of God, and our community considers it a duty to respect and submit to the powers in authority and to pray to God for them (1 Tim. 2:1-4), and this in all matters which are not in opposition to the teaching of Christ.

Article 10

The members of the Christian Nazarene Community do not accept arms but are prepared to serve in the Army even in the most difficult and dangerous posts. Loyalty, honesty and integrity are the holy duty of every member of the church. They do not use the word 'oath', based on the explicit commands of Christ: 'But let your communication be, Yea, yea; Nay, nay'" (Mat. 5:21:33-37).

Article 11

Members of the Christian Nazarene Community are not compelled to any material giving, nor to contribute to the congregation, but may do so of their own free will as a gift from the heart (Col. 3:23), intended for poorer members.

Elders and preachers receive no wage nor recompense; they serve in the ministry from the heart, voluntarily and without pay.

Article 12

The Christian Nazarene Community is a purely religious institution, tasked with preaching and interpreting the Gospel, and in so doing to turn people from sin and towards God through Jesus Christ.

It has no ambition to accumulate earthly goods, but seeks to lay up spiritual treasures in heaven (Mat. 6:19-21).

Article 13

Members of the Christian Nazarene Community have a duty to attend all worship meetings and to apply the teaching of Holy Scripture in their own lives (Heb. 10:25).

Article 14

All members of the fellowship have equal rights.

Acceptance and discipline of members is conducted by the congregation in the presence of the elder/s.

Members under discipline have no right to participate in decision-making in the fellowship.

Article 15

Revocation of membership [is by]: voluntary withdrawal, exclusion for reasons of a disorderly and incorrigible life and violation of Christ's teaching.

Article 16

The Elders' Convention (Elder's Assembly) elects a Council of Elders, which represents it in all administrative affairs, while spiritual authority over all churches is concentrated in the Lord Jesus Christ himself, who is the Head of the Church (Eph. 5:23).

Article 17

The Christian Nazarene Community is convinced that its activity and teaching contributes to the nurture of good and upright people who will be of service to those close to them, and to the state.

Article 18

All movable and immovable property belongs to the Christian Nazarene fellowship in the town in question, while the sale and purchase of property is done by the leadership of the local congregation, through the authorized representative for legal and property matters for the whole territory of the SFRJ, with the agreement of the Council of Elders.

Article 19

Amendments and supplements to these basic articles of the Christian Nazarene Community in the SFRJ may only be made by the Elders' Convention (Assembly).

Article 20

The official stamp of the Christian Nazarene Community bears the title: "Hrišćanska Nazarenska Zajednica u SFRJ – Novi Sad."

Article 21

As the basic articles of the Christian Nazarene Community in the SFRJ enter into force, so the prior administrative title of "Glavni izvršni odbor Hrišćanske nazarenske zajednice u SFRJ" [Chief Executive Board of the Christian Nazarene Community in the SFRJ], which was founded on 30 March 1958 with a one-year mandate, is no longer applicable.

Article 22

The basic articles of the Christian Nazarene Community in the SFRJ were discussed and unanimously approved by the Elders' Convention (Elders' Assembly) of the Christian Nazarene Community in the SFRJ, held 9 April 1966 in Zemun, on which date it entered into force, and the first amendments and supplements to these basic articles have been approved at the general assembly of the brethren in Novi Sad 18 May 1991.

Novi Sad, 18 May 1991

Elders' Convention:

1. Lajoš Paći
2. Bogdan Nikolić
3. Steva Gršić
4. Petar Čikić
5. Veljko Murić
6. Janko Dudaš
7. Miša Supek
8. Miša Murtin
9. Geza Varga
10. Miloš Golubov
11. Jon Valjan
12. Peter Petraš
13. Miša Bilek
14. Pavel Getejanec
15. Janoš Keresteš
16. Ferenc Molnar
17. Laslo Keresteš
18. Karlo Hrubik

Council of Elders:

1. Lajoš Paći
2. Bogdan Nikolić
3. Steva Gršić

Authenticity of document confirmed by
[signature]

Conclusion

Nazarene beliefs originated with the theological leanings of Froehlich in the first twenty years of the emergence of the movement. Froelich succeeded in creating a third model against the two dominant models of the time—the Calvinist model, from which he himself originated, and the Anabaptist model, which he encountered later in life. His model was Anabaptist in terms of decisions of faith and in particular matters such the relationship between church and state, as well as in terms of practice, with the addition of Mennonite conscientious objection. The issue of adult baptism (and the fellowship of the saints) and the rejection of oath-taking and bearing of arms thus became the two dominant issues in the movement. The third issue, which only came somewhat later, regarding care for the elderly and poor, came about as a result of living in the local community, of the difficult living conditions in rural areas in the second half of the nineteenth century and the prevailing crisis of morals and loss of faith in the state church.

Froelich abandoned the state church over his belief that baptism was only for those able to autonomously testify to their faith in Christ (which excluded children), and accepted the common Baptist view that baptism was an external manifestation of belief. But Froelich "supplemented" this, too, with some distinctives of his own. Here the Nazarene movement displays its unique features in relation to other religious communities of similar provenance: the Nazarenes believe that baptism brings about sanctification, regeneration, and renewal in a person. This is why the Nazarenes insist on the maintenance of holiness in the everyday life of its members, and this is achieved through a "changed" life, but also through ongoing public confession and repentance of sin before the entire local congregation. The entire fellowship continues to support the individual in this by closely watching their behavior, their interaction, and their relationships, and any problems are immediately made public. If someone is not yet a member of the congregation and wishes to become one, they are observed over an extended period of time, whilst regularly attending all worship services in the capacity of a "friend."[261] The baptism of believing adults is a key distinctive of the Nazarene movement and is done by full immersion under water. Once the individual becomes a member of the congregation, they are a member of the "fellowship of the saints."

The Nazarenes do not as a rule believe in predestination,[262] rather they seek to witness to others through their deeds and their covenantal life, and this includes their children. The beliefs and practices of the parents have a great influence on the upbringing of their children. However the fact that the Nazarenes do not actively witness to their children has doubtless contributed to their numerical decline, especially during the severe persecution of the twentieth century, when all regimes in this region took an exceptionally negative attitude towards this religious community. The opportunity to join the fellowship of believers later in life was misused (from the Nazarene community's point of view) by some Nazarene elders in order to find an alternative solution to the issue of the military oath, the bearing of arms and military service.

Another very important distinctive of the Nazarenes is their refusal to take oaths, to bear arms or to take life, which probably

---

[261] In friendly conversation with a Nazarene elder, having expressed his faith in God according to Scripture, this author was told with a smile that he could join the community if he were to "attend" for at least three years and if in that period he "proved himself worthy" – then he might be put forward for baptism. After preparation for baptism and an interview with the local elders, at which the readiness of the candidate would be assessed, the actual act of baptism could be undertaken and thus he could become a member of the congregation. The process might last four years.

[262] The doctrine of predestination says that God has already determined those who will be saved, while all others will be judged for all sins, including the original, Adamic sin. Calvinist predestination is distinct in that Calvinists believe that God has predestined not only those who are to be saved (for He has known in advance that they will repent and believe), but also those who are to be punished. Those who are to be saved are also referred to as "the elect." According to this idea, God will not allow anyone to perish but will help them to persevere in their faith in spite of persecution and even death. If a person should fall away and deny the faith, they are deemed never to have been "predestined" for salvation, to never have been a believer, nor elected for eternal life.

has its origins in Froelich's early contacts with Mennonites. Froelich's abandonment of the state Calvinist church also meant the abandonment of state repression against those who believed differently, including Catholics and Anabaptists, which had been going on in the same Canton of Zürich since the time of John Calvin and his followers. This pacifist stance brought much evil and tribulation upon the Nazarenes in those states that had a state religion (Austro-Hungary, Serbia, the kingdom of SCS/Yugoslavia), which can best be seen in the example of Serbia and the Serbian Orthodox Church in the nineteenth and twentieth centuries. Socialist Yugoslavia had a different problem with the Nazarenes—their rejection of the collectivization of land and property in Vojvodina in the post-war period, voting in elections, membership of organizations such as the People's Front and trade unions, and in general their (non)conformance to the new state system, popularly referred to at the time as the "organized people." Socialist Yugoslavia, ever fearing for its security, and despite being familiar with the Nazarenes from the Partisan struggle, in which individual Nazarenes had so distinguished themselves in non-combatant roles that they had even received medals and decorations, maintained the appearance of an evenhanded and measured policy towards all conscientious objectors (including political ones), a policy which included the Goli Otok penal colony, party purges in the army and police, as well as of nationalists such as Gotovac and General Tuđman and many others, and therefore the Nazarenes too. All conscientious objectors were arrested and tried and served long prison terms. The Jehovah's Witnesses and, especially in the first fifteen years or so, the Seventh-Day Adventists, fared no better. The regime equated conscientious objection virtually with high treason.

The latter issue (arms and oath-swearing) led to an eventual schism in the movement. In the period between the two world wars, a division emerged between the "new" and the "old" Nazarenes, and then also, after the Second World War, into the "positive," the "negative," the "loyal" etc. The Nazarene movement invested a great deal of effort, with help from abroad, to overcome both schisms, although seemingly the lines of division can still be seen, especially when discussing the issues with believers on both sides. As far as the authorities are concerned, though, there is only one organization, since the Nazarenes never formalized their internal divisions.

The 1991 articles of faith introduced a number of changes. In addition to a change in the name and registered office of the organization, as well the identity of those authorized to represent it before the state, there were also some changes in the approach to certain issues. The new regulations introduced religious instruction for the children of believers, i.e. Nazarene congregation members, to be held locally. This was a significant departure and change in attitude with regard to the issue of witnessing to one's own children and was indicative of efforts by the Nazarenes to save their movement from likely extinction within a few generations. The pressing need for a change in practices led, among other things, to this significant change in 1991.

According to available information, just in Vojvodina in the late nineteenth century there were more than 10,000 Nazarenes. Data collected by the Gendarmerie in 1925 spoke of more than 16,000 Nazarenes in the kingdom,[263] the state security service also talked of more than 15,000 in Yugoslavia in the 1950s, whereas the last available data suggest 4,000 Nazarenes at most on both sides (positive and negative). Pavle Božić, one of the last Nazarenes to have served prison time for conscientious objection believes that there are no more than two thousand people, in both camps.

The third significant belief and practice of the Nazarenes has been very strongly expressed since the earliest days of the movement in the south of the kingdom of Hungary and later in Serbia – charity towards poor and disadvantaged members of the congregation, and sometimes outside their own circle, too. This issue has been actively addressed in all their statements of faith and enactments from 1919 to the present day. It has been emphasized in every set of rules that the Nazarenes have published, and observation of local congregations reveals how believers have practiced this. In the beginning it involved a small storeroom, close to hand on the church premises,

---

[263] The data relate only to the Belgrade, Podunavlje and Srem districts. A total of 7,900 individuals were of Serbian nationality.

containing the most essential items like heating fuel, flour etc. Of the two rooms in a church building the smaller of the two would be set aside for this purpose, while the larger would be used for worship services. The Nazarenes made voluntary contributions which went into a support fund to help those in need. By joining in shared community "bees" [*moba*] and other ways of helping households in the villages in which they lived, the Nazarenes became something of a model for rural reform, of just the kind some authors were advocating. Their concern for those in need also made them candidates for appropriation by the socialist movement, which was on the rise at that time. In the 1991 rules, the Nazarenes embarked on a new venture in this area with the decision to establish a retirement home for its believers (separate ones for men and women).

In addition to these three basic features of Nazarene belief (adult baptism with regeneration, refusal to swear oaths or bear arms and concern for the poor), which are characteristic of and fairly unique to this movement, we can also mention some other points:

- devotion to Scripture
- the demand for consecrated living on the part of members
- partial rejection of education, especially theological (because of its close ties with the state)
- separation from the world and the insular nature of the community
- the family as the nucleus of the movement
- solidarity in good and evil

Since its emergence in the 1840s the Nazarene movement has brought about many significant changes on the religious stages of Austro-Hungary and Serbia, later Yugoslavia. Their rejection of church-state ties, their dedication to Scripture, their denial of worldly pleasures and their constant persecution are characteristics of the Nazarene movement which make it so unique in this region that it is strange that only one book and just a handful of papers have been published on the subject since the 1950s. Although it would not be right to say that the Nazarenes willingly suffered for their theological

commitments and beliefs, the fact is that they were constantly persecuted for them by all regimes in all periods up until the late 1990s,
even under socialism, where intolerance on the part of the national
churches towards the Nazarenes could not make itself known to the
extent it did in previous times.

In the nearly two centuries since their emergence, and the emergence of the modern state of Serbia, the Nazarene movement has
been the most persecuted religious community in this region.

The persecution of the Nazarenes, the dozens shot and killed,
the thousands convicted and the countless years spent in the jails of
a modern and a supposedly democratic state need to be made public
knowledge so that nothing like it can happen again. The story of
the Nazarenes is a story of a people for whom the Scriptures and its
Gospel message were of greater importance than the things of this
world. With their triumphs and trials, their moral victories and their
theological errors, the elegance of their simplicity and the beauty
of their fellowship, the Nazarenes lived among us (and despite us),
believing as they believed, devoted to the biblical message of salvation and the commandments of Jesus Christ.

Figure 1 – Statement of Faith

This document is used in some Nazarene congregations as the
latest statement of faith, although it is actually a translation from
the English language of the Apostolic Christian Church from the
United States, with whom the Nazarenes in Serbia maintain a sporadic relationship.

The Christian Nazarene Community
WE BELIEVE(Statement of Faith)
Translated from: Church Directory Apostolic Christian Churches of America, 1987.
(Translation and most important amendments made by Z. Lisulov, 1990)[264]

1. We believe that the Bible is inspired by God, that it is the complete and inerrant Word of God. 2 Tim. 3:16; 2 Pet. 1:21; Rev. 22:18-19.

2. We believe that there is one God, who has no beginning nor has He an end. Rev. 1:8; Mic. 5:2.

3. We believe that God is a trinity – Father, Son and Holy Spirit. Matt. 28:19; 2 Cor. 13:13.

4. We believe that Jesus Christ is God incarnate. He was born of a virgin. He lived a sinless life. He died on a cross among sinners and His shed blood is a ransom for our sins. John 20:28; Is. 9:6-7, Heb. 1:1-9; Is. 7:14; Matt. 1:23; Heb. 7:25; 1 John 2:2; 2 Cor. 5:21; Eph. 2:13-20.

5. We believe in his bodily resurrection, that he was raised to the right hand of the Father and that he will personally come to the earth again in power and glory. 1 Cor. 15:4-7; Heb. 7:25; 1 John 2:2; Matt. 25:31; Acts 1:9-11.

6. We believe that God's judgment awaits all those who sin and are lost, but God does not wish that anyone would be lost. Rom. 3:10-23; 2 Pet. 3:7-9.

7. We believe that sinners can find salvation if they repent before God and believe in Jesus Christ. Acts 2:38, 20:21; Rom. 10:8-13.

8. We believe that saving faith will bring fruit through renewal by the Holy Spirit and the Word of God, without which there is no salvation. John 1:12-13, 3:6-8.

---

[264] Since this is not a direct translation of the English version, we have translated it back from Serbian for this edition so that the reader can see the adaptations that the Nazarenes in Serbia have made (t/n).

9. We believe in the baptism of the Holy Spirit who, having come to abide in the believer, gives him strength to live a godly life in spiritual unity with Christ. John 1:33; Acts 8:16-17; Rom. 8:2-17; John 12:23; 1 Cor. 12:13; Eph. 5:20.

10. We believe that both the saved and the lost will be resurrected; the saved unto eternal life, the lost unto eternal destruction. John 5:28-29.

11. We believe that we should speak the truth in all circumstances, and that we should not swear oaths, in submission to the command of Christ: "Swear not at all;... But let your communication be, Yea, yea; Nay, nay." Matt. 5:34-37; Jam. 5:12.

12. We believe that governments have been appointed by God to uphold law and order and prevent evil deeds Governments should therefore be supported and submitted to. Laws and regulations – be they local, state or national – should be obeyed, except when in doing so we would violate a command of God. The call to military service should likewise be honored, and received with humility, but with a biblical limitation to non-combatant roles, as Jesus Christ taught us: "Love your enemies, bless them that curse you, do good to them that hate you, and pray for them which persecute you." Matt. 5:44; Rom. 13:1-10; 1 Pet. 2:13-14; Matt. 22:21.

13. We believe that God commands all people now to repent and be baptized, and that immersion is the manner of baptism that is in accordance with Scripture. However, we believe the baptism may only be performed on those who have believed in Christ and who have been transformed by Him, who have truly died to sin and experienced new spiritual birth. Matt. 3:5-8, 28:19-20; John 3:3; Acts 2:37-38, 26:20; Rom. 6:1-11; Acts 3:19; 2 Cor. 5:17.

14. We believe in the administration of discipline on the part of the church in order to respond to the presence of sin in the lives of church members. 1 Cor. 5:1-13; 2 Cor. 2:5-11;

5:14-18; Gal. 6:1; 2 Thess. 3:6, 14-15; Matt. 18:15-17; Heb. 10:24-25.

15. We believe that the Great Commission of our Lord Jesus Christ is a call to all of us, for His sake, who loved us and gave himself for us, to yield all our personal desires and assets and to whole-heartedly accept the ministry of taking the proclamation of the gospel "into all the world, and to every creature." Matt. 28:19-20; Acts 1:8; Mark 16:16; Luke 24:47; 2 Cor. 5:18; Luke 14:26-27.

16. We believe that the gift of eternal life is the permanent possession of every true disciple of Jesus Christ, and that nothing and no-one can separate him from that; however there is a real possibility that the true believer, once saved, may not remain in the faith and may return to sin, and thus lose the eternal life he once possessed. 1 John 5:11-13; Rom. 8:35-39; Acts 14:22; 1 Tim. 4:1; John 15:1-7; Heb. 3:6, 12-13; Rom. 6:16. Compare John 3:36; 2 Pet. 2:22; Matt. 25:24-30; Mark 13:13; 1 Cor. 9:27, 10:1-12; 1 Tim. 1:18-20; Rev. 2:10, 3:5, 16, 21.

17. We believe that "the bread and the wine of the Holy Supper symbolize the body and blood of Christ." The Holy Supper is served to members only after self-examination. 1 Cor. 10:16, 11:17, 32.

18. We believe that sisters in the Lord wear a shawl or head covering during prayer or worship as a symbol of their submission to God's command at the time of Creation. 1 Cor. 11:1-6.

WE BELIEVE

For they that are after the flesh do mind the things of the flesh; but they that are after the Spirit the things of the Spirit. For to be carnally minded is death; but to be spiritually minded is life and peace. Rom. 8:5-6.

SOURCES

Archive material

Serbia and Montenegro Archive
- Fond 14, fascikla 3, jedinica opisa 10
  - 3-1100 dated 7 Nov 1929, broj 8081/1929.
  - 15407/II dated 24 Jan 1930.
  - May 1940 *o Hrišćanskoj zajednici slobodne braće*
- Fond/faksimil broj: 144-32-324 and 42-389
- Fond 63, fascikla 144
  - Pov. M. broj 8 dated 25 Jan 1923
  - Broj 25320/1924
  - Broj 39684 dated 16 Apr 1925
  - Broj 4859/25 dated 25 Apr 1925
  - Pov. broj 104/1925 dated 22 Jun 1925
  - Pov. broj 380/1925 dated 30 Aug 1925
  - Pov. broj 528/1925 dated 14 Sep 1925
  - Broj 19207/II, dated 6 Mar 1926
  - Broj 6460/236 dated 18 Feb 1927
  - Broj 16919 dated 30 Dec 1927
  - D. Z. broj 1150 dated 10 Feb 1928
  - Broj 3236 dated 9 Mar 1928
  - Broj 157-B dated 20 Mar 1929
  - Broj 8898/29 dated 27 Apr 1929
  - V. broj 16106/29 – XV
  - S. broj 10238 dated 1 Jun 1929
  - V. broj 14451/29-XV dated 11 Jul 1929

- ○ Broj 8850 dated 11 Jul 1929
- ○ Broj 6261 dated 11 Jul 1929
- ○ Broj 11296 dated 12 Jul 1929
- ○ S. broj 869 dated 13 Jul 1929
- ○ Pov. broj 1215 dated 14 Jul 1929
- ○ S. broj 272 dated 15 Jul 1929
- ○ J. B. broj 1283 dated 16 Jul 1929
- ○ S. broj 991 dated 17 Jul 1929
- ○ S. broj 504 dated 18 Jul 1929
- ○ S. broj 489 dated 19 Jul 1929
- ○ S. broj 514 dated 24 Jul 1929
- ○ K. broj 4983 dated 6 Aug 1929
- ○ J. B. broj 1865 dated 10 Aug 1929
- ○ S. broj 14816 dated 12 Aug 1929
- ○ J. B. broj 299 dated 13 Aug 1929
- ○ Telegram (unnumbered) dated 15 Aug 1929 from Skoplje
- ○ J. B. broj 5975 dated 15 Aug 1929
- ○ Broj 920 pov./24 dated 10 Sep 1929
- ○ Broj K. 32/zap. – 1931 dated 4/17 Feb 1931
- ○ Broj 21616/31-XV
- ○ Pov. I broj 1647 dated 24 Jan 1938

Danube Banovina Archive

- - Fond 126 II
  - ○ D. Z. broj 7976 dated 1 Oct 1926
  - ○ 65529/1931
  - ○ 6145/1931 Pov. K. Broj: 278/30 dated 13 Jan 1931.
  - ○ 23430/930
  - ○ 44078/930
  - ○ 18374/930
  - ○ 18881/930
  - ○ 38026/930
  - ○ 6145/931, dopis 39292 dated 31 Dec 1935. godine.

Vojvodina Archive

- F 198/I
  - ○ Informacija Republičke komisije za mart 1961. godine
  - ○ kutija 879. Informacija o delatnosti verskih zajednica Pokrajinske komisije za verska pitanja, Pov. Br. 35 dated 8 Apr 1968.
  - ○ kutija 879. Bilten Savezne komisije za verska pitanja, 29 Mar 1965
  - ○ kutija 879. Bilten Savezne komisije za verska pitanja, 12 Oct 1966
  - ○ kutija 879. Informator o delatnosti verskih zajednica.
  - ○ kutija 877. Savezna komisija za verska pitanja, broj 100/1.
  - ○ kutija 877. 100/1 dated 3 Apr 1967

Serbian National Archive

- ○ Ministarstvo prosvete i crkvenih dela, B-3227, br. 83, 23 Feb 1895
- ○ Zemaljska komisija za verske poslove NRS, G-21, f-14.
- ○ Komisija za verska pitanja NR Srbije, broj 1109, dated 11 Nov 1953
- ○ Komisija za verska pitanja NR Srbije, broj 369 dated 6 Okt 1959
- ○ Komisija za verska pitanja NR Srbije, br 11/1-61.

Pančevo Archive

- Microfilm, rolna 13B
  - ○ Protokol rođenih nazarena 1875-1895.
  - ○ Protokol umrlih nazarena 1876-1893.
  - ○ Protokol venčanih nazarena za 1896.

Archive of the Serbian Academy of Science and Arts

- ○ Folio broj 9830

War Resisters International archive, International Institute of Social History, Amsterdam, The Netherlands
Binder 420
- o   Verzeichnis
- o   Nazarenes imprisoned in Jugo-slavia
- o   Letter to General Pera Zhivkovitch from 29th November 1930
- o   Letter from H. Ruhnam Brown to a "Dear Friend" from 19th November 1930
- o   War resisters in Jugo-slavia: 72 Nazarenes sentenced to 10 years' imprisonment
- o   Koca Popovich to Arl Tatum, letter from 31 October 1958

Archive of the British and International Bible Society, Cambridge University Library, Cambridge, Great Britain
- o   Annual Reports for 1870, 1871, 1877, 1889, 1898, 1922, 1929, 1935 (parts relating to Southern Hungary, Serbia, and later Yugoslavia)
- o   Monthly Reporter

Interviews and correspondence
- o   Birviš, Aleksandar – Belgrade (1998, 1999)
- o   Božić, Pavle – Nova Pazova (1999)
- o   Čizmanski, Miroslav – Bački Petrovac (1999, 2002)
- o   Grulović, Goran – Beška (2011)
- o   Lehn, John, United States (1997)
- o   Lehotsky, Rut – Novi Sad (1999, 2002, 2003)
- o   Marti, Peter, Switzerland (1999)
- o   Ott, Bernhard, Switzerland (1998, 1999, 2011, 2012)
- o   Otto, Harold, Canada (2004, 2005, 2006)

Cited Literature

1. "A Voice from Servia." 1880. *Bible Society Monthly Report.* Vol X, No. 67. December 1, 1880.
2. Alder, Garfield. 1976. *Die Tauf- und Kirchenfrage in Leben und Lehre des Samuel Heinrich Fröhlich, VDM, von Brugg 1803-1857.* Bern. Herbert Lang.
3. Aleksić, Vlad. 1925. "Nazarenstvo i g. Svet. Tornjanski učitelj-upravitelj", *Vesnik,* br. 4.6
4. Aleksov, Bojan. 1999. "The Dynamics of Extinction: The Nazarene Religious Community in Yugoslavia after 1945." MA thesis. Budapest. Central European University.
5. _____. 2006. *Religious Dissent between the Modern and the National: Nazarenes in Hungary and Serbia 1850-1914.* Wiesbaden. Harrassowitz Verlag.
6. _____. 2010. *Nazareni među Srbima.* Beograd. Zavod za udžbenike.
7. "Austria, empire of." 1971. *Encyclopedia Britannica.*
8. Bächtold, Theodor. 1970. "Johann Gerhard Oncken and Baptist Beginnings in Switzerland." BDiv thesis. Rüschlikon, Switzerland. Baptist Theological Seminary.
9. *Biblija ili Sveto pismo Staroga i Novoga zavjeta.* 2001. Beograd. Jugoslovensko biblijsko društvo.
10. Bjelajac, Branko. 2001. "O istoričnosti malih verskih zajednica u Srbiji", *Udar na verske slobode,* zbornik priredili Branko Bjelajac i Dane Vidović, Beograd. Alfa i omega.
11. _____. 2002. "Protestantism in Serbia." *Religion, State and Society.* Vol. 30. No. 3.
12. _____. 2003. *Protestantizam u Srbiji,* I deo. Beograd. Alfa i omega.
13. _____. 2010. *Protestantizam u Srbiji,* II deo. Beograd. Soteria.
14. Birviš, Aleksandar. 2001. "Duhovna kretanja manjeg zahvata u našim krajevima", *Religije Balkana: susreti i prožimanja.* Priredili Milan Vukomanović i Marinko Vučinić. Beograd. Beogradska otvorena škola.

15. _____. 2010. "Tu smo negde bili i mi", uvodnik, *Protestantizam u Srbiji 2*. Beograd. Soteria.

16. Bohus. Karl. 1897. *"Halte was du host." Zur Aufklärung der evangelischen Christen gegenüber den Irrthümern der Nazarener*. Pancsova. Druck v. Brüder Jovanović.

17. Branković, Tomislav.1986. *Politički aspekti učenja i delovanja verskih sekti u SFRJ*. Magistarski rad. Beograd. Fakultet političkih nauka.

18. _____. 1996. "Protestantske verske zajednice u Srbiji." *Gledišta* 3-4.

19. _____. 2006. *Protestantske zajednice u Jugoslaviji 1945-1991: društveni i politički aspekti delovanja*. Niš. JUNIR.

20. Brock, Peter. 1980. "The Nonresistance of the Hungarian Nazarenes to 1914", *Mennonite Quarterly Review*, Vol. 54, No. 1.

21. _____. 1983. "Some Materials on Nazarene Conscientious Objectors in Nineteenth-Century Hungary", *Mennonite Quarterly Review*, Vol. 57, No. 1.

22. _____. 1991. *Freedom from Violence*. Toronto. University of Toronto Press.

23. Buta, Jovan. 1928. "Rascep među nazarenima", *Glas Crkve*. Broj VI. 1-3.

24. Bučar, Franjo. 1910. *Povijest hrvatske protestantske književnosti za reformacije*. Zagreb. Matica Hrvatska.

25. *Cambridge History of the Bible, the*. 1963. Cambridge. University Press.

26. Cerović, Ljubivoje. 1997. *Srbi u Slovačkoj*. Ministarstvo Republike Srbije za veze sa Srbima izvan Srbije.

27. Clark, Elmer. 1949. *The Small Sects in America*. New York. Abingdon/Cokesbury Press.

28. *Conscientious Objection: The Situation in Yugoslavia*. 1987. Religion in Communist Lands. Vol 15, No. 3 (Winter).

29. *Crkva – kalendar SPC za 1939. godinu*. 1939. Beograd. Sveti arhijerejski sinod SPC.

30. Crnković, Nikola. 1985. "Protestantizam u južno-slavenskim zemljama", u Boisett *Protestanitzam, kratka povijest.* Zagreb. Kršćanska sadašnjost.

31. *Cronicle of the Hutterian Brethren, the.* Volume I. 1987. Rifton, USA. Plough Publishing House.

32. Cvitković, Ivan. 1989. *Savez komunista i religija.* Sarajevo. NIŠRO Oslobođenje.

33. Czako, Ambrose. 1925. *The Future of Protestantism: With Special Reference to South-Eastern Europe,* London, George Allen & Unwin Ltd.

34. Ćirković, Sima. 1997. "Srbi i rani protestantizam". *Rabotnici, vojnici, duhovnici: Društva srednjevekovnog Balkana.* Ed. Vlastimil Đokić. Beograd. Equilibrium.

35. Ćorović, Vladimir. 1999. *Istorija Srba.* Niš. Zograf.

36. Daniel, David. 1992. "Hungary". *The Early Reformation in Europe.* Andrew Pettegree ed. Cambridge, UK. Cambridge University Press.

37. Dimić, Paja. 1870. "O nazoreima". *Pastir, list za nauku i književnost duhovnog sadržaja.* Vol III. Beograd.

38. Dimić, Pavle. 1880. *O nazarenima, preštampano sa dopunom iz Pastira.* Velika Kikinda. Izdanje knjižare Jovana Radaka.

39. Dimitrijević, Vladimir. 1894/1. *Nazarenstvo: njegova istorija i suština.* Novi Sad.

40. _____. 1894/2. "Obred pri krštenju i još neki drugi običaju nazarenski", *Srpski Sion,* god 4, broj 48, od 27.11.

41. _____. 1903/1. *"Pobožni"- rasprava.* Budimpešta. Srpska štamparija J. Krnjca.

42. _____. 1903/2. *U nazarenskoj skupštini.* Budimpešta. Štamparija Srpskih novosti.

43. Dinić-Knežević, Dušanka. 1962-3. "Prilog proučavanju pokreta Jovana Nenada". *Godišnjak Filozofskog fakulteta u Novom Sadu.* Knjiga 7. Novi Sad. Filozofski fakultet.

44. Draganović, Krunoslav. 1938. "Izvješće apostolskog vizitatora Petra Masarechija o prilikama katol. naroda u

Bugarskoj, Srbiji, Srijemu, Slavoniji i Bosni g. 1623. i 1624." *Starine XXXIX*, Zagreb, JAZU.

45. Đ.S.R. 1958. "Gavrilo Svetogorac". *Enciklopedija Jugoslavije III tom*. Zagreb. Leksikografski zavod FNRJ.

46. Đorđević, Sanja. 1996. *Hrišćanska nazarenska zajednica u Zemunu*. Neobjavljen diplomski rad. Odeljenje za etnologiju i antropologiju Filozofskog fakulteta u Beogradu.

47. _____. 2003. *Hrišćanska nazarenska zajednica*. Niš. Junir-Punta.

48. Đorđić, Petar. 1971. *Istorija srpske ćirilice*. Beograd. Zavod za izdavanje udžbenika.

49. Đurić-Milovanović, Aleksandra i drugi. 2011. *Rumunske verske zajednice u Banatu: prilog proučavanju multikonfesionalnosti Vojvodine*. Vršac. Visoka škola strukovnih studija za obrazovanje vaspitača "Mihailo Palov".

50. Eotvos, Karoly. 1997. *The Nazarenes*. Rewritten from the 1908 original, translated by Perry A. Klopfenstein. Fort Scott, Kansas, USA. Sekan Publications.

51. Erofeyev, Victor. 2010. "The Secret of Leo Tolstoy". *The New York Times*. November 19, 2010.

52. E.S. 1939. "Četiri sekte ili pogrešna verska učenja kojih naš narod treba da se čuva" *Crkva – kalendar SPC za 1939. godinu*. Beograd. Sveti arhijerejski sabor SPC.

53. Filozof, Konstantin. 1970. "Život despota Stefana Lazarevića". *Stara srpska književnost*. Novi Sad. Matica srpska.

54. Flere, Sergej i drugi. 1986. *Male verske zajednice u Vojvodini*. Novi Sad. Institut društvenih i pravnih nauka.

55. Friedmann, Robert. 1961. *Hutterite Studies*. Editor Harold Bender. Goshen, USA. Mennonite Historical Society.

56. Fröhlich, S. H. 1978. *Meditations on the Epistle to the Hebrews*. Writings of S.H. Froechlich. Illinois, USA. Apostolic Christian Publications.

57. Gardašević, B. 1971. "Organizaciono ustrojstvo i zakono-davstvo pravoslavne crkve između dva svetska rata", *SPC: 1920-1970*. Beograd. Srpska pravoslavna crkva.

58. Glišić, Venceslav. 1969. "Zločini nacista i kvislinga u Beogradu 1941-1944." *Godišnjak grada Beograda*, broj XVI.

59. Gnjatović, Dragana dr. 2010. "Zemljoradničke kreditne zadruge: prve institucije za finansiranje razvoja poljop-rivrede u Srbiji". *Bankarstvo 3-4*. Beograd.

60. Golubić, Mirko. 1970. *Istorija hrišćanske crkve*. Beograd. Adventistička viša teološka škola.

61. Graham, John W. 1992. *Conscription and Conscience*. London. George Allan and Unwin.

62. Grujić, Rad. M. 1931. "Jedan papski inkvizitor 15. Veka u Vojvodini". *Glasnik istorijskog društva u Novom Sadu*. Knjiga 4, sveska 3. Sremski Karlovci.

63. Grulich, Rudolf. 1983. "The Small Religious Communities of Yugoslavia". *Occasional Papers on Religion in Eastern Europe*. Vol.3, No. 6.

64. Hadži, Kosta dr. 1896. "Nazarenstvo kao socijalna pojava". *Budućnost*. Broj 19.

65. "Hadžija". 1936. *Nazareni*. Beograd. Štamparija Živka Madžarevića.

66. *Historical Catalogue of the Printed Editions of Holy Scripture, in the Library of the British and Foreign Bible Society*. 1963. New York. Kraus Reprint Corporation.

67. Horak, Josip dr. 1970. "Protestantizam i ekumenizam". *Verske zajednice u Jugoslaviji*. Zagreb. NIP Binoza.

68. Horvat, Rudolf. 2000. *Srijem, naselja i stanovništvo*. Slavonski brod. Hrvatski institut za povijest.

69. Hrizostom, episkop. 1991. *Tihi glas: besede i članci*. Požarevac. Eparhijski upravni odbor.

70. Hutten, Kurt. 1967. *Iron Curtain Christians: The Church in the Communist Countries Today*. Translated by Walter G. Tillmans. Minneapolis, USA. Augsburg Publishing House.

71. Ilić, Sava. 1925. "Nazarenstvo", *Vesnik*, br. 2. 10. oktobra.
72. *Istorija srpskog naroda*. 1906. Knjiga II. Beograd. Srpska književna zadruga.
73. Ivić, Aleksa. 1914. *Istorija Srba u Ugarskoj, od pada Smedereva do seobe pod Čarnojevićem (1459-1690)*. Zagreb. Privrednikova knjižara.
74. _____. 1929. *Istorija Srba u Vojvodini, od najstarijih vremena do osnivanja Potisko-Pomoriške granice (1703)*. Novi Sad. Matica srpska.
75. Ivić, Pavle. 1971. *Srpski narod i njegov jezik*. Beograd. Srpska književna zadruga.
76. Jambrek, Stanko. 1999. *Hrvatski protestantski pokret XVI i XVII stoljeća*. Zaprešić. Matica Hrvatska Zaprešić.
77. _____. 2007. "Pentekostni pokret u Hrvatskoj 1907-2007". *Kairos* broj 2. Zagreb.
78. Janjić, Vojislav. 1924. "Versko pitanje u našoj zemlji". Beograd. *Politika* 5.1.1924.
79. Jeftić, Miroljub. 1990. "Vojna obaveza i male verske zajednice", *Vojno-politički informator*. Broj 3.
80. Jireček, J. 1885. *Duchovni styky Cechuv a Maďaruv za XIV a XV veku*, C.C.M.
81. Jovanović, Radosav. 1910. *Pokret pod carem Jovanom 'Nenadom' i politički problem postanka Austrije kao velike sile*. Doctor thesis – unpublished manuscript. Beograd. Arhiv SANU, folio 9830.
82. *Južnoslovenski filolog*. Knjiga 6. 1927. Beograd.
83. Kabiljo-Šutić, Simha. 1989. *Posrednici dveju kultura: studija o srpsko-engleskim književnim i kulturnim vezama*. Beograd. Institut za književnost i umetnost.
84. *Karakter i rad Đure Daničića*. 1923. Novi Sad. Matica srpska.
85. Kašanin, Milan. 1966. "Sudbine i ljudi". *Letopis Matice srpske*. Knjiga 398, sv. 2-3.
86. Kàtona, Stephano. 1872. *Historia pragmatica Hungariae XII*, Budae.

87. Kilgour, R. 1939. *The Bible throughout the World*. London. World Dominion Press.
88. Klaić, Vjekoslav. 1980. *Povijest Hrvata, knjiga 5*. Zagreb. Nakladni zavod MH.
89. Klem. F. 1952. "Yugoslavia". *European Baptists Today*. Edited by J.D. Frank. Nashville, USA. Broadman Press.
90. Knežević, R. 2001. *Pregled povijesti baptizma na hrvatskom prostoru*. Zagreb. Savez baptističkih crkava u Republici Hrvatskoj – Baptistički institut.
91. Kojić, I.M. 1906. "Subotinački nazareni", *Vesnik Srpske crkve*, godina XVII, avgust 1906.
92. Korać, Stanko. 1982. *Književno delo S. Matavulja*. Beograd. SKZ.
93. Kraljik, Vladimir. 1995. *Ekklesia sada*. Unpublished undergraduate final dissertation. Novi Sad. Biblijsko-bogoslovski centar "Logos".
94. Kuburić, Zorica. 2011. *Verske zajednice u Srbiji i verska distanca*. Novi Sad. Centar za empirijska istraživanja religije.
95. Kušej, Rado dr. 1922. *Verska anketa u Beogradu i njeni zaključci: S kritičnim primedbama i praktičnim predlozima za popravljanje materijalnoga položaja svećenstva*. Ljubljana. Author's edition.
96. Kuzmič, Peter. 1983. *Vuk-Daničićevo Sveto Pismo i Biblijska Društva na južnoslovenskom tlu u XIX stoljeću*. Zagreb. Kršćanska sadašnjost.
97. Lanović, dr. Mihajlo. 1920. *Izvestiteljev predlog Zakona o međuverskim odnosima u Kraljevstvu SHS*, Beograd.
98. Lebl, Arpad dr. 1963. *Politički lik Vase Stajića: izabrani ideološki i politički spisi*. Novi Sad. Progres.
99. Leđenac, Maja i Jelica Nikolić. 2011. "Male verske zajednice u Vojvodini: bajka o verskim slobodama". *Dijalozi vojvođanskih kultura*. Beograd. EU delegation in Serbia.
100. Lilić, Stevan i Kovačević-Vučo, Biljana. 2001. *Prigovor savesti*. Beograd. Jugoslovenski komitet pravnika za ljudska prava.

101. Lončar, Dušan. 1981. "Uticaj verskih zajednica i kultura u SAP Vojvodini". *Savremenost* 11, br. 9/10.

102. Lukić, Branko. 1984. *Početak nazarenstva u Srbiji: kako je preneta vera preko Milana Luke Lukića u Donju Srbiju.* Unpublished manuscript.

103. Makaji, Jakov. 1975. *Istorijat i nauka nazarena.* Undergraduate final dissertation – unpublished manuscript. Zagreb. Biblijsko-teološki institut.

104. Makenzi, F. 1892. *Radi opravdanja ili objašnjenja svega što se odnosi na nedeljnu školu za hrišćansku nauku u Sali mira na Englezovcu.* Beograd. B.i.

105. Makovický, Dušan. 1896. *Nazarénové v Uhrách,* Praha. Knihtiskarna B. Grunda a V. Svatoné na Král. Vinohradech.

106. Maksimović, Jovan. 1911. *Zmajevo nazarenstvo.* Beograd. Sava Radenković i Brat

107. Malušev, Jovan. 1887. "O nazarenima". *Glas istine*, br. 24.

108. Maričić, Slobodan. 1995. *Folksdojčeri u Jugoslaviji: susedi, dželati, žrtve.* Beograd. Connect + Media Marketing International.

109. Märki, Albert. 1995. *Die Gründung der Gemeinschaft Evangelisch Taufgesinter.* B.i.

110. Marković, Slobodan. 2006. *Grof Čedomilj Mijatović: Viktorijanac među Srbima.* Beograd. Pravni fakultet Univerziteta u Beogradu i AIZ Dosije.

111. Marković, Živa. 1996. *Despot Stefan Lazarević.* Despotovac. Narodna biblioteka "Resavska škola".

112. Markovski, Venko. 1984. *Goli otok: The Island of Death. A Diary in Letters.* Boulder, Colorado, USA. Social Science Monographs.

113. Matić, S. 1934. "Pismo Gavrilovo o Luteru (Petstogodišnjica Gavrilovog pisma)". *Bogoslovlje.* Broj 9. Sveska 1.

114. Mayer, F.E. 1958. *The Religious Bodies of America.* 3rd edition. Saint Louis, USA. Concordia Publishing House.

115. Mead, Frank. 1988. *Handbook of Denominations in the United States.* 8th edition. Nashville, USA. Abingdon Press.
116. Medaković, Dejan. 1958. *Grafika srpskih štampanih knjiga XV-XVII veka.* Beograd. Srpska akademija nauka.
117. Mijatović, Čedomilj. 1895. "†Fransis H. Makenzije", *Male novine*, Beograd, 5.9.1895
118. _____. 1898. "Predgovor prevodiočev", *Komentari k Jevanđeljima*, from the foreword by David Braun, Novi Sad, Štamparija Đorđa Ivkovića.
119. Mijatovich, Chedomille Count. 1917. *The Memoirs of a Balkan Diplomatist.* London. Cassell and Company, Ltd.
120. Mijatović, Chedo. 1908. *Servia and the Servians.* London. Sir Isaak Pitman & Sons. Retrieved from https://archive.org/details/serviaandservia00mijagoog.
121. Milin, Lazar. 1986. *Naučno opravdanje religije, knjiga 6: Crkva i sekte.* Beograd. Prosveta.
122. Millard, Edward. 1896. "A Tribute". *The Bible Society Reporter.* February 1896.
123. Miloradović, Živoslav. 1994. "Nazareni – snaga kroz trpljenje". *Novi Pančevac.*
124. Miz, Roman. 2002. *Religijska slika Evrope.* Novi Sad. MBM-plas i EHO.
125. Močnik, Albin. 1925. *Adventizam.* Novi Sad. B.i.
126. Nedić, Svetlana. 1995. "Sala mira". *Godišnjak grada Beograda.* Beograd. Muzej grada Beograda.
127. Nenadov, Kathleen R. 2006. *Choosing to Suffer Affliction: The Untold Story of Nazarene Persecution in Yugoslavia.* San Diego, USA. Published by the author.
128. *Neue Zionsharfe: Eune Sammlung von Liedern für die gemeinde der Glaubenden in Christo.* 1855. Zurich. Druck von Zürcher u. Furrer.
129. Nikolaj, episkop i Milin, Lazar. 1997. *Pravoslavna vero-nauka i delovanje verskih sekti.* Beograd.

130. Nikolić, Jovan protojerej. 1991. "Biblija u pravoslav-noj crkvi". *Bogoslovska smotra, Ephemerides Theologicae Zagrebienses.* Broj 1-4. Zagreb.

131. Nikolić, Rada I Milovančev, Zora. n.d. *Odakle je u Aranđelovac (Srbija) došla nazarenska vera.* Unpublished manuscript.

132. Njistor, Zoltan dr. 1940. *Nazareni.* Pančevo. Štamparija "Napredak". Publisher, priest Vladimir Nenadov of Opovo.

133. Makaji, Jakov. 1975. *Istorijat i nauka nazarena,* under-graduate final dissertation (unpublished). Zagreb. Biblijsko-teološki institut.

134. Milivojević, Dragoljub. 1925. "O adventistima i naza-renima", *Bratstvo, list za vjersko i narodno prosvjećivanje.* Sarajevo. Brojevi 1 i 3.

135. "O suzbijanju nazarenstva". 1912. *Zbornik zakona, ure-daba i naredaba Ministarstva prosvete i crkvenih poslova od 1881-1912.* Beograd. Štamparija Vlade Stanovića i Druga.

136. Oljhovski, V. 1905. *Nazareni v Vengrii i Serbii: k istorii sektantstva,* Moskva, Posrednik.

137. _____. 1922. *Iz mira sektantov: Sbornik statei.* Moskva. Gosudarstvenie izdatelstvo.

138. Ott, Bernhard. 1996. *Missionarische Gemeinde werden: Der Weg der Evangelischen Täufergemeinden.* Liestal. Verlag ETG.

139. Palaret, Majkl. 1992. "Čovek koji je izgradio Englezovac – Fransis Makenzi u Beogradu (1876-1895)". *Istorijski časopis,* XXXIX, str. 137-164

140. Pavković, Nikola i Dušan Bandić, Radomir Rakić. 1978. *Male verske zajednice u opštini Pančevo.* Beograd. B.i.

141. Pavković, Nikola. 1998. "Religijski pluralizam u Vojvodini – istorijski pregled". *Zbornik za društvene nauke MS.* Br. 104-105.

142. Pavlica, Branko. 2001. "Najveći (nemački) uticaj na naš jezik". *Helsinška povelja.* God IV. Novembar.

143. Petrović, Dušan. 1906. *O nazarenima u Nadalju*. Sremski Karlovci. Srpska manastirska štamparija.

144. Petrus, Levi ed. 1939. *Europeiska Pingstkonferensen i Stocholm*. Stockholm, Sweden. Förlaget Filadelfina.

145. Podgradski, Josif. 1871. *Otvorena knjiga dru Miletiću u Vac via Pest. O žalosnom stanju narodno-crkvenog života kod Srba*. Novi Sad. N.p.

146. Popović, Dragutin. 1903. "Stanje nazarena u Šabačkoj eparhiji", *Vesnik Srpske crkve*, godina XIV, sveska 1.

147. Popović, Dušan. 1990. *Srbi u Vojvodini*. Knjiga 1. Novi Sad. Matica srpska.

148. Popović, Jevsevije. 1992. *Opšta crkvena istorija*. Knjiga 2. Phototype edition. Novi Sad. Prometej.

149. "Prisoners for Peace in Servia". 1881. *Bible Society Monthly Reporter*. Feb 1 1881.

150. Prohaska, Dragutin dr. 1922. "Husiti i bogumili", *Jugoslavenska njiva*, br. 3, broj 28.

151. Purković, Miodrag. 1934. *Avinjonske pape i stare srpske zemlje*. Požarevac. B.i.

152. Puzović, Predrag dr, protojerej. 1997. *Prilozi za istoriju Srpske pravoslavne crkve*. Ogledalo. Niš.

153. Radenić, Andrija. 1961. "Metodi nemačke i kvinsliške strahovlade u Beogradu 1941. Godine". *Godišnjak grada Beograda*. Knjiga VIII.

154. Radić, Radmila. 2002. *Država i verske zajednice 1945-1970*, knjige I i II. Beograd. Institut za noviju istoriju Srbije.

155. Radojičić, Đorđe Sp. 1962. *Razvojni luk stare srpske književnosti*. Novi Sad. Matica Srpska.

156. Radonić, Jovan. 1923. "Prilozi za istoriju braće Jakšića". *Spomenik srpske kraljevske akademije*. LIX. Drugi razred. Broj 50. Beograd. SKA.

157. _____. 1950. *Rimska kurija i južnoslovenske zemlje od XVI do XIX veka*. Beograd. Srpska akademija nauka: Odeljenje društvenih nauka.

158. Rakić, Lazar dr. 1986. *Jaša Tomić (1856-1922)*, Novi Sad, Matica srpska.

159. Revesz, Imre. 1956. *History of the Hungarian Reformed Church.* Translation George Knight. Hungarica Americana 5. Washington D.C., USA. The Hungarian Reformed Federation of America.

160. Rotar, Janez. 1983. "Rad Primoža Trubara na glagoljskim i ćirilskim knjigama". Prevod M. Mitrović. *Književna istorija*, XV (60).

161. Rüegger, Herman sen. 1962. *Aufzeichnungen über entstehung und bekenntnis der gemeinschaft Evanglish Taufgesinnter (Nazarener).* Biel. Graphische Anstalt Shüler AG.

162. _____. 1985. *Apostolic Christian Church History.* 2nd edition in English, Eureka, IL, USA. Apostolic Christian Publications, Inc.

163. Ruvarac, D. 1923. "Korespondencija Jovana Saskog, rektora protestantske škole u Đuru". *Godišnjica Nikole Čupića.* Knjiga XXXV. Beograd. Čupićeva zadužbina.

164. Sabo, Josip. 1960. "Istorijat Kristovih duhovnih crkava". *Okružnica Saveza Kristovih Crkava u FNRJ.* Broj 1.

165. Saria, Bogdan. 1928. "Protestantske crkve". *Narodna enciklopedija.* Beograd.

166. Sava, episkop šumadijski. 1996. *Srpski jerarsi od devetog do dvadesetog veka.* Beograd-Podgorica-Kragujevac. Evro-Unireks-Kalenić.

167. Samardžić, Radovan. 1976. *Sulejman i Rokselana.* Beograd. Srpska književna zadruga.

168. _____. 1981. *Religious Comunities in Yugoslavia.* Beograd. Jugoslovenska stvarnost.

169. *Sbornik zakonah i naredabah valjanih za kraljevine Hrvatsku i Slavoniju.* 1895. Komad XX. 12.12.1895.

170. "Servia". 1868. *Bible Society Monthly Reporter.* Feb 1 1868.

171. *Seventh Day Baptists in Europe and America; a series of historical papers written in commemoration of the one hundredth anniversary of the organization of the Seventh Day*

Baptist General Conference, celebrated in Ashaway, Rhode Island, August 20-25, 1902. 1910. Plainfield, USA. American Sabbath Tract Society.

172. Skerlić, Jovan. 1923. *Srpska književnost u XVIII veku.* Reprint 1966. Beograd. Napredak.

173. Slijepčević, Đoko dr. 1943. *Nazareni u Srbiji do 1914. godine.* Beograd. Izdavačko i prometno a.d. "Jugoistok".

174. *Slovačka evangelička augsburške veroispovesti crkva u SFR Jugoslaviji.* 1980. Novi Sad. Slovačka evangelička crkva.

175. Smajls, Samjuel. 1908. *Karakter.* Beograd. Published by Lazar S. Marković.

176. Smith, George. 1891. *A Modern Apostle: Alexander Somerville.* London. John Murray, Albemarle Street.

177. Smrekar, Milan. 1905. *Priručnik za političku upravnu službu u kraljevinah Hrvatskoj i Slavoniji.* Knjiga peta. Zagreb. Tiskom i nakladom Ignjata Granitza.

178. *Spomenica na cara Jovana Nenada subotičkog 1527-1927.* 1927. Subotica. Akcioni odbor za proslavu.

179. Spremić, Momčilo. 1989. "Despot Đurađ Branković i papska kurija". *Spomenica Svetozara Radojčića: Zbornik Filozofskog fakulteta.* Knjiga XVI. Beograd.

180. Srkulj, S. 1913. *Izvori za povijest.* Knjiga III. Zagreb. Nakl. Kr. Hrv.-Slav.-Dalm. zemaljske vlade.

181. Stanikić, Jug. 1897-1899. "O nazarenima i njihovom učenju". Karlovci. *Srpski sion: nedeljni list za crkve-no-prosvetne i avtonomne potrebe.* U 1897 brojevi 11-51, u 1898 brojevi 2-44, u 1899 brojevi 8-51.

182. Stanković, Milan. 1952. *Uspomene iz socijalističkog pokreta 1893-1914.* Beograd. Narodna knjiga.

183. Stanković, Sanja. 2007. "Dijalog sa nazarenima", *Teološki časopis.* Broj 7. Novi Sad. TFNS.

184. Stanojević, St. 1928. "Bogumili i husiti u Sremu i Bačkoj". *Glasnik istorijskog društva u Novom Sadu.* Knjiga 1, sv. 1. Sremski Karlovci.

185. "Stanovništvo Srbske Vojvodine po veri i narodnosti". 1863. *Letopis Matice srpske.* Sveska 108.

186. Stäubli, C. 1928. *Nazarenes in Jugoslavia*, Syracuse, NY, Apostolic Christian Publishing.

187. Steele, David. 1995. "Configuration of the Small Religious Communities in the Former Yugoslavia", *Religion in Eastern Europe XV*. No. 3 (June).

188. Sterlemann, Karl. 1988. *Studien zur Kirchengeschichte der Reformierten Christyichen Kirche in Jugoslawien, Kroatien und Sudungarn (von der Ansiedlungszeit bis 1944)*. Winnenden/Wurttemberg. Eigenverlag des Verfasserrs.

189. Stojanović, Irinej jeromonah. 1927. "Nazaren", *Pravoslavna hrišćanska zajednica*. Broj 8. Avgust 1927.

190. *Studies in Anabaptist and Mennonite History: The Hutterian brethren 1528-1931*. 1931. A Story of Martyrdom and Loyalty. Edited by Harold Bender et al. Goshen, USA. The Mennonite Historical Society.

191. Šelmić, Leposava. 1979. "Prilog proučavanju srpskog nazarenskog slikarstva". *Zbornik za likovne umetnosti*. Broj 15. Matica srpska.

192. Šidak, Jaroslav dr. 1932. "Heretički pokret i odjek husitizma na slovenskom jugu". *Zbornik za društvene nauke Matice srpske*. Sveska 31.

193. Šušljić, Milan. 1980. "Propovedaće se ovo evanđelje". *Glasnik hrišćanske adventističke crkve*. Broj 4.

194. _____. 1981. "Hrišćanska adventistička crkva u SFRJ". *Savest i sloboda*. Sveska III. Zagreb. Znaci vremena.

195. Taube, Fridrih Vilhelm von. 1777. *Istorijski i geografski opis kraljevine Slavonije i vojvodstva Srema kako s obzirom na njihove prirodne osobine tako i na sadašnje ustrojstvo i novo uređenje u crkvenim, građanskim i vojnim stvarima*. Reprint 1998. Novi Sad. Izdavačko preduzeće Matice srpske.

196. Tejlor, Alen. 2001. *Habzburška monarhija*. Beograd. Clio.

197. Tolstoy, Leo. 2006. *The Kingdom of God is Within You*. Constance Garnett translation. UK. Dover Publications.

198. Trotter, Edward Mrs. 1914. *Lord Radstock*. London. Hodder and Stoughton.

199. Ustav Kraljevine Jugoslavije. 1931. Beograd. *Službene novine*. Broj 200.
200. *Ustav Kraljevine Srba, Hrvata i Slovenaca.* 1921. Beograd. Izdavačka knjižarnica Gece Kona.
201. Ustav Republike Srbije. 2006. Beograd. *Službeni glasnik RS.* Broj 96.
202. *Yugoslavia: Prisoners of Conscience.* 1985. London. Amnesty International UK.
203. Vajta, Vilmos ed. 1977. *The Lutheran Church: Past and Present.* Minneapolis, USA. Augsburg Publishing House.
204. Vekić, Tihomir. 2003. "Osvjetljenje početka pentekostne crkve u Slavoniji, Srijemu i prekumurju". Final undergraduate dissertation. Osijek. Evanđeoski teološki fakultet. Unpublished manuscript.
205. *Verske zajednice u FNRJ.* Knjige I i II. 1953. Beograd. Institut za bezbednost.
206. Wilbur, Earl Morse. 1951. *A History of Unitarism: In Transylvania, England and America.* Canbridge, USA. Harvard University Press.
207. Williams, George Huntington. 1962. *The Radical Reformation.* Philadelphia, USA. The Westminster Press.
208. Williscroft, Paul. 1968. "A Day of Opportunity in Yugoslavia". *Pentecostal Evangel.* 24.3.1968.
209. *Writings of S.H. Froelich.* 2009 (version 29), Fairbury IL, USA. The Heritage Center Foundation. Retrieved from https://www.apostolicchristian.org/uploaded/bookstore/bookstore_downloads/0400_Complete_Set_of_Froehlich_Writings.pdf
210. Wyllie, J.A. 1877. *The History of Protestantism.* Volume III. London, Paris & New York. Cassell Petter & Galpin.
211. *Zbornik: Rukopisne i štampane knjige.* 1952. Beograd. Muzej primenjene umetnosti.
212. Žujović, Gordana i Ljubisav Vojinović. 1990. *Episkop Hrizostom: život i rad.* Belgrade Sveti arhijerejski sinod Srpske pravoslavne crkve.

CPSIA information can be obtained
at www.ICGtesting.com
Printed in the USA
BVHW041105260319
543499BV00006B/8/P